TROUBLE IN PARADISE

TROUBLE IN PARADISE

Uncovering the Dark Secrets of Britain's Most Remote Island

KATHY MARKS

HARPER PERENNIAL

London, New York, Toronto, Sydney and New Delhi

Harper Perennial
An imprint of HarperCollins*Publishers*
77–85 Fulham Palace Road, Hammersmith
London W6 8JB

www.harperperennial.co.uk
Visit our authors' blog at www.fifthestate.co.uk

This Harper Perennial Original edition published 2008
1

First published in Australia as *Pitcairn: Paradise Lost*
by Fourth Estate in 2008

Copyright © Kathy Marks 2008

Kathy Marks asserts the moral right to be
identified as the author of this work

A catalogue record for this book is
available from the British Library

ISBN 978-0-00-728614-0

Map by Shelly Communication

Printed and bound in Great Britain by Clays Ltd, St Ives plc

For my parents

Contents

Map   ix

Cast of characters   xi

Christian clan   xv

Brown family   xvi

Warren clan   xvii

Young family   xviii

Prologue   1

Part 1 — On the island

1 A surreal little universe in the middle of nowhere   7

2 Mutiny, murder and myth-making   18

3 Opening a right can of worms   34

4 No amnesty   48

5 The fiefdom and its leader   61

6 The propaganda campaign starts   78

7 Key witnesses evaporate   94

8 The trials begin   112

9 Let's make-believe 136

10 Judgement day 157

11 'You can't blame men for being men' 174

Part 2 — Viewing Pitcairn from a distance

12 How the myth was forged 197

13 Politics, poison and power plays 216

14 Britain's 'ineffective long-range benevolence' 230

15 'I just did my job and minded my own business' 245

16 Interdependence + silence = collusion 259

17 Making legal history 275

18 The final trials 290

19 Reaping a sad legacy since *Bounty* times 316

20 *Lord of the Flies?* 333

21 The last throw of the dice 351

Epilogue — Isobel's story 367

Acknowledgements 375

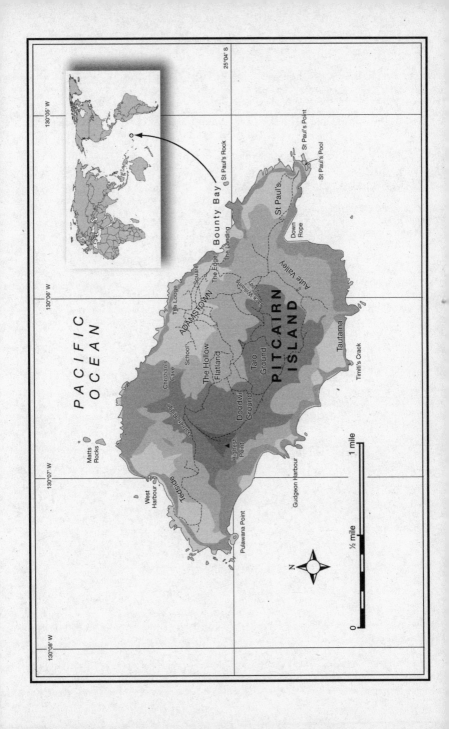

Cast of characters

Historical figures

Edward Christian (Fletcher's brother)

Edward Young (mutineer)

Fletcher Christian (mutineer)

Harry Christian (hanged in 1898 for murder of wife and baby)

John Adams (mutineer and community leader)

Maimiti (Fletcher Christian's Tahitian 'wife')

Matthew Quintal (mutineer)

Peter Heywood (mutineer court-martialled then pardoned)

William Bligh (captain of *Bounty*)

William McCoy (mutineer)

Media

Claire Harvey (*The Australian*; *The Times*)

Ewart Barnsley (Television New Zealand)

Kathy Marks (*The Independent*; *New Zealand Herald*)

Neil Tweedie (*The Daily Telegraph*; Press Association)

Sue Ingram (Radio New Zealand)

Zane Willis (TVNZ)

Officials and diplomats

Baroness Patricia Scotland (Former Overseas Territories Minister)

George Fergusson (Governor at time of writing)

Grant Pritchard (former Governor's Representative)

Harry Maude (British colonial official in 1940s)

Jenny Lock (former Governor's Representative)

Karen Wolstenholme (former Deputy Governor)

Leon Salt (former Commissioner)

Leslie Jaques (Commissioner at time of writing)

Martin Williams (former Governor)

Matthew Forbes (former Deputy Governor)

Richard Fell (former Governor)

Police and legal personnel

Adrian Cook QC (defence)

Allan Roberts (defence)

Charles Blackie (Chief Justice)

Charles Cato (defence)

Christine Gordon (prosecution)

Christopher Harder (former barrister)

Dennis McGookin (Kent Police)

Fletcher Pilditch (prosecution)

Gail Cox (Kent Police)

Graham Ford (court registrar)

Grant Illingworth QC (defence)

Gray Cameron (magistrate)

Jane Lovell-Smith (judge)

Karen Vaughan (New Zealand Police)

Kieran Raftery (prosecution)

Lord Hoffman (Privy Council)

Max Davidson (Kent Police)

Paul Dacre (defence)
Peter George (Kent Police)
Robert Vinson (Kent Police)
Russell Johnson (judge)
Simon Moore (prosecution)
Simon Mount (prosecution)
Vinny Reid (British Military Police)

Teachers and Church figures
Albert and Jane Moverley (teachers)
Albert Reeves (teacher; charged with indecent assault and rape)
Allen Cox (teacher)
Barrie Baronian (teacher)
Hannah Carnihan (teacher's daughter)
Lyle Burgoyne (lay pastor and nurse)
Neville Tosen (pastor)
Pippa Foley (teacher)
Ray Coombe (pastor)
Rick Ferret (pastor)
Roy Sanders (teacher)
Sheils Carnihan (teacher)
Tony Washington (teacher)

Victims (pseudonyms)
Belinda
Carla
Caroline
Catherine
Charlotte
Elizabeth
Fiona

Gillian
Isobel
Janet
Jeanie
Jennifer
Judith
Karen
Linda
Marion
Susan
Suzie

Various

Bill and Catherine Haigh (communications expert and his wife)
Caroline Alexander (historian)
Dea Birkett (author of *Serpent in Paradise*)
Herb Ford (California-based director of Pitcairn Islands Study Center)
Maurice Allward (friend of Pitcairn Island)
Maurice Bligh (descendant of William Bligh)
Nigel Jolly (skipper of the *Braveheart*)
Ricky Quinn (step-grandson of Terry Young)

Christian clan

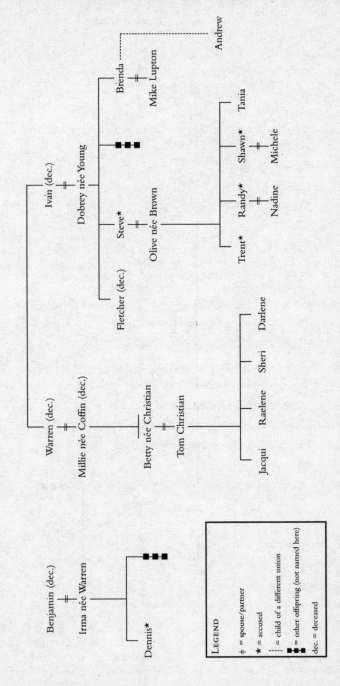

NOTE: The following diagrams are not complete family trees, but visual representations of the relationships between key protagonists in this book.

LEGEND

╪ = spouse/partner

★ = accused

---- = child of a different union

■■■ = other offspring (not named here)

dec. = deceased

Brown family

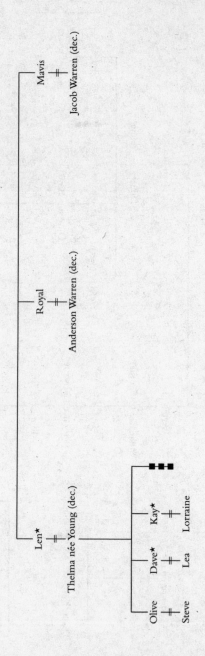

Warren clan

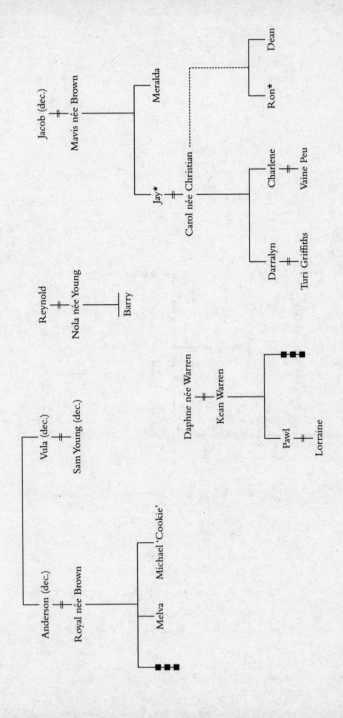

Young family

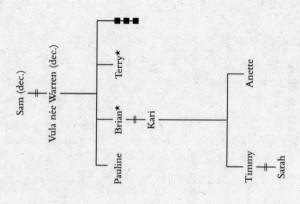

Prologue

Pitcairn Island, a British outpost floating in a remote corner of the South Pacific, was until recently considered a tropical paradise. Seldom visited, it is a place of extreme isolation, with no airstrip and limited sea access. The rocky outcrop is inhabited by about 50 people, most of them descended from Fletcher Christian and his fellow *Bounty* mutineers.

The sailors fled to the island to evade British law, but for the next two centuries Pitcairn was, to all appearances, trouble-free — stabilised by religion, with negligible crime, and largely capable of running its own affairs. Just before the dawn of the new millennium, that perception was turned on its head.

In December 1999 several Pitcairn girls claimed that they had been sexually assaulted by a visiting New Zealander. By chance, a British policewoman was on the island, and one of the girls confided that she had also been raped by two local men in the past. An investigation into those allegations developed into a major inquiry that saw British detectives criss-cross the globe, interviewing dozens of Pitcairn women. Their conclusion was that nearly every girl growing up on the island in the last 40 years had been abused, and nearly every man had been an offender.

I first read about the investigation — codenamed, quite coincidentally, Operation Unique — in 2000, when snippets surfaced in the British and New Zealand media. At that time I was a relative newcomer to Sydney, where I am based as Asia–Pacific Correspondent for *The Independent*. The story had immediate appeal, combining Pitcairn's mutinous history with a glimpse of life darkly played out on a far-flung island — an island that also happened to be a British colony, one of the final vestiges of Empire.

What struck me, even at that early stage, was that sexual abuse seemed to have been part of the fabric of life on Pitcairn. I tried to visualise what childhood must have been like for the victims, living there with no means of escape from their alleged assailants.

At the same time, certain Pitcairners — including women on the island — were loudly denying that children had ever been mistreated. They claimed that Pitcairn was a laid-back Polynesian society where girls matured early and were willing sexual partners. Britain, they claimed, was trying to cripple the community and force it to close, thus ridding itself of a costly burden. Who was telling the truth, I wondered: the women describing their experiences of abuse, or those portraying the affair as a British conspiracy?

For Britain, the case raised embarrassing questions about its supervision of the colony, now known as an Overseas Territory. Confronted with such serious allegations, however, the government had no choice but to act robustly. Judges and lawyers were appointed, and in 2003, after a series of legal and logistical hurdles had been surmounted, 13 men were charged with 96 offences dating back to the 1960s.

The plan was to conduct two sets of trials: the first on Pitcairn, the second in New Zealand. Preparations got under way on the island, where the accused men helped to build their own prison.

The locals wanted the press excluded; as a compromise, and to prevent the place from being swamped, Britain decided to accredit just six journalists. Media organisations around the world were invited to make a pitch.

On holiday in Japan at the time, I submitted a rather hurried application, pointing out my long-standing interest in the story. I also mentioned that I would be able to file for *The Independent*'s sister paper, the *New Zealand Herald*. Shortly afterwards, I was informed that I had been chosen as a member of the media pool.

In 2004 I spent six weeks on the island, reporting on one of the most bizarre court cases imaginable. Outside court, I bumped into the main protagonists every day, which was inevitable, since I was living in the middle of their tiny community. Some of those encounters were civil; others were less so, but I was able to observe at close quarters how Pitcairn functioned: the gossip, the feuding, the claustrophobic intimacy — and the power dynamics that had allowed the abuse to flourish.

The legal saga did not end with the verdicts and sentences handed down on the island by visiting judges. It continued until late 2007, with further trials held in Auckland and the offenders appealing to every court up to the Privy Council in London. As I followed these twists and turns in both hemispheres, my mind buzzed with unanswered questions.

Why was it that many outsiders persisted in defending men who were guilty of a crime that was normally reviled: paedophilia? Why did they continue to mythologise Pitcairn, although it had failed, in such a dramatic way, to live up to its Utopian image? How far back, I asked myself, did the sexual abuse stretch — to the time of the mutineers? Why had parents not denounced the perpetrators and kept their children safe? Had anyone outside the island realised what was going on?

There were bigger questions, too. What did Pitcairn tell us about human nature and life in small, remote communities? Is this how all of us would behave if left to ourselves, with no one looking over our shoulder?

Is Pitcairn a cautionary tale — a real-life version of *Lord of the Flies*, that chilling story of a group of schoolboys who descend into savagery on an imaginary island?

Are there more Pitcairns out there?

Part 1

On the island

CHAPTER 1

A surreal little universe in the middle of nowhere

Balancing on the deck of the *Braveheart*, I glanced down at the longboat rolling alongside us in the vigorous swell. Between the two vessels lay churning ocean, and a gap that narrowed and yawned alarmingly. 'Jump,' urged a voice behind me. Heart pounding, I leapt. A pair of muscular arms caught me and propelled me onto a wooden bench.

It was September 2004, and for the next six weeks, along with other journalists, I would be living on a lump of volcanic rock in the middle of the South Pacific. Our group had been travelling for eight days and was still some way off, separated by seas whipping themselves into furious peaks. But we could see our destination ahead of us: Pitcairn Island, the legendary home of Fletcher Christian and the *Bounty* mutineers.

One of Fletcher's heirs was slouched in the back of the longboat: Randy Christian, black-bearded and massively built. Limbs that looked like gigantic steel girders sprouted from his black shorts and singlet.

When you first clap eyes on a person charged with serious crimes, they are generally seated in the dock of a court, flanked by prison guards. Randy was skippering the boat that was conveying us to shore so we could report on his trial for five rapes and seven indecent assaults. Next to him stood Jay Warren, another big man, with a dark moustache and Polynesian features. Jay, too, would soon be facing justice, for allegedly molesting a 12-year-old girl.

Looking back, it was a fitting introduction to the surreal little universe in which we were about to be immersed: a place where the sexual abuse of children is shrugged off, and not even a legal drama generating international headlines can disrupt the rhythms of daily existence. Randy and Jay, expert at picking their way through Pitcairn's spiked collar of rocks, were in charge of the longboats, and the locals saw no irony in them coming out to fetch us. As for us, we had blithely placed our lives in the hands of men who surely did not wish us well.

Pitcairn is a crumb of land, roughly 2 miles square, and probably the most inaccessible spot on Earth. Before leaving my home in Sydney, I had found it on the map, with some difficulty: a pinprick in a vast expanse of blue, 3300 miles from New Zealand and 3600 miles from Chile. In an era when you can fly from Australia to London in a day, the journey to Pitcairn is a powerful reminder of the size of the planet. The island is one of the few places in the world without an airstrip. Too remote to be reached by helicopter, it does not even have a scheduled shipping service. Most visitors charter a yacht out of Tahiti, or hitch a lift on a trans-Pacific container ship, which takes more than a week to get there from Auckland or Panama.

As the island does not have a safe harbour, ships must heave to a mile or so offshore, where the community-owned longboats collect passengers and goods. If the seas are rough, which they often are, the captain may decide to press on without stopping. Then it can be months before another vessel passes.

Travelling in an official British party, I had taken a slightly different route, flying from Auckland to Tahiti, then waiting three days for the once-weekly connection to Mangareva, a beautiful island in the outermost reaches of French Polynesia and the nearest inhabited land to Pitcairn. The four-hour flight was broken by a refuelling stop in Hao, the atoll where the French agents who blew up the Greenpeace flagship *Rainbow Warrior* were briefly imprisoned. A few days later, in Mangareva's tiny, threadbare port of Rikitea, our party boarded the *Braveheart*, a 110-foot former scientific research vessel, for the final leg of our odyssey: a 30-hour ocean voyage. As well as the six-person media pool, there were two British diplomats, two English police officers, and an Australian Seventh-day Adventist pastor and his wife.

Some 300 miles of open sea lie between Mangareva and Pitcairn; having been warned that the passage could be extremely choppy, I was armed with seasickness tablets, including 'Paihia bombs', a New Zealand remedy. What I was not prepared for was quite how lonely it would feel in that distant corner of the world's largest ocean. We saw no other ships, just flying fish, and seabirds skimming the waves, and fields of whitecaps stretching to infinity in every direction. Only an occasional dusting of coral atolls relieved the sensation of dizzying emptiness.

On our second day, at about midday, a grey smudge appeared on the horizon: Pitcairn. The sight of it made my flesh tingle. It was quiet on deck. For the next five hours we watched as the island's distinctive silhouette emerged and the smudge turned into a solid chunk of rock.

This was exactly what Fletcher Christian would have seen from the *Bounty* as he combed the South Pacific for a bolthole from the

British Navy in 1790. Pitcairn proved to be ideal, and the sailors settled on the island with their Polynesian 'wives' and companions. Two centuries later, their descendants lived on there — just 47 of them, mostly related and sharing four surnames. And now the heirs of the famous mutineers were famous for quite different reasons.

Thirteen men had been charged as a result of a police investigation into child sexual abuse, and seven of them lived on Pitcairn, where they accounted for nearly half the adult males. Those men had insisted on their right to be tried at home; however, the last major court case on the island had been in 1898, when Harry Christian was convicted of murdering his wife and child. The island had no legal infrastructure, only a local court that had not been used for years, even for minor offences. On top of that, it had little accommodation and very few amenities.

All the key players — including judges, lawyers and court officials — were having to be shipped in, along with supplies to feed them for six weeks. British officials had chartered the *Braveheart* to carry everyone, together with their luggage, and a dozen crates of legal documents and evidence. With the trials due to start in four days, my group was on the boat's final run.

After dropping anchor, we waited for the longboat, the only vessel which — unless conditions are exceptionally calm — can execute the tricky landing at Bounty Bay. The loaf-shaped island stretched out before us, silent and aloof, its shores hammered by the relentless waves. Bounty Bay, a small, rock-strewn cove, was a mere chink in an armour of tall cliffs that enclosed Pitcairn almost completely. The island was surprisingly green, with thick vegetation and ochre-red rock exposed by gashes in the escarpments.

The *Braveheart* hovered. Ten minutes passed. Then another ten. We chatted and joked, affecting a nonchalance that none of us felt. We scanned the scene ahead. The smile on the face of Matthew

Forbes, the British diplomat with day-to-day responsibility for the territory, looked strained. Surely the islanders wouldn't refuse to bring the boat out?

I knew that many of the locals were deeply resentful about the trials, and the consequent influx of strangers to the island. The Pitcairners were protective of their privacy and turned down most requests to visit; if the British diplomats and police officers on the *Braveheart* were undesirable guests, the media representatives were perhaps even less welcome. Touchy about the way they had been depicted by writers and film-makers, the islanders had more or less banned journalists since the publication in 1997 of a travel memoir, *Serpent in Paradise*, a closely observed study of Pitcairn life, which they detested, along with its English author, Dea Birkett.

I had been given a flavour of what lay in store for us after emailing Mike 'Cookie' Warren, one of the more outspoken islanders, while we were *en route*. I asked Cookie how the community felt about the impending trials, and expressed the hope that we journalists would be able to present a balanced picture. Cookie replied, 'Let me begin by asking you why you are coming here when you don't have permission from the islanders? Let me suggest that you are no different to any other reporter and journalist I know. That is, most are out to print what sells and to make money. I couldn't care less whether what you report is balanced or not. We have already been humiliated and the presence of the press pool will only serve to reinforce that fact further.'

He added, 'A family in trouble best deals with its troubles and problems privately and discreetly. How would you like it if your family disputes were aired on television for the whole world to see? Would you call this justice?'

The stand-off, if that was what it was, ended abruptly. A boat materialised in the distance, slicing through the waves at a hectic pace, and a few minutes later drew up beside us with a flourish. A fearsome-looking figure was planted on the prow: hulking and shaven-headed, with a bandana, a shark's tooth necklace and several dozen earrings and studs. It looked like a pirate; it was, in fact, Pawl Warren, whom we would come to know as one of the nicest men on the island.

Randy and Jay, the two defendants, watched impassively as others helped us aboard, stowing our baggage beneath a tarpaulin. There was an awkward silence as we sat down. What does one say in that situation? 'Hello Jay, hello Randy, hope your trial goes well'? Among the boat's other occupants I recognised Tom Christian, tall and rangy, in a battered Panama hat: he had been Pitcairn's radio operator for decades.

The longboat bounced off across the breakers. No one spoke to us; most of the islanders kept their gazes firmly averted. I felt ill at ease, and I sensed that my colleagues — all seasoned operators, some with experience in war zones — did too. Soon we were approaching Bounty Bay, where we shot in through a narrow entrance after veering sharp left to dodge some nasty-looking rocks.

Our reception party was modest and consisted mainly of outsiders. A handful of Pitcairners, including Tom Christian's wife, Betty, were waiting on the concrete jetty; one or two others stood at the far end, well away from the boat, and they left after photographing our arrival. We clambered ashore and milled around uncertainly, amid the bustle of greetings and boxes being unloaded. Jay and Randy, still at work, winched the longboat up a slipway and into the boatshed, which was crowned by a big sign stating 'Welcome to Pitcairn Island'. Another sign pointed to the 'last resting place of H.M.S Bounty' — the spot where the skeleton of the ship, which the mutineers scuttled and burnt, lies submerged in shallow water. Long-beaked frigate birds flapped overhead, swooping down to seize fish guts from the outstretched hand of an islander who was cleaning her catch.

Snatches of the locals' curiously cadenced language drifted over to us. Pitkern reflects their mixed roots, combining the sailors' 18th-century English with some Tahitian words. Others around us were speaking English, but with the characteristic drawl of England's West Country. The origins of that accent are something of a mystery.

A couple of us briefly interviewed Tom, who declared, 'I can't wait to get this whole mess behind us.'

Then it was time to move, and that meant up.

Pitcairn, the tip of an extinct volcano, has little flat land. Overshadowing The Landing, as it is known, is a 300-foot cliff, at the top of which Adamstown, the one settlement, crouches on a slender plateau. It is reached via a steeply winding track, aptly called the Hill of Difficulty, which in 2004 was still ferociously rutted and suitable only for quad bikes, the sole vehicles used on the unsealed roads. A dozen quad bikes were parked near the jetty, like a herd of exotic animals congregating around a waterhole. I climbed onto the back of one driven by the island's New Zealand doctor.

I took the doctor for an islander and he did not enlighten me, apparently enjoying a little game of who's who. As I tried to draw him into conversation, we passed a pink bulldozer on a hairpin bend; inside it was a dark-haired man with a moustache and swarthy features, who was busily repairing a stretch of road. I did not realise then, but it was Steve Christian — Randy's father, mayor of Pitcairn, and the principal defendant in the child abuse trials. Steve had not been on the longboat, nor at The Landing. But there he was, watching events from on high and asserting himself as a person of importance as he carried out vital maintenance work completely unconnected with our arrival.

The quad bike laboured uphill, with spectacular views of the bay unfolding beneath us. At the top, the ground suddenly levelled out, and we forked right along the 'main road', a dusty red trail that snakes through the village, fringed by a dense tangle of bush — hibiscus, frangipani, banana and coconut palms, pandanus trees, bamboo and towering banyans. Turning down a side lane, we headed back towards the ocean, and after passing a cemetery stopped outside the Government Lodge, the rather grandly named dwelling allocated to the media.

The Lodge, generally occupied by official visitors, was a pre-fabricated four-bedroom house, rather basic, with spartan furnishings. It reminded me of my student days 20 years earlier, and the comparison was fitting, for we six adults, aged from late 20s to late 50s, were about to revert to precisely that kind of communal set-up. I agreed to share a room with Claire Harvey, a reporter with *The Australian* newspaper. Ewart Barnsley, the Television New Zealand (TVNZ) correspondent, took up residence with his cameraman, Zane Willis. Neil Tweedie, of Britain's *Daily Telegraph*, was to have his own room, as would Sue Ingram from Radio New Zealand.

The Lodge was not only our new home, but a workspace. Media interest in the forthcoming trials was intense; TVNZ's footage would be broadcast around the world, and our syndicated press stories and photographs would be published widely. I was acutely aware that we were all filing for different time zones, and mostly for more than one outlet — in my case, newspapers in the UK and New Zealand. Television, radio and print each had its own demands. I wondered how we would fare, all cooped up together and confronting Pitcairn's peculiar logistical challenges.

Laptops were quickly arranged on the dining-room table and

hooked up to the relatively new internet system. Zane and Ewart set up an editing suite in their bedroom. Satellite phones were lined up on a grassy bank behind the house, antennae pointing optimistically skywards: the island had no landline telephones and mobiles had not functioned since we had left Tahiti. Satphones would be our only means of speaking to anyone in the outside world.

We had brought with us every conceivable piece of technical equipment, as there was no question of getting anything repaired or replaced on Pitcairn. For the other necessities of life, only limited items would be available in the local shop. Packing for the trip had involved trying to envisage every eventuality — and we had only been allowed 20 kilograms of luggage.

After briefly settling in, Claire and I set off to explore. A back lane wound up past the Mission House, usually inhabited by the resident Seventh-day Adventist pastor but temporarily assigned to the three trial judges from New Zealand. The islanders were all Adventists, having converted *en masse* in the late 19th century. Beyond the Mission House, past a tall mango tree, stood Pitcairn's newest building: a large, L-shaped prison, elevated on stilts above a dirt yard, with six double cells fronted by a wide wooden deck. The prison, which looked quite attractive, had been built by men who were at risk of becoming its first inmates — no one had wanted to miss out on the work, even in the circumstances.

The lane spat us out in the village, Adamstown, which appeared to be deserted. Scattered along the main road were houses of weatherboard and corrugated iron, somewhat ramshackle-looking; other homes, all single-storey, were found off a jumble of tracks that meandered further up the hillside. Although there was, notwithstanding the steep terrain, quite a bit of space on which to build, people seemed to be living almost on top of each other.

Above the main road was the square, the heart of the community, where a few mainly timber buildings clustered around a patch of roughly laid concrete. The brick Adventist church faced the public hall, with its graceful white verandah; between them were squeezed the pint-sized library and post office. A bench ran along the fourth side.

In front of the hall, which was also the courthouse, was an imposing sight: the *Bounty*'s anchor, mounted on a plinth. Outside the hall, among several notices pinned up on a board, was one that warned the islanders about 'personal incidents that could be sensationalised in the media'. It was signed by Steve Christian. Another reminded the locals that 'malicious gossip' was an offence.

As we wandered back to the Lodge, I was struck by the stillness in the lanes and a heaviness in the air. Dusk was falling, but it was still humid, and everything around us seemed exaggerated: the spring flowers were too vivid, as if daubed from a child's palette, the bees buzzing around them were a little too loud. Perhaps I was affected by thoughts of why we had come here. But I smelt a definite whiff of menace.

My other lasting impression was the sheer ordinariness of the place. While the island had a kind of wild beauty, Adamstown looked like a run-down rural village in England or New Zealand. And it was tiny. Already I felt hemmed in, and unsettled by the omnipresent ocean, an immense blue blanket swaddling and smothering us, a wall separating Pitcairn from the world. The sense of isolation was overpowering.

Back home, we were greeted by the aroma of something burning. Baking was one of the new skills we would have to learn, for bread, like so many everyday commodities, could not be bought. A colleague had gamely put a loaf in the oven, but then forgotten about it, distracted by deadlines.

At 10 p.m. the living room went dark, prompting a chorus of groans and curses. Public electricity, supplied by a diesel generator, was rationed to ten hours a day. Most homes had a back-up system, with a bank of 12-volt batteries providing a few hours of extra power. However, in our ignorance we had already drained our batteries, and had to carry on working by candlelight.

Hours later, after everyone else had gone to bed, I paced up and down outside the house, trying to send my first day's copy via satellite phone. The temperature had dropped, and I was surrounded by a darkness more complete than I had ever experienced. With no moon or stars, and no artificial light for hundreds of miles, I would not have found our back door again without a torch.

As I waved my phone around like a conductor's baton, searching for a signal, I reflected on the weeks that lay ahead of me. Pitcairn would be no run-of-the-mill assignment, that was clear. And it was clear, too, that the story was about more than just the child abuse trials. It was about a strange little community, marching to its own tune in the middle of nowhere — and at the core of which we were now ensconced, rather uneasily.

CHAPTER 2

Mutiny, murder and myth-making

The next morning I got up and took a hot shower. Only later did I realise that, on Pitcairn, hot water does not simply arrive through the tap. A wood fire in a little shed near the house heats a copper boiler, which in turn heats cold water pipes leading to a storage tank. But in order for this to happen, a fire has to be built. And firewood has to be chopped.

Fortunately for the rest of us, Ewart Barnsley, the TVNZ journalist, was an early riser with a practical disposition. Shortly after dawn, he had chopped wood and lit the fire. From then on, he made that his daily chore.

We were discovering some of the other quirks of Pitcairn life. The 'duncan', for instance, which is an outside pit toilet. Ours was situated about 30 feet from the Lodge. The island does not have a sewerage system, and its only source of water, for drinking and washing, is rain.

Then there were the land crabs that lurked around, some the size of a dinner plate, turning a night-time trip to the duncan into a hair-raising ordeal. These fearsome-looking creatures usually tucked their soft bodies inside a coconut shell for protection, but we heard tales of crabs seen wearing a sweetcorn tin, a plastic doll's head, and a Pond's Cold Cream jar.

Should any of us encounter a particularly aggressive crab, or one of Pitcairn's formidable spiders, help was close by, and it had an English accent. Three British diplomats — among 29 outsiders who had recently descended on the island, nearly doubling its population — were installed next door to us in the Government Hostel, another pre-fabricated dwelling for visitors. For the trials, just one new house had been put up, called McCoy's after one of the mutineers, and it had been assigned to the prosecution team of three lawyers and two police officers. They found themselves living next door to Steve Christian, the Pitcairn mayor, who was facing court on six counts of rape and four of indecent assault. And the defence lawyers? They were sleeping in cells in the new jail.

At the Lodge, our other next-door neighbour was Len Brown, the oldest of the seven defendants. Len, who was charged with two rapes, was 78 and quite deaf, but still cut a physically imposing figure. Soon after we arrived, we saw him sitting in his garden, working on a carved replica of the *Bounty* — one of the wooden souvenirs that the islanders sell to tourists. For reasons unclear, a rusting cannon from the real ship stood on Len's front lawn.

The mutiny on the *Bounty* is one of the most notorious events in British maritime history. Yet it was only one of a series of rebellions against the British Navy in the late 18th century. One uprising in 1797 involved dozens of ships and a blockade of London. Another led to the murder at sea of a captain and eight of his officers.

That few people are familiar with these incidents, while nearly everyone knows about the drama on board the *Bounty*, can be explained in one word: Hollywood. The mutiny inspired five films between 1916 and 1984, three of them made by American studios, with Fletcher Christian played by matinée idols such as Clark Gable, Marlon Brando and Mel Gibson. Studio bosses loved the story, with its exotic South Seas setting, scenes of swashbuckling adventure and cast of semi-naked Polynesian maidens, and so did generations of cinemagoers, who warmed to Christian and sided with him against the apparently cruel and sadistic Captain William Bligh. The mutineers' descendants mostly shared that view of Bligh as the villain and Christian as the dashing young hero; to this day, they will not hear a word against their infamous ancestor.

The historical background is more complex than Hollywood has allowed. And it all began with breadfruit, a large, globe-shaped fruit.

Breadfruit trees had been discovered in Tahiti in 1769 by Sir Joseph Banks, the English naturalist, who urged King George III to introduce them to the West Indies as a cheap food source for slaves on the sugar plantations. The King appointed Bligh, a Royal Navy lieutenant, to lead an expedition, and in December 1787 a 220-ton former merchant ship, His Majesty's Armed Vessel *Bounty*, set sail from Portsmouth with 46 officers and men. Among them was Fletcher Christian, the master's mate and, effectively, Bligh's chief officer.

Bligh was an ambitious 33-year-old, and an outstanding navigator who had accompanied Captain James Cook on his final voyage. Christian was 23, equally ambitious, and from a genteel — albeit no longer wealthy — family with strong links to the Isle of Man. He had sailed twice previously under Bligh, who regarded him as a friend and protégé.

The plan was to head to Tahiti via South America, collect some breadfruit saplings and transport them to the Caribbean. However, the *Bounty* ran into atrocious weather at Cape Horn, after which

Bligh elected to go east, taking the longer route. The ship reached Tahiti's Matavai Bay in October 1788.

Early European visitors had called the island an earthly paradise, and after nearly a year at sea the Englishmen could only agree. Tahiti's white beaches were caressed by warm breezes; its trees hung heavy with fruit and its lagoons teemed with fish. The native men treated the sailors as 'blood brothers', while the beautiful, uninhibited women showered them with attention. Six months later, when it was time to depart, no one except the puritanical Bligh was keen to resume the rigours of shipboard life.

Bligh was convinced that it was Tahiti's charms, so reluctantly relinquished, that triggered the events of 28 April 1789. Most historians now agree that, far from being a brutal despot, Bligh was an enlightened captain who kept his crew healthy and flogged only sparingly. But he was also prone to fly into rages. After the *Bounty* left Tahiti, he humiliated the thin-skinned, volatile Christian, branding him a coward and accusing him of stealing coconuts from a stash on deck. Their relationship had broken down — although probably not as a result of a gay liaison gone sour, as some have speculated.

Three weeks out of Matavai Bay, as the *Bounty* approached the Friendly Islands (now called Tonga), five men burst into Bligh's cabin at dawn. With Christian pointing a bayonet at his chest, Bligh was made to climb into the ship's launch, along with 18 loyal officers and men. He appealed to Christian, reminding him, 'You have danced my children upon your knee.' The latter, reportedly in a delirious state, replied, 'That, Captain Bligh, that is the thing . . . I am in hell . . . I am in hell.'

Bligh and his followers were set adrift with no charts and only meagre supplies. In a remarkable feat of navigation, Bligh guided the launch across 3618 miles of open sea, landing on the island of

Timor 48 days later. Amazingly, only one life had been lost: that of a quartermaster, killed not at sea but in a skirmish with Tongans. In Batavia (now Jakarta), Bligh found a berth on a Dutch East Indiaman, and in March 1790 he arrived back in England, where he recounted his tale to an astonished nation.

The mutineers, meanwhile, were searching for a refuge. They could not go home to England, and an attempt to settle on Tubuai, 400 miles south of Tahiti, was abandoned after clashes with the locals. The men split into two factions. Sixteen of them decided to chance their luck on Tahiti; the other nine, led by Christian, would continue their quest. The *Bounty* dropped the first group at Tahiti, but picked up some new passengers: 12 Polynesian women, six Polynesian men and a baby accompanied Christian's band on their journey.

Two months later, while flicking through a book in Bligh's library, Christian noticed a reference to 'Pitcairn's Island'. The island sounded promising, but it had been incorrectly charted, and another two months passed before he finally sighted it in January 1790. Christian led a party ashore, and when he returned he was smiling for the first time in weeks. Pitcairn was not only off the map, but it was also unpopulated, and it was a natural fortress — thickly forested, with towering cliffs and no safe anchorage. Yet it had fertile soil, fruit trees and (unlike now) a water source. The mutineers ran the *Bounty* aground and prepared to establish a new community far from civilisation.

The sailors divided the cultivable land into nine plots, one for each of them. The proud Polynesian men, who had been their friends and equals on Tahiti, received nothing; instead they were to be their servants. The Englishmen also took one 'wife' apiece, with the other three women shared among the six Tahitians. These actions created a deadly stew of sexual jealousy and racial resentment, which boiled over two years later.

22

After the wives of John Williams and John Adams died, the pair commandeered two of the Polynesians' women. Enraged, the native men hatched a plot to murder the mutineers. But the latter were tipped off, and it was two Tahitians who were killed, one of them by his former wife.

In 1793 violence flared again. The four remaining Polynesian men stole some muskets, and within the space of one day murdered five Englishmen, including Fletcher Christian. Only John Adams, William McCoy, Matthew Quintal and Edward Young survived. Tit-for-tat killings followed, by the end of which all the Tahitian men were dead.

Calm then descended on the community — until 1798, when McCoy built a still and began producing a powerful spirit from the roots of the ti-plant. The men, and some of the women, spent their days in a drunken stupor, and it was in such a state that McCoy threw himself off a cliff. Quintal grew increasingly wild, and tried to snatch Young's and Adams' wives; the pair decided that they had no option but to kill him. They hacked Quintal to death with a hatchet. At last the cycle of bloodshed was over.

In 1800 Young died from an asthma attack. It was ten years since the mutineers had first spied Pitcairn. Of the 15 men who had settled there, only Adams was left.

Carved into a cliff high above Adamstown is Christian's Cave, reached by a vertiginously sheer trail trampled by the wild goats that roam the island's ridges and escarpments. It was to this windblown spot, a dark slash in the volcanic rock face, that Christian would retreat, so it is said, to scan the Pacific Ocean for British naval ships — and to reflect, perhaps, on the reckless act that had exiled him for eternity.

Once the *Bounty* was stripped and burnt to the waterline, the mutiny stopped being Christian's story. He was no longer a leader, and little is known about his life on Pitcairn, apart from the fact that his Tahitian wife — called Maimiti, or sometimes Mauatua — bore him two sons and a daughter. There is still debate about whether he really died there, or somehow managed to return to England — stoked by a 'sighting' of him in Plymouth, and the failure ever to locate his burial site.

The only mutineer with a preserved grave is John Adams, and it is he, not Christian, who was the father of the Pitcairn community, who set it on the course it was to follow for the next 200 years.

Adams, an ambiguous figure, signed up for the *Bounty* as Alexander Smith, reverting to his real name on the island. Rough and ready, like the average working-class salt, he played a prominent role in the seizing of the *Bounty* and subsequent racial warfare. Then, after the killings, he underwent a miraculous conversion — at least, that was his account, and there was no one left alive to challenge it.

Adams claimed that Edward Young taught him to read, using a Bible retrieved from the *Bounty*, and that he was so affected by the Bible's teachings that he repented of his misdeeds and embraced Christianity. After Young's death he was left alone with nine women and the 24 children born to the mutineers during those violent early years; strangely, no children were fathered by the Polynesian men. And, according to Adams, all of them led lives of spotless integrity under his patriarchal guidance.

The outside world, meanwhile, was gripped by the mystery of the mutineers' whereabouts. The men on Tahiti had been quickly tracked down and shipped home, then court-martialled, after which three of them were hanged. Fletcher Christian and his followers, though, seemed to have vanished.

The little society headed by Adams lived in complete isolation until 1808, when an American whaler, the *Topaz*, stumbled across it; the *Topaz*'s captain, Mayhew Folger, was astounded to be greeted by three dark-skinned young men in a canoe, all of whom spoke perfect English. Adams related his tale of sin and redemption to Folger who, after just a few hours on shore, left convinced that Pitcairn was 'the world's most pious and perfect community'. He informed the Admiralty about his incredible discovery, but the news was received with indifference; Britain was at war with France, and the mutiny was no longer of much interest in naval circles.

To each visitor after Folger, Adams gave a slightly different version of events, and few visitors interviewed the women, who were the only other witnesses. It was the start of the myth-making that was to obscure the reality of Pitcairn for the next two centuries.

By 1814 Adams was out of danger, following another chance visit, this time by two British naval captains. Enchanted by the new colony, they advised the Admiralty that it would be 'an act of great cruelty and inhumanity' to repatriate Adams and put him on trial.

Pitcairn's period of seclusion was over. A stream of ships called, mainly British men-of-war, but also whalers and merchant vessels. All of them found a peaceful, devout society whose young people were healthy, modest and well educated. The legend of an island populated by reformed sinners, the offspring of murderers and mutineers, spread across the English-speaking world.

To outsiders, the idea of a Western-style community flourishing in such a faraway spot was compelling. Missionary groups dispatched crateloads of Bibles; other well-wishers, including Queen Victoria, sent gifts such as flour, guns, fishing hooks, crockery and an organ. Pitcairn was many things to many people. It was a religious fable. It was a fairy tale. It was the fulfilment of a Utopian dream.

The island's fame grew in the late 19th century, after the locals rescued foreign sailors from a series of shipwrecks. Then in 1914 the opening of the Panama Canal put Pitcairn on the main shipping route to Australia and New Zealand. Liners packed with European emigrants would pause halfway across the Pacific so that their passengers could glimpse the island, and even meet its inhabitants, for — then as now — the islanders would board the ships to sell their souvenirs.

Jet travel destroyed the glamour of the ocean voyage, but while the rest of the world shrank, Pitcairn remained tantalisingly inaccessible, thus retaining much of its original allure. Children still scoured atlases for it; adults projected their escapist fantasies onto it; armchair travellers daydreamed about stepping ashore. The islanders, meanwhile, cultivated their own mystique, nurturing the romantic aura that drew tourists — and their American dollars — to their door.

The day after we arrived on Pitcairn, Olive Christian, Steve's wife, invited members of the media to Big Fence, her sprawling home overlooking the Pacific. Like the rest of my colleagues, I had absolutely no idea what to expect.

When we got there in the early afternoon, 15 women — almost the entire adult female population — were assembled on sofas and plastic chairs arranged around the edge of the living room. The room, which had a lino floor, was as big as a barn; the walls were decorated with family photographs and a large mural of fish and dolphins. Through the front window we could see tall Norfolk pines clinging to slopes that tumbled steeply to the ocean.

The women represented all four of Pitcairn's main clans: the Christians and Youngs, still carrying mutineers' surnames, and the Browns and Warrens, descendants of 19th-century sailor settlers. The other English lines — Adams, Quintal and McCoy — had died out, although not in New Zealand or on Norfolk Island, 1200 miles east of Australia, where most people with Pitcairn roots now live.

At the time of the Big Fence gathering, the names of the seven Pitcairn-based defendants were still suppressed by a court order. However, we were privy to this poorly kept secret. Every woman in the room was related to one or more of the men — as a wife, mother, sister, cousin, aunt or stepmother-in-law.

Looking around, I saw that, with a few exceptions, the women were solidly built. While some were dark-haired, with striking Polynesian features, others, with their fair skin and European looks, would not have stood out in an English village. All of them were casually dressed, many in shorts and singlets: practical choices, given the heat and ubiquitous Pitcairn dust.

We had been summoned to Big Fence, it turned out, to be told that their menfolk were not 'perverts' or 'hardened criminals': they were decent, hard-working family types. No islander would tolerate children being interfered with, and no one on Pitcairn had ever been raped. The 'victims' were girls who had known exactly what they were doing. It was they who had thrown themselves at the men.

As I digested this notion, which was being put forward with some passion, I noticed that a handful of people were dominating proceedings. These particular women were speaking over the top of each other, impatient to get their point across. Others said little, and looked ill at ease. Steve Christian's mother, Dobrey, sat quietly, weaving a basket from pandanus leaves.

The talkative ones explained that under-age sex was the norm on Pitcairn. Darralyn Griffiths, the daughter of Jay Warren, one of the defendants, told us in a matter-of-fact way that she had lost her virginity at 13, 'and I felt shit hot about it too, I felt like a big lady'. She was partly boasting, partly censorious of her younger self, it seemed to me. Others clamoured to make similar admissions. 'I had it at 12, and I was shit hot too,' said Jay's sister, Meralda, a woman in her 40s. Darralyn's mother, Carol, 54 years old, agreed that 13 was 'the normal age', adding, 'I used to be a wild thing when I was young and single.' Olive Christian described her youth, with evident nostalgia, as a time when 'we all thought sex was like food on the table'.

The British police had misunderstood Pitcairn, they claimed: it was a South Pacific island where, to young people, sex was as natural as the ocean breeze. Olive said, 'It's been this way for generations, and we've seen nothing wrong in it. Everyone has sex young. That's our lifestyle.' Darralyn echoed her. 'It was just the way it was. No one thought it was bad.'

We must have looked surprised. They were surprised we were surprised. Well, at what age did we start having sex, they demanded. It was clear, in this company and at this particular juncture, that the question could not be avoided. Some of our responses met with howls of derision. The women of Pitcairn did not believe that anyone could have lost their virginity at 18; the idea of being that old was simply preposterous.

The serious point of this was to persuade us that the criminal case was based on a misconception — and, furthermore, that it was all part of an elaborate plot. Britain was determined to 'close the island down', they said, because it had become a financial burden — a 'thorn in the arse', as Tania Christian, Steve and Olive's daughter, put it. What better way to achieve that than to jail the men who were the very backbone of the community?

Why, though, we wondered aloud, would the women who had spoken to police have fabricated their accounts — accounts that, despite them growing up on the island in different eras and now living thousands of miles apart, were remarkably alike? At this point the Pitcairners produced their trump card: Carol Warren's daughters, Darralyn and Charlene.

Charlene, 25 years old, with long, curly hair and a diffident manner, spoke up first, egged on by her mother. Charlene revealed that she had been one of the women who made a statement in 2000, alleging sexual abuse by Pitcairn men. But, she added, as others sitting around her clucked approvingly, she had only done so because she had been blinded by greed. She explained, 'The detectives . . . dragged me to the police station. I didn't know what I had done. I was ignorant. I was offered good money for each person I could name. They said I would get something like NZ$4000 (£1,500) for every guy. After I had added it up in my head, I was, like, "Whoa!" I just blurted everything out to them.'

Then it was her sister's turn. Darralyn was 27; well built, with a fair complexion, she resembled Charlene physically, but was more self-assured. Darralyn told us that she had also made a statement — but, she said, only after being browbeaten by police. She claimed that detectives had asked her to 'make up a false allegation against a guy here, because they didn't have enough evidence to put him under'.

A New Zealand detective and child abuse specialist, Karen Vaughan, who had joined the British inquiry team, told Darralyn's partner, Turi Griffiths, that if they had a baby daughter and brought her to the island, she would get raped too, Darralyn alleged. 'I was shit scared. They told me if I tell the truth, everything will be fine. They said they'd heard from other people about my past. They asked me disgusting personal questions.'

Both sisters were living in New Zealand at the time of the investigation, and both told police that they were prepared to go to court. But 'after I really thought about it, it was half and half ... I wanted it just as bad as them. It was very much a mutual thing,' said Charlene, referring to the men whom she had named as abusers. That re-evaluation took place after Charlene returned to Pitcairn. Darralyn changed her mind shortly before she, too, went home.

By now my head was spinning. We had had middle-aged matrons bragging about their sexual exploits. We had had Charlene and Darralyn outing themselves as victims, but not really victims. Now their mother, Carol, was declaring that no Pitcairn girl had ever been abused — and, almost in the same breath, telling us that *she* had had an unpleasant experience as a child. 'It didn't affect me,' she said. 'I was probably luckier than some I've read about. It was tried but nothing happened. I was ten at the time. But even at ten I knew it was wrong, it's a bad thing. I screamed like hell.'

When she heard that Darralyn had spoken to police, Carol said, 'I thought, what on earth is that girl thinking about? The silly idiot ... Well, if that's what she's gone and done, I'll have to stand by her.' She went on, 'I told the cops, not one of these girls went into this with their eyes shut. They knew exactly what they were doing. They weren't forced by anyone. The women here are loose, and it's not the men's fault. What are they supposed to do?'

Carol then hinted at 'some really bad stuff that I know about that's happened on the island that's a heck of a lot worse [than under-age sex] ... That's sick sex I'm talking about, between adults'. She was referring to adultery, it transpired, and as she uttered the word, Carol growled like an alley cat. 'Maybe I'm old-fashioned, but to me that's taboo,' she said. 'Some people don't care. They don't have morals.'

Like the others, Carol had a way of looking at you without meeting your eye. It was disconcerting. The women, with their permanently distant expressions, all seemed to be wearing masks. The outspoken ones laughed a lot, particularly at coarse jokes. They came across as both manipulative and naïve. They were not the type to be easily intimidated. They were feisty and opinionated: people who would be able to look after themselves.

But when conversation moved to the prospect of their male relatives being jailed, the women suddenly appeared vulnerable. 'I wouldn't want to be without the men,' Meralda said softly. Carol interjected, 'We're lost as hell without them.' Olive reckoned that, without the men, 'you might as well pick Pitcairn up and throw it away, because no one is going to survive ... We can't look after ourselves.' With the population already at crisis point, they claimed, if even a couple of men were locked up, there would be too few to crew the longboats and maintain the roads. Meralda questioned why Britain had singled out the able-bodied men. Olive said, 'There's no one who can replace them. They can't bring outsiders in to run the boats. They've no idea what to do.'

Of all those present, Olive stood to lose most. Among the seven defendants on the island, she counted her husband (Steve), her son (Randy), father (Len) and younger brother (Dave). The six men facing court in New Zealand included her other brother, Kay, and her two other sons, Trent and Shawn. Like certain women in the room, Olive also had connections with some of the alleged victims. She lamented, 'We live as one big family on this island, and nothing will ever be the same ... Right now, with all this going on, maybe they should have hanged Fletcher Christian.'

We had been at Big Fence for several hours, and no one was showing any sign of moving. The women, it seemed, were willing to stay for as long as it took to win us over. When we got our cameras out, they smiled, repeatedly. We could take as many pictures as we wanted.

We had not, though, been offered so much as a glass of water. It was a hot afternoon, and my tongue was sticking to the roof of my mouth. After a few more photographs, the six of us left. We would never set foot inside Steve Christian's house again. And some of those women would never again speak to us, or even acknowledge our existence.

The next day, two of those who had remained in the background invited us to talk to them privately. They did not wish their names to be used, and we met them on neutral ground; even so, the other islanders knew within hours that the interview had taken place.

The two were anxious to dispel the impression that Pitcairn was a hotbed of under-age sex. That had not been their experience when they were growing up, they claimed. I asked why they had kept quiet at Big Fence. 'There's no point in one little voice speaking up,' one woman replied. She told us that the Pitcairners usually avoided confrontation. 'If you're opposed to something, you tend to defer. We all have to get along together. We're a community. None of us can survive here on our own.'

The pair were already unpopular because they had not condemned the prosecution outright. One observed, 'If you try to give a balanced view, you're regarded as disloyal.' The other had been called a 'Pommy supporter' and 'puppet of the Governor' while going about her business in the Adamstown square.

The women believed that the sexual abuse had to be stopped. 'If it's as bad as it's been made out to be, then it needed to be addressed,' said one. She added, 'But I'm not condemning the guys. I don't personally want to see them jailed. I feel very sorry for the guys. Yet we're hurting for the girls. It's a double-edged sword.

We're all related. We're related to the victims. We're related to the offenders. And whatever decision is made, it's going to hurt everybody. The ripples are so widespread.'

One woman alluded to victims within her own family, and said that she admired the courage of those giving evidence. However, she went on, 'I don't know who's done what to whom, and I don't really want to know, because then I'll have to live with that for the rest of my life. You go to bed at night, you can't sleep for thinking about it. No one wants to take that on board.'

This off-the-record conversation, I remember, left me feeling like Alice in Wonderland. The women at Big Fence had promised us the real story. The two dissidents had given us another perspective. But theirs, too, was clouded by ambiguity.

Walking home, as we passed little groups of people chatting in the road, I was struck by a sense of life unfolding in parallel universes. On the surface, the island seemed innocuous, even banal. Then every so often you glimpsed something hard-edged and sinister. Which was the real Pitcairn?

CHAPTER 3

Opening a right can of worms

While exploring my surroundings in those early days before the trials began, I poked my head into the public hall, which doubled as Pitcairn's courthouse. A familiar figure gazed back at me: Queen Elizabeth II, in a hat and pearls, clasping a bunch of flowers. There were, in all, three photographs of the Queen at the front of the hall, as well as one of the Duke of Edinburgh and one of the royal couple. On the same wall hung a Union Jack, together with a Pitcairn flag and a British coat of arms.

It was an overt display of patriotism of a kind rarely seen nowadays, and it was in striking contrast to the anti-British sentiments expressed at Big Fence, where most of the women seemed to agree with Tania Christian, Steve's daughter, when she declared that 'Britain can go to hell as far as I care.'

The reality was that, until Operation Unique started, barely a subversive murmur was heard around Adamstown. Pitcairn was Britain's last remaining territory in the South Pacific, and its inhabitants were — as visitors often remarked — among Her Majesty's most loyal subjects. Until not so long ago, 'God Save the

Queen' was sung at public meetings, school concerts, even the twice-weekly film shows, while the British flag was flown on the slightest pretext. A number of islanders were MBEs, and several, including Steve Christian, Jay Warren and Brian Young, one of the 'off-island' accused, had been invited to Buckingham Palace.

Pitcairn's origins were emphatically anti-British, of course; in Fletcher Christian's day, there were few acts more heinous than mutiny. So it was an ironic twist when, a couple of decades later, the British Navy became the islanders' guardian and lifeline. The captains of British warships that patrolled the South Seas in the 19th century, keeping an eye on that corner of Empire, felt responsible for the minuscule territory. They developed a senti-mental attachment to the place and stopped there regularly, delivering gifts and supplies. They also found themselves settling disputes and dispensing justice in the fledgling community.

Russell Elliott, the commander of HMS *Fly*, who visited in 1838 after a difficult decade for the islanders, is recalled with particular fondness. Following John Adams' death in 1829, the Pitcairners had emigrated to Tahiti, where many of them died of unfamiliar diseases. The rest, after limping home, spent five years under the despotic rule of an English adventurer, Joshua Hill, who convinced them that he had been sent out from Britain to govern them. When Hill left, they were then terrorised by American whalers, who threatened to rape the women and taunted the locals for having 'no laws, no authority, no country'. Demoralised, the islanders begged Elliott to place them under the protection of the British flag, and he agreed, drawing up a legal code and constitution that gave women the vote for possibly the first time anywhere.

Pitcairn was now British, although for the next 60 years its only connection with the mother country was to be the visiting navy ships. In 1856, concerned about overpopulation, the islanders decamped again, this time to the former British penal colony of Norfolk Island; however, a few families returned, and the population — the origin of the modern community — climbed back to pre-Norfolk levels. Then in 1898 Pitcairn was taken under the wing of the Western Pacific High Commission, based in Fiji, which oversaw British colonies in the region. The WPHC did not trouble itself greatly with its newest acquisition: during a half-century of administrative control, only one High Commissioner visited — Sir Cecil Rodwell, who turned up unannounced in 1929.

In the meantime, the warships stopped calling, although the vacuum was partly filled, following the opening of the Panama Canal, by passenger liners. The captains and pursers of the merchant fleet took over the Royal Navy's paternal role, ordering provisions for the islanders, carrying goods and passengers for free, and donating items from their own stores.

With the liners came emigration, and intermarriage with New Zealanders. While strong ties were forged between Pitcairn and New Zealand, the relationship with Britain remained fundamental, and one of the colony's proudest hours came in 1971, when the Duke of Edinburgh and Lord Mountbatten arrived on the Royal Yacht *Britannia* and were transported to shore in a longboat flying the Union Jack from its midships. Official visits, to the disappointment of the locals, continued to be fleeting and infrequent, though.

There were, obviously, practical obstacles hindering more effective colonial scrutiny. Pitcairn, 3350 miles from Fiji, was hard to get to and even harder to get away from. In order to visit for 11 days in 1944, Harry Maude, a Fiji-based British official, had to be away from home for nearly six months. Communications were also primitive. Until 1985 the only way

36

to contact the island was to send a radio telegram by Morse code.

But logistics were not the only issue. Pitcairn was tiny and remote, with no resources worth exploiting, and — unlike, say, the Falkland Islands in the South Atlantic — it was of no strategic importance. When responsibility for the island was transferred from Fiji to New Zealand in 1970, the British Foreign Office reassured the High Commissioner to Wellington, who would now be supervising the colony, that 'the duties of the Governor of Pitcairn are not onerous'.

If recent governors heard that statement, they would sigh. In the past, their role as the Queen's representative on Pitcairn was mainly ceremonial, although they did have the power to pass laws and override the local council. But since allegations of widespread sexual offending came to light, the island has taken up an inordinate amount of their time.

While the scandal broke in 2000, the first hint of it actually came in 1996, with an incident that not only foreshadowed what was to follow, but set off a chain of events that led inexorably to Operation Unique, and the women of Pitcairn breaking their silence. An 11-year-old Australian girl living on the island with her family — let us call her Caroline* — accused Shawn Christian, Steve's youngest son, of rape. Her father reported it to the Foreign Office, and Kent Police, based in southeast England, offered to investigate.

Dennis McGookin, a freshly promoted detective superintendent and genial ex-rugby player, was given the case. Accompanied by Peter George, an astute detective sergeant, he flew to Auckland in

---

* **The names of all victims in this book have been changed.**

September 1996, where the pair met Leon Salt, the Pitcairn Commissioner, and the British official in charge of servicing the practical needs of the remote territory. (Among other things, the Commissioner organises the delivery of supplies.) The three men travelled to Pitcairn on a container ship, the *America Star*; arriving in a big swell, they descended the ship's wildly swinging Jacob's ladder into the waiting longboat.

Despite Pitcairn having been a British possession for 160 years, McGookin and George were the first British police to set foot there. They were nervous about their reception; yet the islanders, including 20-year-old Shawn, could not have been friendlier. Shawn readily admitted to having sex with Caroline, saying that it had been consensual. He showed them love letters from her, and even escorted them to the sites of their encounters, which included the church.

Caroline's family had already left the island. She had been questioned by police in New Zealand, and was said to be very tall for her age, physically mature and 'quite streetwise'. She had made the rape allegation after her parents caught her coming home late. Despite her age, the detectives decided just to caution Shawn for under-age sex.

The inquiry was over in a day, but the Englishmen had to wait to be picked up by a chartered yacht from Tahiti. They resolved to spend their time addressing the issue of law enforcement.

Pitcairn had never had independent policing. The island, theoretically, policed itself. The Wellington-based British Governor appointed a police officer, and the locals elected a magistrate, who was the political leader as well as handling court cases. Until Dennis McGookin and Peter George appeared, the only law was another islander.

The police officer in 1996 was Meralda Warren, a sparky,

extrovert woman in her mid-30s. (Meralda was one of the vocal participants at the Big Fence meeting.) While she was bright, Meralda had no qualifications for the position, nor had she received any training. 'Everyone on the island had a job, and that just happened to be hers,' says McGookin. Meralda was also related to nearly everyone in the community. If a crime was committed, she might have to arrest her father, or her brother, or one of her many cousins.

History indicated, though, that she was unlikely to find herself in that delicate situation. Her predecessor, Ron Christian, who had been the police officer for five years, had never made a single arrest. Neither had the two previous incumbents, of seven and 21 years' service respectively. No one had been arrested since the 1950s. The Pitcairners, it seemed, were extraordinarily law-abiding. All Meralda did was issue driving licences and stamp visitors' passports. To be fair, that was all her predecessors had done.

The magistrate in 1996 was Meralda's elder brother, Jay, later to go on trial himself. Jay, who was on the longboat when we arrived, had occupied the post for six years. Like Meralda, he had no qualifications or training, and was related to nearly everyone on the island. That could have been tricky, but fortunately for Jay, not a single court case had taken place during his time in office. And previous magistrates had been similarly blessed. The Adamstown court had not sat for nearly three decades.

Not that the locals would have feared the prospect of jail. The size of a garden shed and riddled with termites, the prison — a white wooden building — had never held a criminal. Lifejackets and building materials were stored in its three cells.

The British detectives were unimpressed with Meralda and Jay. According to Peter George, whom I interviewed in the Kent Police canteen in Maidstone in 2005, 'It was glaringly obvious, bluntly speaking, that their standard of policing was not really adequate.'

When the police left Pitcairn at the end of their ten-day stay, the islanders, including Shawn Christian, waved them off at the jetty. Soon afterwards, the Governor, Robert Alston, wrote a letter to the Chief Constable of Kent Police, David Phillips. Thanks to McGookin and George, he said, the matter — which 'had the potential to turn into a long, drawn-out and complicated legal case' — had been satisfactorily resolved. Alston added that the visit had 'had a salutary effect on the islanders and one which will remain with them for a long time'. As a token of gratitude, he sent Phillips a Pitcairn coat of arms, to be displayed at Kent Police headquarters.

Dennis McGookin was not so convinced about the salutary effect. Back in London, he informed the Foreign Office that the island needed to be properly policed. Britain was not prepared to fund a full-time police officer for a community of a few dozen people. Instead, it decided to recruit a community constable to travel to Pitcairn periodically and train the local officer.

In 1997 Gail Cox, who had been with Kent Police for 17 years, was selected for the job. Cox was easygoing and gregarious; she had worked in the traffic section, in schools liaison and on general patrol duties. The *Daily Telegraph* newspaper, which interviewed her before she left, reported that she was 'a practised hand at dealing with pub brawls and squabbles between neighbours', and 'highly regarded for her ability to defuse situations before they turn nasty'. Cox told the paper that 'if the line needs to be drawn, it will be drawn, and I am not frightened to draw it'. Those words were to prove prophetic.

Leon Salt, the Auckland-based Commissioner, accompanied Gail Cox to the island and introduced her to the locals. 'I put on this jokey persona, and they seemed to like that,' she told me when I met her in Auckland in 2006. 'They were very accepting of me. I became part of the community.'

Cox spent 12 weeks on Pitcairn, and established a good rapport with the islanders — perhaps too good. 'A lot of people are romanced by the place, and I fell for it,' she says. 'I saw the community through rose-coloured glasses. I thought it was this really idyllic place, and everybody was really nice.'

The Englishwoman was not scheduled to go back to the island until 1999. Between her visits, Pitcairn underwent some changes. A new Deputy Governor, Karen Wolstenholme, was appointed. Wolstenholme took more interest in the place than some previous incumbents, and visited soon after taking up her post. Another fresh face was Sheils Carnihan, a forthright Scot brought up in New Zealand, who started teaching at the school in early 1998.

Carnihan and her husband, Daniel, had been attracted by the idea of living in such an isolated spot. But they found life on the island numbingly ordinary. 'All the stuff we were told about it being such a wonderful, caring place turned out to be rubbish,' she told me in 2005. 'There's no real community spirit. And it's not exotic: it's like any small town. The only difference is you can't escape.'

From the start, the teacher had a nagging sense that something was 'not quite right' with the children. Six- to eight-year-olds in her class talked about boyfriends and girlfriends in a way that seemed, to her, precocious. When Carnihan's own family got to Adamstown, a boy slightly younger than her 11-year-old daughter, Hannah, told the girl, 'You're mine.' Another boy said the same thing to Carnihan's other daughter, nine-year-old Adie.

About halfway through her two-year posting, she overheard a snippet of conversation between two schoolgirls, aged 11 and 13, who were sitting on a verandah outside the classroom. 'You'll be 12 next week, you know you'll be old enough for it?' the older pupil asked her friend.

From what she had seen and heard, Sheils Carnihan already suspected that girls on Pitcairn were considered 'fair game' once they turned 12. This little exchange seemed to confirm that. 'I was appalled,' she says. 'The older girl knew her friend would be expected to have sex. She was making sure she understood what her birthday meant.'

Carnihan was particularly worried about two 13-year-old girls, Belinda and Karen, who seemed extremely troubled. They would 'talk about sexual things and then giggle and be secretive, or make quite blunt sexual comments', she says. Soon after the teacher's family arrived, Belinda jumped onto Daniel's knee and snuggled up to him in a suggestive fashion.

Once Carnihan had occasion to reprimand Karen for bullying, and the girl's emotional reaction startled her. 'She was really angry with me, she was crying and told me that I didn't understand. She said I didn't know what it was like to be made to be friends with someone or else they would beat me up.' Perturbed by these incidents, she confided in Meralda Warren, the police officer, and in the Seventh-day Adventist pastor, John Chan, the only other outsider. Meralda, she says, dismissed her concerns, while Chan's response was that 'the morals [on Pitcairn] are quite loose, but you don't do anything about these things'.

During Sheils Carnihan's stay, Chan, an Australian, was succeeded by a South African-born pastor, Neville Tosen. Before long, Tosen came to share her unease. 'But we didn't know what to do about it,' she says. 'We didn't have any evidence. It was just a gut feeling. And we didn't feel we could ask the girls yet.'

Even as Carnihan agonised about what to do, her own

daughters were forming friendships that would be crucial to this case. Hannah and Adie got to know Belinda and Karen, as well as other girls, and went on camping trips with them around the island. During those trips, the adolescents shared their secrets.

Just as for the Carnihans, Pitcairn was not what Neville Tosen had expected. Brought up on tales of a beacon of faith in the Pacific, he had been looking forward to ministering to a community of committed Adventists. However, when he arrived in late 1998 with his wife, Rhonda, he discovered that only a few people went to church — and they were not exactly glowing advertisements for the religion they professed to practise. Tosen was dismayed to learn that adultery was rife, and that churchgoers were also involved in dubious financial dealings. He delivered a few blunt sermons, 'and we weren't too popular as a result', he says. 'No one had ever told Church members to pull their socks up before. It caused quite a stir. But nothing changed.'

One islander warned him, 'There's more to come.' And Tosen feared that he knew what the man meant. 'I've been a teacher most of my life, and we immediately picked up mood swings,' he says. 'One day a certain student will be friendly to you, the next day totally withdrawn. It took me three months. I said, "Wait a minute, these kids are being abused." When I tried to talk about it, everyone just clammed up, including the kids themselves.'

He and Carnihan agreed to keep a careful eye on the situation; meanwhile, Tosen examined the birth records that were kept in the island secretary's office. They revealed a pattern: most Pitcairn women had their first child between 12 and 15. The pastor, who spoke to me at his home in Queensland in 2005, raised the subject at a meeting of the island council. One councillor, Tom Christian, who had four daughters, replied, 'The age of consent has always been 12, and it's never hurt them.' Neville Tosen, who had worked all over the Pacific, says, 'I remember getting quite hot and saying that even the Kanakas of Western Guinea had 16 as an age of consent. Tom got very angry. He called me a racist, and accused me of interfering in island politics.'

Tosen went on, 'Steve [Christian] also spoke up, saying it was their Tahitian culture and sometimes the girls couldn't even wait until they were 12. Everyone else at the meeting was very quiet, including Jay, who was mayor then. The only person who supported me was Brenda [Steve's sister]. She said, "Any man that does that to a 12-year-old deserves to be knackered."'

When Gail Cox returned to Pitcairn in October 1999 to conduct her second block of training, she found a community at war with itself. Things were very different from her first visit, and she was different, too. Dennis McGookin, her boss, had instructed her to be a police officer, not the islanders' friend.

The first problem she had to deal with was theft, particularly of government property, which she discovered was widespread and had been going on for years. Diesel fuel was siphoned off into quad bike tanks; timber, roofing iron and fuse boxes vanished as soon as they were unloaded at the wharf; cement for the slipway ended up as a swimming pool in someone's garden. Electrical equipment and a computer had been stolen. People jokingly referred to one Adamstown home, which was built entirely from pilfered materials, as 'Government House'. 'They don't see it as stealing,' one outsider told me later. 'In their minds, everything that arrives on the island is Pitcairn property.'

British officials ordered the policewoman to crack down. She questioned all of the islanders, and nearly everyone, even the elderly folk, owned up to something. One man confessed to stealing

NZ$20,000 (£7,500) from the co-operative store. At the suggestion of diplomats in Wellington, Cox offered the locals an amnesty, which they accepted. 'But they weren't happy with me challenging them like that,' she says.

Six weeks or so after Gail Cox returned, Sheils Carnihan's two-year posting was up. Two days before the family left, 13-year-old Hannah spoke to her mother, disclosing the explosive information that Belinda and Karen, her friends on the island, had confided months earlier. Both girls, allegedly, had been sexually assaulted by Randy Christian, the burly 25-year-old who was Steve's middle son. Carnihan straight away told Gail Cox, who notified British diplomats in Wellington as well as the Commissioner, Leon Salt.

According to Hannah, Belinda, in particular, was 'dying to tell' her mother about Randy, but could not summon up the courage. She even begged her friends to speak to her mother on her behalf, and wrote her a letter, which she then burnt. Belinda was anxious about damaging the friendship between her family and Randy's, and was sure her mother would not believe her. Hannah told Sheils, 'She wanted to write to her mum saying what had happened, and that she wanted it to stop. I mean, if her mum knew, maybe it would.' To which Neville Tosen comments, 'How the mother didn't already know about it — I've never answered that question. Because from my rather limited access to the girl, I was aware that she'd been interfered with.'

Gail Cox was supposed to leave in late November, on the same ship as the Carnihans, but agreed to stay on longer to deal with the fallout from the thieving revelations. By chance, then, she was still on Pitcairn when Ricky Quinn, a visitor from New Zealand, turned up.

The step-grandson of Vula Young, one of Pitcairn's matriarchs, Quinn struck Pitcairn like a tropical storm. A good-looking

23-year-old, he had past convictions for possession of LSD, morphine and heroin, which, to the local teenagers, gave him an exciting aura of danger. Quinn had brought with him a stash of marijuana, and he slotted straight in with the minority of islanders who formed the 'drinking crowd'.

A visiting policewoman on the alert; a handsome newcomer with drugs in his pocket; young girls tired of being preyed upon and itching to talk. All the elements were in place. Now all that was needed was the spark.

The drinkers got together most Friday nights. Two weeks before Christmas, Pawl Warren had a party. Most of the young people on the island attended. They stole some alcohol from their parents, and also some Valium tablets.

Gail Cox was still awake at 1.10 a.m. when Dave Brown, one of the partygoers, knocked on her door. 'There's trouble at Pawl's house,' Dave announced. At Pawl's, Cox found several frightened and sobbing youngsters, who admitted that they had been drinking. The police officer went on to Belinda's house, where Belinda and Karen had taken refuge; once inside, she got the feeling that Belinda wanted to tell her something. But when Cox tried to speak to her, the teenager's mother stood up and blocked out her husband, who was lying behind her. 'Not now,' she mouthed.

Belinda's mother took Cox aside and told her what the two 15-year-olds, both very distressed, had confided in her. They had been sexually assaulted by Ricky Quinn — and also, in the past, as Hannah had signalled, by Randy Christian. (A third girl, 12-year-old Francesca, had accused Quinn of similar behaviour.)

At 3 a.m. Gail Cox telephoned Dennis McGookin. It was Saturday daytime in England, and he was on his way to watch his favourite rugby team, Gillingham. Cox explained that she needed a specially trained officer to take a complaint from a child. 'I knew that wasn't practicable,' he told me over a pub lunch in Kent in 2005. 'I told her to take down a detailed statement, making sure an adult was present, and then fax that over to me.'

Cox also emailed Leon Salt to inform him about the weekend's events, including the allegations against Randy. As I later found out, Salt's response was swift. 'If we dig into this, we'll open a right can of worms, and we'll have every man on Pitcairn locked up for life,' he warned her.

CHAPTER 4

No amnesty

The morning after Pawl Warren's party, Gail Cox had an uproar on her hands. Ricky Quinn had admitted to assaulting Belinda and having under-age sex with Karen, and the Pitcairn community was furious with him. Cox had to intervene to prevent Karen's father from attacking him, and Quinn was so afraid for his safety that Cox installed him in the schoolhouse.

The islanders appeared disgusted by the New Zealander's behaviour. Yet within a few days, public opinion had swung in his favour. Brenda Christian, Steve's sister, told Cox that some of the locals were saying 'the girls had asked for it'. Olive Christian's sister, Yvonne Brown, who was visiting Pitcairn, claimed that Quinn was being 'treated disgracefully'.

Now the community turned against Gail Cox. Only Brenda Christian and her husband, Mike Lupton-Christian, supported her. The others — as well as resenting an outsider 'interfering' in their business — regarded Ricky Quinn as an extremely hard worker and therefore 'above the law'. Moreover, news had spread that the girls were accusing local men of similar offences — and who knew where that would lead? It was the start of the community resistance that was to characterise the sexual abuse case for years to come.

Despite opposition, Cox was determined to prosecute Quinn, and she scheduled a trial for ten days after the party. In the interim, she found herself undermined by the locals. On one occasion she agreed that Quinn could go home with Meralda Warren, the island police officer, and work with her on her wooden carvings. She was incensed to learn that he had spent several hours with Meralda's brother, Jay, the magistrate who would be deciding Quinn's fate, and had also gone fishing with another Pitcairner.

Jay, meanwhile, telephoned Quinn's father, Richard, in New Zealand and, according to Richard, informed him that he was 'looking after Ricky'. It subsequently emerged that Jay was hoping to buy a cheap motorbike that Quinn planned to import.

At his trial, Quinn surprised Gail Cox by denying the indecent assault against Belinda that he had earlier admitted. She discovered afterwards that he had acted on advice from Meralda, who knew that Cox was unwilling to call Belinda as a witness. Forced to drop the charge, the policewoman was livid: Meralda had betrayed her confidence and 'perverted the course of justice', she says. (Meralda denies it.) The complaint by Francesca had been dropped, at her parents' request. Quinn pleaded guilty to 'unlawful carnal knowledge' in respect of Karen, and was sentenced by Jay to 100 days in prison. As pre-arranged between Cox and British officials, the Governor, Martin Williams, then ordered him to be deported and remitted his sentence. In essence, he was let off.

A few days later, just before Christmas, the young New Zealander left on a ship, carrying two letters addressed to his parents — one from Meralda, the other from Yvonne Brown. Meralda apologised to Richard and Diane Quinn 'for this whole mess', saying their son had been 'a great asset to our island', and it was 'our loss that he is leaving'. Yvonne wrote, 'We have a British policewoman here and boy is she a "pig" . . . the policewoman blew everything out of proportion.'

Commissioner Leon Salt wrote to Meralda and Jay, admonishing them for unprofessional conduct. He asked Jay, 'If it is so difficult bringing a case against an outsider, how on earth could a case be brought against a local?' Of Meralda he inquired, 'How can we have any confidence that the law is being upheld on Pitcairn?'

With Ricky Quinn gone, Gail Cox was finally able to address the other matter that had arisen from Pawl Warren's party: the allegations against Randy Christian. And there was a second man in the picture. Belinda had approached Cox three days after the party to divulge that Randy's younger brother, Shawn, had also raped her. The Englishwoman urged her to let her mother know. Belinda said, 'Thank you for believing me.'

Cox informed Salt about the development relating to Shawn, and Salt phoned Randy and Shawn's father, Steve. 'Tell the boys to get a lawyer,' he told him.

Belinda's friend, Karen, had already left Pitcairn for New Zealand, where she would be finishing her schooling, as many local teenagers did at 15. Before departing, she had spoken to Gail Cox informally about one relatively minor assault by Randy. Cox had the strong sense that she had more to tell; however, that was all Karen would say — and she was desperate to get off the island.

Belinda had plenty to say, but she found it difficult to say it. It took her four hours to describe the first time she was raped, at the age of ten, and seven hours to recount all the incidents involving Randy and Shawn — including one where they allegedly raped her in tandem. That was the episode that was hardest to talk about. 'She was so halting, it was painful,' Cox told me much later in an Auckland café, speaking for the first and only time about her role in the case.

Never before in her career had the Kent constable interviewed a rape victim. Her investigative experience was limited to traffic accidents. But she was compassionate and sensible. She took an 'old-fashioned statement', making sure to record every detail. Then she asked Belinda and her mother to read the statement through and sign it. 'Those boys should hang for what they've done to my daughter,' her mother declared.

Belinda's father, though, feared for his family. 'I don't like this,' he told Cox.

She replied, 'Don't worry, it'll be alright.'

'No,' he said. 'There'll be trouble.'

He was correct. Belinda's allegations against Steve Christian's sons would blow the island community apart.

Cox sent the statement to Dennis McGookin in England in January 2000. Her work was over, but it would be another three weeks before she could get off the island. She was almost friendless in a hostile community — a fact that had become plain on New Year's Eve, when she stayed in, but someone, apparently assuming she would ring the bell in the square at midnight, had rigged up a surprise for her. One of the locals, Dennis Christian, took her place, and a load of fish oil and guts fell on his head.

Soon after midnight, as the fireworks went off, Cox heard an intruder trying to get in through her office window. They did not succeed, for she had taken to locking her doors and windows, after a document had disappeared. That person, presumably, had expected her to be in the square.

The community made it almost impossible for her to do her job. Jay refused to hold a council meeting to discuss policing, saying he was too busy. Meralda sabotaged her plans to stage a mock court case, as a training exercise. With black humour, Gail Cox told Leon Salt that she would 'need to wear a stab-proof vest' for the rest of her stay.

The night before she left, Cox went to see the pastor, Neville Tosen, and his wife, Rhonda. 'She put her head down and cried,' Tosen told me later, 'and said she was sorry she'd ever come to this such and such island, and she was never coming back.'

Cox says that, after that second visit, 'I felt dead inside … emotionally numb. I really loved that community and I cared about them. I felt so disappointed, so deeply betrayed.'

Two months later, in April, Belinda followed her off the island. Since making her statement, Belinda's situation had been uncomfortable, to say the least; now police learnt that Randy Christian, who had been living on and off on Norfolk Island, was intending to return. There were fears that she might not be safe once he was back, so Leon Salt made clandestine arrangements to book her on a ship to New Zealand. Belinda's father was bitterly opposed to the events she had set in train. As he said goodbye to her at the jetty, he told her, 'It'll be your fault if the islanders are arrested and the island breaks apart. If you go ahead with this, you'll never be able to come back to Pitcairn and you'll be out of this family.'

In Auckland, Belinda was re-interviewed on video by Karen Vaughan, the Wellington detective with child abuse expertise. The British Governor, Martin Williams, told the Foreign Office that she and her mother were adamant that they wanted charges brought. However, he forecast, 'Their determination could waver, as the family of the alleged perpetrators is very high in Pitcairn's informal pecking order.'

In Wellington and London, British officials were finally giving Pitcairn their undivided attention. Although they only had Belinda's and Karen's allegations so far, they seemed to recognise straight away that these hinted at a wider problem.

Martin Williams wrote to his superiors at the Foreign Office in London, 'I have no doubt that these are not unique cases. It is far more likely that they are a continuation of a pattern that has been going on for 200 years ... If we now launch charges against the two suspects, this may well kindle feuds and resentments about similar cases which have occurred over the years ... about which ... nothing has ever been done.'

It was clear that, notwithstanding this apparent inaction in the past, something had to be done now. A prosecution, however, would entail massive expense, and the logistics were almost unthinkable. As for a court case, with all the attendant publicity, it would be highly divisive, and potentially devastating, for the community.

Nevertheless, the allegations had to be investigated, and Kent Police agreed to take on the new inquiry. It would be funded by the Foreign Office, with detectives reporting to a Pitcairn Public Prosecutor, soon to be appointed. By April 2000 Peter George, who had worked on the 1996 Shawn Christian case, and Robert Vinson, a high-flying detective inspector in his 30s, were in Australia. Operation Unique was under way.

In Newcastle, 100 miles north of Sydney, the pair interviewed Shawn Christian, who was living there with his Australian partner; three days later, they flew to Norfolk Island to question his brother, Randy. Both men denied raping Belinda, but each of them admitted to having under-age sex with another woman, Catherine, who had moved to Auckland — and so began a domino effect.

In New Zealand, on their way home, George and Vinson decided to call on Catherine. They knocked on her door at about 8 p.m. What Catherine had to say took them aback. As Robert Vinson recalls it, she told them, 'I can't help you with what you're investigating, but I was raped myself when I was ten, by [Belinda's] father.'

Catherine gave detectives a lengthy statement, listing a number of Pitcairn men who she said had assaulted her during her childhood. She added that this was 'a common thing on Pitcairn', remarking, 'You won't get a girl reaching the age of 12 that's still a virgin.' Although the islanders all knew it went on, she said, it was seen as 'part of life', and no one complained about it.

According to Peter George, by now a detective inspector, that statement 'changed the whole course of it'. Back in the UK, he and Vinson told senior officials that a broader inquiry was needed. The reaction was lukewarm. In Wellington, the worry of Karen Wolstenholme, the Deputy Governor, was that a prosecution might fail and the island would become ungovernable. Britain was also apprehensive about likely criticism of its supervision of the territory. Wolstenholme warned in a memo, 'Pitcairn has a great deal of followers internationally and however the investigation proceeds I think we can expect negative publicity and condemnation for our actions.'

Ultimately, the Foreign Office had no choice: Catherine's allegations were too serious to disregard. The parameters of the wider inquiry were set. George and Vinson would trace every woman who had grown up on Pitcairn since 1980. Leon Salt, the Commissioner, gave them names and addresses. There were 20 women in all.

Salt, although helpful, was gravely concerned. In his view, the criminal behaviour was 'a cultural issue', he told Wolstenholme, probably involving 'most males on the island' and 'going back many generations'. If the men were brought to trial, he prophesied, 'the inevitable outcome will be the collapse of the community ... and its abandonment of the island'. Families, he said, 'would have great difficulty co-existing ... Healing differences between families would be impossible.'

The Governor's legal adviser proposed a radical solution: a general amnesty, conditional on offenders admitting their guilt. Karen Wolstenholme was among those who welcomed the idea, describing the situation as 'partly of our own making'. She commented that it was 'not altogether surprising if the community does not see the laws as applicable to them'. However, a decision was about to be taken over diplomats' and lawyers' heads.

Baroness Patricia Scotland, the British minister responsible for the Overseas Territories, had been following developments in the Pitcairn case closely. In May 2000 Governor Williams met with Scotland in London. He reported back that she wished the legal process to take its course, 'no matter the cost or the implications for Pitcairn's future'. 'No question of an amnesty,' Williams' hurriedly faxed note to Wolstenholme concluded, with those words underlined.

In August 2000 Peter George and Robert Vinson, the detectives assigned to Operation Unique, returned to the Antipodes to start tracing the 20 women on their list: most of them lived in Australia or New Zealand, with a few in Britain and the United States. Accompanied by two New Zealand detectives, Karen Vaughan, the sharp-witted willowy blonde with child abuse expertise, and Paula Feast, police worked at a hectic pace — flying into a city, hiring a car and often just turning up on people's doorsteps. Yet 'every door we knocked on,' George told me, 'we got the same response ... Every Pitcairn girl, and I mean every single one, a 100 per cent hit, had been a victim of sexual abuse to varying degrees.' Vinson remembers, 'We got disclosure after disclosure. It was staggering. It was like opening the floodgates for some of these women.'

The victims, by then in their late teens to late 40s, described incidents covering the whole gamut of abuse, from relatively minor assaults to violent rape. Some recalled blighted childhoods during which they were targeted by half a dozen or more Pitcairn men. The majority named more than one offender. In numerous instances, the abuse had started when they were three to five years old.

Most had kept their experiences to themselves, confiding in no one, not even their husbands. Now their husbands were hearing for the first time about the horrors of growing up as a girl on Pitcairn. Reliving it all was traumatic for the women, some of whom went into long-term counselling after telling their stories. Relationships and families were placed under enormous strain.

The first group of women told detectives about older victims, including friends and relatives, who had also been abused. Abandoning their 20-year time limit, police interviewed those women too, drawing a new line at 1960; before then, the relevant sexual offences law did not apply on the island.

By the end of the investigation, 31 victims — including two men — had spoken to police, naming 30 offenders, 27 of them native Pitcairners. Nearly every island male from the past three generations had been implicated; almost a third of those named were dead. Among the outsiders alleged to have taken part was a New Zealand teacher posted to Pitcairn in the 1960s, Albert Reeves.

Nearly a dozen women had made accusations against brothers, uncles or first cousins. But incest was not the only reason why Operation Unique at an early stage became, in Robert Vinson's words, 'very messy'. With every victim who was tracked down, the connections between those involved grew ever more excruciatingly tangled.

Belinda and Karen had been the first to disclose abuse. Next police spoke to Catherine, who claimed that Belinda's father had raped her. Detectives then questioned a woman called Gillian, who — as well as recounting her own experiences — suggested that they contact two sisters, Geraldine and Rita. The pair told police that they had been raped as little girls. Their assailant, they said, was Gillian's father.

Gillian's uncle was allegedly an offender also, and so was her grandfather. Her first cousin was a victim. So was a relation of Geraldine's and Rita's. Their brother was said to be an abuser.

As the layers of secrecy that had enclosed Pitcairn for decades were peeled away, a picture emerged of almost systematic abuse. Many families allegedly contained both offenders and victims. How would those families cope with the fallout?

News travels fast along Pitcairn's 'coconut grapevine'. Just from the engine noise, the islanders can identify the driver of any quad bike that passes their house. They claim to know what everyone else is up to, at any hour of the day or night. 'The jungle drum of Pitcairn is unbelievable,' says Mary Maple, a former teacher on the island.

The grapevine extends across New Zealand, Australia and Norfolk Island, and during 2000 it buzzed with stories of English police questioning Pitcairn women. So when Peter George and Robert Vinson arrived at Pitcairn aboard a 48-foot yacht in September, no one was in any doubt as to why they had come.

After interviewing the island women, detectives were questioning the men. They had already spoken to suspects in New Zealand and Australia. Now it was the turn of those who lived on Pitcairn. Vinson and George set up video-recording equipment at the Lodge, where they were staying, and invited the men in one by one. While they were questioning Dave

Brown, Len's son and Olive's brother, the power went off. Dave obligingly helped them to start up the generator, enabling them to resume his interview.

Despite the circumstances of their visit, the two Englishmen were received hospitably. 'We were greeted with open arms, even by the accused,' says Peter George, who recalls people 'bringing us fish and freshly baked cakes ... It was surreal.'

Beneath the surface, though, the community was in turmoil. When police began to ask questions, 'everyone got the fright of their lives', says Neville Tosen, the pastor. 'Some of the men were quite clear that they were going to go to jail. They started cutting firewood for their mothers and wives, laying in stocks for a long period. They thought they were going to be taken off the island.'

Terry Young, who had promised his father, Sam, on his deathbed that he would look after his mother, Vula, was especially anxious. So was Dave. 'I'm in trouble, no question,' Dave told several people. 'I'm going to jail ... They're going to lock me up and throw away the key.' Even men who were not under scrutiny were alarmed. One older islander told an outsider, 'They [the police] are going back 20 years. If they went back further, there'd be others.'

Elderly women who depended on their sons saw their whole future at risk, says Neville Tosen. 'One mother was telling her son to come clean. Another was beside herself with worry. She said, "The police have come, and they're going to take my boy away and hang him."'

While Tosen had long had his suspicions, he was appalled to find out the scale of the alleged abuse. Above all, he was at a loss to comprehend how the older women, the mothers and grandmothers, could have allowed it to happen. It seemed obvious to him that they must have known. He and Rhonda spoke to the matriarchs. 'We said to them, "Where were you when this was going on? You're the elders of the island, surely you must be unhappy?" And they replied that nothing had changed. One of the grandmothers said, "We all went through it, it's part of life on Pitcairn." She said she couldn't understand what all the fuss was about.'

The couple were feeling increasingly isolated. The communal satellite phone never seemed to be working when Tosen tried to reach Adventist regional headquarters. 'We couldn't get a message out of Pitcairn,' he says. 'We couldn't even contact our kids. I also wrote letters to the Church administration, saying I was concerned about things on the island. They never arrived.'

Accompanying police on their visit was Eva Learner, an English social worker, who was sent out to support the locals and assess the impact of the investigation. In a report to the Foreign Office, Learner said that the men were 'in [a] distinct state of shock and fear ... very weepy ... depressed and withdrawn'. Within the wider community, she encountered 'general disbelief ... about the nature and extent of the alleged abuse': the islanders could not grasp 'why the matters being investigated were of concern ... or how they might be damaging to young women and children'. Mothers, Learner wrote, 'professed difficulty in understanding that this had happened to their daughters'.

When the police departed, the locals thanked them. 'They thought we were going to go away and never come back,' says Peter George. Six months later, in March 2001, some of the team returned for more interviews; in October that year they visited yet again. By then, according to Karen Vaughan, who went on the two latter occasions, 'it was clear they wished we'd go away ... They thought we'd go there once and then realise how difficult, logistically, it was to pursue. The men just thought they could get away with it.'

By mid-2001 police had finished their inquiries and built up an extensive file of evidence. But Leon Salt was deeply sceptical, and predicted that they would get no further. Salt, who had opposed a prosecution from the outset, told detectives, 'The women may speak to you, they may give you statements, but you'll never get them to go to court and give evidence. You'll never get the Pitcairners to testify against each other.'

Now that I was on the island, with the trials starting shortly, I was about to find out whether or not he was right.

CHAPTER 5

The fiefdom and its leader

It was Tuesday morning, which meant that Pitcairn's one shop, situated on the main road, a couple of banana groves down from the square, was open for business. But you had to be quick, for it would be closed by 9 a.m. — and if you missed it, you had to wait until Thursday, when it opened for another solitary hour of trading.

The small shop was crowded, although probably no more than a dozen people were browsing the dusty shelves, stacked with tins of lambs' tongues and condensed milk. Olive Christian, a grandson on her hip, was inspecting bottles of bleach, while her mother-in-law, Dobrey, chatted animatedly in Pitkern to another elderly islander. Olive's son, Randy, and several other men who were about to go on trial stood around, laughing loudly at some private joke. They were mostly barefoot, and carried fishing knives in their belts. As Claire and I roamed the aisles, a figure in a baggy grey T-shirt leant over a freezer of meat. 'We don't like reporters here,' said Dave Brown, with a half-smile.

Short and stocky, with a bushy moustache, Dave was charged with 16 offences, including indecent assault and gross indecency with a child. But, like the other defendants, he was free on bail, and for now he was just gassing with his mates.

Behind the till, entering purchases in tattered account books labelled simply 'Dobrey' or 'Olive', was Darralyn Griffiths, née Warren. Darralyn had withdrawn from the case, claiming that she had been coerced into giving a statement; it was common knowledge, however, that she and Dave had had an 'affair' that began when he was 34 and she was 13. It had prompted many a sly wink at the time, although not from Dave's wife, Lea, or Darralyn's mother, Carol, whose main objection had been that Dave was married.

Also open that morning, again for the blink of an eye, was the minuscule post office, presided over by Dennis Christian. Dennis, the postmaster, was charged with three sexual assaults. Considerably more forthcoming than Dave, he explained to us politely that Pitcairn's once booming stamp business was in decline. 'Hardly anyone mails any more,' he said. 'Everyone jumps on the internet nowadays.'

The library, too, had unlocked its door for an hour, revealing a closet-sized space and shelves piled haphazardly with *Bounty*-related books, airport novels and travel guides. All could be borrowed indefinitely, without risk of a fine. Next door, the island secretary, Betty Christian, was sweeping out her office, which had another picture of the Queen on the wall. Outside, a few of the older women were swapping gossip on the wooden bench, which was known as the 'bus shelter'.

I had now met, or at least laid eyes on, all seven of the Pitcairn-based defendants: Randy Christian and Jay Warren on the longboat; Steve Christian in the pink bulldozer; Dave Brown at the shop; Dennis Christian at the post office; and Len Brown, our next-door neighbour, in his garden. The seventh man was Terry Young, who lived near the store with his mother, Vula. I had passed him in the main road, a large, lumbering figure. Terry was charged with one rape and seven indecent assaults.

Within two or three days of landing, we knew who was who among the 40 or so Pitcairn residents. (Half a dozen were away.) And they, of course, knew who we were: six despised reporters tramping around their island. We could not have avoided the locals if we had tried. Every time we stepped out, we bumped into them; often as we walked along the dirt tracks, they would overtake us on the quad bikes that they hopped on even for short trips. I was never sure whether to wave: it seemed rude not to, but sometimes the only response was an icy stare.

Not everyone was unfriendly. Outside the medical centre, I met a chatty, baby-faced Englishman: Mike Lupton-Christian, who is married to Brenda Christian, Steve's sister. Mike and Brenda had met in England, and had moved to the island in 1999 with her son from a previous marriage, Andrew. Mike, who had added Brenda's surname to his, appeared to be well suited to Pitcairn life. A former manager of retail and leisure services for the British military, he had a practical nature and was not afraid to get his hands dirty. But his attempts to muck in had so far been frustrated.

Mike, who was qualified to drive heavy machinery, was keen to use Pitcairn's big red tractor. He needed a local licence, but when he applied to the council's internal committee, chaired by Randy Christian, nothing happened. He made inquiries. Still nothing happened. 'They kept saying things like "After the next ship's been",' said Mike.

Vaine Peu, an amiable Cook Islander and the partner of Charlene Warren, told a similar story; Turi Griffiths, Darralyn's husband, also from the Cooks, could not get a licence either. As for Simon Young, an Englishman who had settled on Pitcairn with his American–Filipina wife, Shirley, he had managed to secure a licence — but only for an old blue tractor, and only for collecting rubbish, which was his job. Mike, Vaine, Turi and Simon had one thing in common: they were all outsiders. Meanwhile, two local teenagers were being trained to drive the big red tractor.

Those who could not drive the tractor, which was used in countless chores, most notably to plough the islanders' gardens, were dependent on those who could. And those who could were men who had been born on Pitcairn and spent their lives there: the 'Big Fence gang', as they were called.

If the big red tractor was a symbol of power from which outsiders were excluded, it was eclipsed by the longboat — Pitcairn's umbilical cord, and the sole preserve of Steve Christian and his followers.

Such is the aura surrounding the longboat that it was an anti-climax to discover that it is just a large open boat with an outboard engine and an aluminium hull. The boat's mystique dates from the days when it was made of wood, powered by oars, and hauled up the slipway by hand. But while less muscle may be required now, its significance has not diminished: without it, Pitcairn could not function. The boat — or boats, for there are two of them — collect people and supplies from the ships in all weather. Cargo, including fuel drums and timber, is lowered in a net; for those standing underneath, it can be dangerous work. The heavily laden vessel is then guided back into shallow, surf-lashed Bounty Bay, and it is their skill in accomplishing that task in the wildest conditions that gives Pitcairn's men their intrepid reputation.

The longboat slows down as it approaches the cove and pauses, with its motor idling. The engineer turns round to face the open sea; when he spots a suitable wave, he opens the engine up at full throttle. The boat is swept forward and *surfs* into the bay through a slender, rock-studded channel, skidding to a halt by the jetty — which, for passengers, is like landing at the bottom of a helter-skelter. There is little room for error, though, and islanders have been killed or seriously injured on occasions when the swell has seized the boat and dashed it against rocks.

For the local boys, joining the crew is a rite of passage, and they long to be skipper or coxswain, just like other boys dream of driving a train. The coxswain has the most kudos of anyone on the island. In an exceptionally macho society, he is the most macho figure of all.

Steve has been a coxswain since the age of 17. Randy — the only one of Steve's sons living on the island, and thus seen as the heir apparent to his political power — is a coxswain. So is Dave Brown. So is Jay Warren. Those men were always at the back of the boat, in charge of the tiller or engine. Len Brown, who in his day headed one of Pitcairn's leading families, was among the island's most capable engineers and coxswains.

Vaine Peu, Simon Young and Mike Lupton-Christian had all asked to be trained for the key roles. But the locals were unenthusiastic, for according to them, you had to have grown up on Pitcairn. So 'the boys', as they were known, continued to control the longboat — and, with it, the community's access to resources, its economy, its very survival.

As of 2004, Steve and Randy occupied the highest-ranking official positions on Pitcairn. As mayor, Steve was the community leader and chairman of the local council, which administers the island day to day. (The Governor wields overall authority.) Randy was chairman of the influential internal committee, which, among other things, allocated jobs. The pair also headed the unofficial hierarchy, for the real power base on the island was not the public hall, where the council met monthly, but Big Fence, Steve's family home, where important decisions were made by his 'inner circle', and the same men gathered on Friday nights for rowdy drinking sessions.

Only native-born Pitcairners were part of the gang. Outsiders, particularly men, were regarded with hostility and suspicion. Steve and his mates, it is said, saw them as a threat to their jobs, and to the cosy way they ran the place for their own benefit. 'They hate outsiders with a vengeance,' a former Pitcairn teacher told me. 'It's their rock, and they don't want anyone else on it.'

At the same time, Pitcairn is desperate for new blood. From a high of 227 in 1937, the population has dropped to around 50. Yet as much as newcomers are needed, they are feared and disliked, and also looked down on, because they lack the *Bounty* lineage. The locals ridicule them for breaking invisible protocols, and say of them in Pitkern that they 'cah wipe' — do everything wrong.

According to Mike Lupton-Christian, as an outsider, 'you're actually treated quite badly … They don't like people coming in with new ideas or doing anything better than them. You become very unpopular if you disagree with them.' Mike's house, built high on a hillside overlooking the Pacific, is derisively called 'Pommy Ridge' by other islanders.

In the past, some newcomers have turned up starry-eyed and then left, unable to deal with the hardships of Pitcairn life. But outsiders are expected to fail. Nola Warren, one of the matriarchs, says, 'People from outside can't live here. They'll never settle down. They wouldn't be able to cope.'

Some are not given much of a chance. Nicola Ludwig and Hendrik Roos, from the German city of Leipzig, were ideal immigrants: young, strong and fit, with small children. They loved the outdoors, and were eager to adopt a self-sufficient lifestyle. Nicola, whose family is now in New Zealand, told me recently, 'We went to Pitcairn for an adventure and to get away from the outside world. We were absolutely naïve about the place. We thought it was this little community full of greenies, where everyone is nice to each other.' Although Hendrik pitched in, particularly on the boats, the Pitcairn men ostracised him and subjected him to anti-German insults. Eighteen months after the family arrived, a container ship offered them a free passage to Auckland. They packed up and left.

Some islanders are treated as outsiders, too. Brenda Christian — small, but very strong and fit — is always in the thick of it with the men, flitting around the boats and shouldering heavy loads. Yet Brenda is not considered a true Pitcairner. She left the island at the age of 18 and did not return until 30 years later.

Like Brenda, Pawl Warren has an obvious rapport with island life. Shaven-headed Pawl, who gave us a fright when we first saw him on the longboat, left Pitcairn as a baby and grew up in New Zealand. In 1993, inspired by the Hollywood films about the mutiny, he moved back with his wife, Lorraine, and three children. Pawl describes the island as 'a magical place', but adds, 'It's not been easy to fit in here, because the hierarchy was already established.'

Even locals who have not lived away may experience similar problems. Tom and Betty Christian — elders of the Church, well travelled, well read and relatively affluent — are envied and distrusted by many of their fellow islanders. The couple, who have pioneered most of Pitcairn's commercial ventures and undertaken overseas trips sponsored by the Adventist Church, find themselves increasingly isolated in their own community.

In the early 1990s, in an effort to boost the population, British administrators introduced a scheme to attract young Norfolk Islanders. A few people took up the offer of work and cheap housing; none of them ended up staying for long. Even Randy Christian's wife, Nadine, who has married into the island's most powerful family, confides, 'The Pitcairners have their own way of doing things. I've had to try and do stuff the Pitcairn way, but it's very difficult.'

I asked Matthew Forbes, Karen Wolstenholme's successor as Deputy Governor, who, in his opinion, had been the last outsider to settle successfully on the island. After a long pause, Forbes suggested Samuel Warren, an American whaler who arrived in 1864.

Nadine, Steve Christian's daughter-in-law, had been one of the talkative women at the Big Fence meeting; for the time being, she and other female relatives were as close as we would get to Steve. However, we soon came to know his voice well, thanks to the VHF radio system that is Pitcairn's domestic telephone network. Every house and public building has a VHF unit. If you want to speak to someone, you holler out their name three times on the main frequency, Channel 16. (Only a first name is needed.) When they respond, the two of you switch to another channel — and everyone else adjusts their sets, in order to eavesdrop.

The radio in our living room crackled into life dozens of times a day, as the islanders got in touch with each other to chat or make plans. Steve's rich tones rang out frequently. He might have been about to go on trial, but he was, unmistakably, still in charge. It was he who made public announcements, informing people when the next ship would be calling, or telling them not to worry if they saw smoke rising — 'We're just burning rubbish.'

While Steve was elected mayor in 1999, unofficially he had been a leader since his teens. Good-looking, self-confident and powerfully built, he had always stood out: cleverer than his peers, a bit more articulate, and possessing a certain raw charm. His late father, Ivan, had been magistrate for eight years, and his mother,

Dobrey, remains a formidable woman. Despite a strict upbringing, Steve was described as a tearaway by a Royal Air Force team stationed on Pitcairn in the 1970s, when he was in his early 20s. In a report to British authorities, the team also tipped him as a 'future strongman', and said that he would be a 'severe loss' if he decided to emigrate. Steve never did leave, except for limited periods, and that has been a source of strength.

In his youth, Steve had the pick of the local girls, and he eventually married Olive Brown, Len's eldest daughter, although — much to people's amusement — he reportedly also had affairs with her two younger sisters; he was referred to as 'the man with three wives'. The birth of three sons, Trent, Randy and Shawn, consolidated his status. In addition, Steve has a multitude of talents. It is said of him that he can fix anything, and that he is a person who gets things done. A few years ago, when the islanders were heading home in a gale and rough seas, a rope got caught in the longboat's propeller. Steve dived overboard, cut the rope and was back in the boat before some of its occupants had realised anything was amiss.

On another occasion, when a woman was seriously ill, her husband contacted a specialist in California via ham radio. (Until recently, the only health professional on Pitcairn was a nurse.) The doctor proffered a long-distance diagnosis, and Steve, on his instructions, fashioned two surgical instruments which the nurse then used to perform an emergency procedure. The woman believes that Steve saved her life. 'It was a miracle, and he was part of that miracle,' she says.

Steve himself walks with a limp, the legacy of a teenage accident that has required two hip replacements. Nevertheless, he is physically equal to Pitcairn's tough environment. He is said to be good company, and an entertaining host. He has something else, too — an 'X-factor', one outsider calls it, saying, 'You can feel it as soon as he walks in. He carries himself like a leader.'

The Adventist Church filmed a series of documentaries about Pitcairn; watching them while on the island, I was struck by the way that Steve dominated nearly every scene — leading a group of young men off on motorbikes to hunt wild goats; debating the design of a new longboat with New Zealand engineers; driving around in a Mini Moke, the island's one car; and giving the signal for Christmas presents to be distributed in the square. Steve even built the Pitcairners' coffins.

To his fellow islanders, he was the linchpin of the community. Nothing happened without Steve's say-so, and if he was away temporarily, on Norfolk Island, for instance, the others would still consult him. 'Steve liked to be boss,' says Tony Washington, a New Zealander who taught on Pitcairn in the early 1990s. 'He had more say than Jay [Warren], although Jay was magistrate. When we went on a trip to Henderson [a neighbouring island], it was Steve who decided when we should come back.'

Neville Tosen describes him as 'the evil genius who ruled Pitcairn'. He adds, 'And yet I came to recognise him as a person of ability. He was smart. He understood the island and the way things were done. He could think his way through problems and come up with a solution. He was the brains of the place.'

Others say that Steve surrounded himself with yes-men and treated Pitcairn as his personal fiefdom. He would turn up late to communal dinners, knowing that no one else would start eating without him. 'Pitcairn was an oligarchy,' says Leslie Jaques, who has succeeded Leon Salt as Commissioner. 'Steve ruled, and everyone else did what they were told. The way the community was run was medieval.'

There was an in-crowd, but not everyone in it was equally favoured. The island's pecking order was quite intricate, it seems, and was reflected in the jobs that people did, and even by their positions in the longboat. As one British official observes, 'It was almost like an Indian caste system. You had your place in society, and you never moved from it.'

For six decades the mainstay of the Pitcairn economy was stamps. First issued in 1940, they became the cream of many a collection, coveted because of the island's colourful history and exotic location. So popular were they, in fact, that within a few years the community was able to build a new school and, for the first time, hire a professional teacher from New Zealand.

The proceeds from stamps went into a Pitcairn Fund that until a few years ago met the island's running costs, as well as subsidising freight charges and the price of diesel fuel and building materials. The fund — latterly bolstered by sales of coins, phonecards and the .pn internet domain suffix — enabled the islanders to travel to New Zealand for further education and health care, and be paid salaries for carrying out 'government jobs'. Capital items, such as longboats, tractors and generators, have always been provided by Britain, which is also responsible for maintaining the infrastructure.

As stamp collecting and letter writing fell out of fashion, the fund dwindled. Thanks to British subsidies, Pitcairn has nonetheless continued to enjoy full employment, in a manner reminiscent of a Cold War-era Communist state. The government jobs, equivalent to a public service bureaucracy, include deputy postmaster, trainee tractor driver, second assistant forester and keeper of John Adams' grave. While there may be a whiff of absurdity about some of the jobs, who gets what is a serious matter, for the small stipends — NZ$500 (£200) a month for the island's engineer, for instance — can go a long way on Pitcairn. And, until recently, who got what depended on your connections.

When Steve Christian's daughter, Tania, arrived for an extended visit, she was promptly given two positions: museum keeper and librarian. Simon Young, the English newcomer, who had a horticulture degree and wanted to work in biosecurity, was made garbage collector. That had been the job of Hendrik Roos, the German settler. His wife, Nicola Ludwig, had been gardener of the cemetery.

Steve was not only mayor; he was chief supervising engineer — probably the most significant post on Pitcairn. (Randy was his deputy.) He was also the island's dentist, having completed a course in New Zealand that qualified him to perform extractions. He was the radiographer. He was the number one tractor driver. He was the explosives supervisor, and a heavy machinery operator. He was a longboat coxswain. Steve had eight paid jobs.

The Christian clan has traditionally been the aristocracy on Pitcairn, but not all Christians are equal, and in Steve's day his branch has been pre-eminent. The Warren clan also plays a prominent role in island affairs, securing some of the best jobs for family members. Despite lacking Steve's force of personality and charisma, Jay is regarded as his main rival for power.

The mayor — or magistrate, as the office was formerly called — has always been a man. Betty Christian once nominated a woman. 'Everyone laughed. They thought it was the biggest joke they'd ever heard,' she says. Many women thought so too. When an outsider asked one older islander, Nola Warren, *why* a woman could not be in charge, she replied, 'Because it's never been, and it just can't be.'

One of Pitcairn's attractions is that people do not pay tax. Instead, they carry out 'public work': painting buildings, repairing the slipway, clearing the roads of undergrowth. They can go fishing if the weather is good, or tend their gardens and orchards. The islanders grow, among other things, mangoes, pineapples, passionfruit, strawberries, avocadoes, watermelons, pumpkins, peppers and sweet potatoes. Everything thrives in the volcanic soil and semi-tropical climate.

The locals trade their produce with the crews of passing ships, swapping fruit and fish for items such as timber, frozen chickens and cans of Coke. Their most valuable commodity, however, is the wooden carvings to which they devote most of their free time. The carvings are sold to passengers on the cruise ships that visit Pitcairn during summer, and also through the islanders' websites. A *Bounty* replica can fetch US$120. Not long ago, on a cruise ship, a Pitcairn family made US$10,000 in one day.

Souvenirs account for three-quarters of the Pitcairners' earnings. Most homes have a workshop equipped with power tools, and the carvings — while no longer produced by hand — are still made from the richly veined miro wood harvested locally or on Henderson Island, 15 hours away by longboat. (Henderson is one of three other islands, all uninhabited, in the Pitcairn group; the other two are Oeno and Ducie.)

Most of the Big Fence crowd are drinkers. For a long time Pitcairn was a dry island — in theory, at least. Alcohol is banned by the Seventh-day Adventist Church. In 1997 the locals voted to legalise its importation, but a licence is still required and drinking in public remains outlawed; in the outside world, Pitcairn retains its teetotal image. You cannot buy alcohol on the island, any more than you can buy cigarettes or ice cream or a carton of milk.

Seventh-day Adventism replaced John Adams' idiosyncratic brand of Anglicanism in 1876, after the American-based Church posted a box of literature to Pitcairn, then dispatched a missionary to argue its cause. The islanders were baptised in a rock pool, and since pork was now a forbidden food, they killed all their pigs — pushed them off a cliff, so the story goes.

Adventism, an evangelical Christian denomination, has 14 million members worldwide. Followers believe that Saturday is the Sabbath, and that the Second Coming of Christ is imminent; they are expected to dress modestly, and avoid shellfish as well as pork; tobacco is another prohibited substance. Dancing, gambling and the theatre are frowned on, along with works of fiction and music other than hymns.

The Seventh-day Adventist Church has been a generous benefactor to Pitcairn, raising funds for the community and sending out teachers and pastors. It is not clear, though, how deeply the faith implanted itself, or to what degree the islanders ever observed its precepts. Certainly, they called themselves Adventists, and until a few years ago the pews were always crowded on Saturdays. But going to church was, like elsewhere, the done thing, and on Pitcairn the church was also very much a social focus.

Outsiders were struck by the locals' earthy language, peppered with innuendo and swear words, and by their relaxed sexual morals. Roy Sanders, a New Zealand teacher, described a Sabbath service in the 1950s that was punctuated by heckling and jeering, and 'intermittent spitting out of the windows'. Ted Dymond, a visiting British official, reported in the 1970s, 'The lengthy and rambling sermon was soporific and I counted seven islanders in deep slumber.' Some believe that Pitcairn's history has been characterised by cycles of moral decay and religious renewal. Others are doubtful about the renewal part.

Nowadays Seventh-day Adventism is no longer a spiritual anchor. Yet Saturday is still 'the Sabbath', and everybody has a quiet day. Even some of the least pious islanders continue to pay a tithe, and the pastor is deferred to, outwardly at least. Council meetings, market days and communal meals begin with a prayer. 'They all look so bloody sincere, with their heads bowed,' remarks Bill Haigh, an Englishman who has spent long periods living on Pitcairn, modernising its communications on behalf of Britain.

'Sacrificial living', it seems, has never been embraced by local people, despite being a central plank of Adventism. Carol Warren has five freezers, and most households own at least three, among an array of white goods and electrical appliances: fridges, deep-fryers, microwaves, video cameras, stereo systems, DVD players, television sets, video recorders. The Pitcairners are defensive about their material possessions — more so, perhaps, than about any other aspect of their lives. It certainly feels odd, in such a remote, rugged spot, to find homes stuffed with the emblems of Western-style wealth. Paradoxically, the houses themselves are relatively basic, with concrete floors and unpainted walls, and the furniture is plain.

The multiple freezers and fridges, the islanders point out, are a necessity — and after opening a bag of flour infested with weevils, I could see what they meant. Moreover, the hoarding instinct is ingrained, for no one is ever quite sure when — or if — the next ship will come. The video and DVD players, too, are crucial in a place with no television, cinema or theatre, and no restaurants, pubs or cafés. Such goods are also status symbols, though, and in that respect Pitcairn is not much different from anywhere else. I suppose I had expected, rather naïvely, to find people living the simple life.

Carol told Sue Ingram, the Radio New Zealand reporter, 'We've had it really good for a long time, and I don't think a lot of our people in New Zealand could live like we do. We do live quite extravagantly. I have everything they have, plus.'

Pitcairn has been fairly prosperous for decades. Roy Sanders, the teacher in the 1950s, was taken aback to find children with gold watches and expensive fountain pens. A British official in that era reported that the islanders were reticent about their earnings; however, he added, 'Judging from the manner in which some of them journey up and down to New Zealand — even to England — they cannot be too badly off.'

Not everyone benefits equally from the spoils of the island. Take the share-out, which is one of Pitcairn's more charming traditions. Based on an old naval custom, it takes place in the square and is used to distribute the catch from a communal fishing trip or goods donated by a ship. The fish (or flour, or clothing, or whatever) is divided into piles equivalent to the number of households. Everybody turns their back, except for one person, who points to a pile; another person, facing away, calls out the name of a family. The process is repeated until every family has been allocated a ration — with everyone, in theory, receiving equal.

Mike Lupton-Christian told us that the share-out had become a joke, with Steve Christian and Dave Brown often siphoning off the prime items beforehand: bottles of beer, for instance, or the best cuts of meat. As Mike put it, 'The stuff is shared out equally, only Steve's family gets a bigger share.' It was the same when a ship wanted to buy a consignment of fish or produce. 'The order only goes to those in the know,' he said.

As for the general dishonesty that Gail Cox, the Kent constable, had tried to address, Mike's belief was that 'everyone in the community had something on everyone else ... Nobody was prepared to shop anyone else ... It was a bit like the sexual abuse thing.'

The 'sexual abuse thing' was now plunging the island into its worst crisis since the mutineers' day. Pitcairn's leading men stood accused of paedophilia, a crime so abhorrent that it sometimes causes vigilante-style reprisals. Not only had they preyed on children, it was alleged, they had done so within their own small, introverted community, targeting girls who lived a few doors away — the daughters of cousins and neighbours, or, in some cases, family members.

If a prosecution was launched, though, the island's name would be blackened, and relationships in this most interdependent of societies ruined. The community was already in a precarious state, thanks to the fragile economy and falling population. Could it survive this latest and most devastating blow? And how would fans of the legendary *Bounty* island react?

CHAPTER 6

The propaganda campaign
starts

By mid-2001 Pitcairn was making international headlines, although the scale and true nature of the problem uncovered by English police were not yet known. '"Mutiny on the Bounty" island faces first trial in history,' proclaimed *The Independent* in London, trumpeting a story written by one of my colleagues. 'End of a legend as Pitcairn Island meets the modern law,' announced the *New Zealand Herald*.

None of the stories running then quoted anyone on Pitcairn. The islanders, not slow to use the media in the past, refrained from making any public comment — at least for the time being. Others spoke up on their behalf, however, and chief among them was Dr Herbert Ford, an ordained Seventh-day Adventist minister and director of the Pitcairn Islands Study Center, located on the campus of Pacific Union College, California.

'Herb' Ford had worked in public relations and as a journalism professor at the college, which was funded and administered by the Adventist Church. He had a lifelong fascination with Pitcairn: he had met Tom and Betty Christian in California in the 1960s and visited the island briefly in 1992; he had also raised money for it, securing donations from, among others, Robert Redford and Jordan's late King Hussein. After he retired, the college gave him some office space for a study centre, and when the child abuse story broke, Ford made himself available to media worldwide. He spoke well and could spin a good quote. He also communicated with the island weekly by ham radio, which qualified him to pronounce on the community's 'mood'.

In 2001 he told me, referring to the investigation, that 'the sum of it all is pure speculation, and whether you want to call it rape, I don't know'. He added, 'There's been an awful lot of Polynesian blood put into the island. The girls resorted to sexual activity at a very early age, and that was carried on by the women into Pitcairn.' Ford claimed that Gail Cox, the English constable, had 'ingratiated herself' with the locals, 'wheedling' information out of the girls during informal 'kitchen table' chats, and precipitating a 'sweep' by police of Pitcairn women. In his view, it would not be surprising if the inhabitants of a remote tropical island were 'out of harmony with the laws of downtown London'.

Also quoted in those early days was Glynn Christian, a former television chef and author of a biography of Fletcher Christian, *Fragile Paradise*. Accessible and articulate, Glynn was a seventh-generation descendant of Fletcher, and had grown up in New Zealand. In a telephone interview, he spoke of the 'goodness and niceness' of the Pitcairners, whom he met in 1980 while conducting research on the island, and, in a remarkable observation, said that 'to be there makes you think there's no such thing as original sin'. Glynn ascribed the current crisis to British neglect, which he claimed had left the Pitcairners in a social timewarp. In his opinion, the Pitcairn men had known no better. 'It's not wilful badness,' he said. 'You can't punish a child for doing something wrong if he's not been told that it's wrong.'

* * *

Once the British Foreign Office had resolved to act on the child abuse allegations, it set about addressing a problem identified by its advisers many years earlier: Pitcairn's lack of a legal infrastructure, which, given recent developments, needed to be rectified swiftly. A series of appointments were made, among the most important of which was the naming of Simon Moore as Pitcairn Public Prosecutor. Moore was already Crown Solicitor for Auckland, the chief prosecuting counsel in New Zealand's largest and most crime-ridden city; now he was to take on a similar job for an island of a few dozen people.

Christine Gordon, a senior colleague, was appointed Deputy Public Prosecutor. The pair regarded themselves as a formidable team. Moore, an effervescent character with a mane of golden-brown hair, rode with the Auckland hunt and belonged to that city's exclusive Northern Club. He was a master of courtroom theatrics. Gordon, a petite blonde with a ferocious grasp of detail, smiled sweetly while asking the killer questions.

Having prosecuted a previous case of child abuse in a closed community, Gordon correctly predicted that the allegations would proliferate. By mid-2001 the two lawyers had enough evidence to charge 13 men; Moore, though, paused to consider another factor — the public interest. How would a prosecution affect the tiny, isolated society? Would it really collapse if men were put in jail? He and Gordon realised that they could not answer these questions while sitting in an office block in central Auckland. They would have to make the journey to Pitcairn, to see for themselves how the community operated.

In October 2001, accompanied by Karen Vaughan, the Wellington-based detective, the prosecutors travelled to Pitcairn on a container ship, the *Argentine Star*. The Deputy Governor, Karen Wolstenholme, was already on the island, as were several new resident outsiders, British authorities having belatedly acknowledged the need for some external supervision. Two New Zealand social workers were watching over the half-dozen children, while two British Ministry of Defence police officers — known as MDPs and licensed to carry firearms — were monitoring the suspects and keeping communal tensions in check. The two pairs, sent out on rotating three-month tours of duty, were resented by the majority of islanders, who grumbled that Pitcairn had become a police state and accused Britain of planting spies in their midst.

Standing on the deck of the *Argentine Star*, Christine Gordon had 'a knot in my stomach when I saw the dot on the horizon, because we didn't know what the situation would be there'. As it turned out, and just as Peter George and Dennis McGookin had experienced, the Pitcairners went out of their way to be friendly, even if these latest visitors found them a little overwhelming at first. Simon Moore recalls, when the longboat came out, 'the assortment of humanity, wearing different coloured T-shirts, some carrying huge frozen fish on their shoulders, clambering aboard just like pirates and swarming around the ship in all directions'. He also observed the efficiency with which the locals stocked up on duty-free cigarettes and alcohol. 'We'd been told they didn't drink,' says Moore, whom I interviewed in his oak-panelled office in 2005. 'So I was astonished to see the quantities of booze unloaded, and boxes of eggs and frozen meat, and anything else you can imagine — wads of cardboard, mattresses, chairs — all dropped down into the longboat.'

The next morning the visitors were invited on a community fishing trip. At one point Simon Moore found himself in a small boat driven by Dave Brown, one of the alleged child abusers. Dave instructed him to lie flat, then he revved up the engine and the boat shot forward. 'I looked up and saw that we were hurtling towards this solid rock face,' says Moore. 'Just as we were about to hit it, or so it seemed, the swell dropped and exposed the mouth of a cave.' Dave deposited him on a patch of sand deep inside the cave, where the other visitors had already been dropped off. 'I thought perfect,' says Moore, rolling his eyes. 'If they wanted to abandon us, this is the way to do it.' A little later, though, they were picked up, and everyone proceeded to fish for a local species, nanwe. Despite the rough seas, the islanders hauled up hundreds of fish.

The catch was destined for a 'fish fry' that afternoon at The Landing, in celebration of Dave's birthday. The fish were cleaned and the guts thrown off the end of the jetty, attracting a reef shark, which Randy Christian, another of the accused men, caught. Then, as one witness tells it, 'Randy got a sledgehammer and hit the shark so hard that the hammer went right through its head and came out the other side. The shark was writhing in agony, the women were gagging, and Randy just stood there grinning, with the bloody sledgehammer in his hand.'

By coincidence, it was also Simon Moore's birthday; so after regaling Dave with a rendition of 'Happy Birthday', the Pitcairners sang 'Happy Birthday' to their Public Prosecutor. Dave later complained to someone, 'That prick Moore, we put on a birthday party for him the first time he came, and I thought he'd go easy on us as a result of that, the bastard.'

The fishing expedition was the first of numerous communal events, including dinners and sports days, that were staged for the visitors' benefit during their fortnight on Pitcairn. At a tennis tournament, Karen Vaughan found herself partnering Dave in a doubles match. Simon Moore played cricket in a team skippered by Dave, and at a picnic later on chatted amicably with Randy, the rival captain. The prosecutors also attended a 'cultural day' at the school, where Christine Gordon was taught basket weaving, and Steve Christian, the mayor and another child abuse suspect, showed Moore how to carve a wooden dolphin.

That must have been weird, I say. Moore leans back in his hair, hands behind his head. 'Yes. But then everything was weird on that trip. Normally we never see the people we're prosecuting until we get into court, but here we were mixing with them quite closely.'

Some of the outsiders on the island voiced cynicism about the community activities, saying they had never seen the Pitcairn people display such unity and goodwill. Then, just before the visitors left, the islanders sang them their traditional farewell song, 'Sweet Bye and Bye', in the public hall. Moore says, 'I was genuinely quite moved by it, but others, apparently, were not, because they saw it as yet another show for us.'

While they enjoyed sampling the local cuisine and learning new sports such as Pitcairn rounders, the lawyers had serious business on the island. At a public meeting soon after he arrived, Simon Moore explained the role of a public prosecutor, emphasising that his job was to serve the islanders' interests. Privately he was optimistic that the men would plead guilty, enabling the matter to be settled with minimum damage to family relationships. The locals warmed to Moore, a man of considerable natural charm. But, according to one person present, 'they didn't get it ... They saw him as their friend, even the suspects did. When he talked about the good of the island, they thought that meant that nothing would happen to them, whereas he was talking about the law being upheld.'

Moore had been told there was a widespread belief that the alleged crimes were minor, even though police had spelt out exactly what they were investigating. At the meeting, therefore, he took care to stress that some of the offending was exceedingly serious. 'I could see some of the older people gasp,' he says, 'and I was told later that a number of islanders were quite upset.'

During their stay, he and Christine Gordon spoke to nearly every Pitcairn resident. Many expressed fears for the community's future if men were imprisoned. But no one suggested that the allegations were untrue, and the overwhelming message the lawyers received was that prosecutions ought to go ahead. This was unexpected, since the islanders had previously resisted the notion that sexual abuse even existed, let alone needed to be tackled. Yet according to Moore, 'The feeling was, if these are crimes elsewhere in the world, then we shouldn't be treated differently. That came through really loud and clear. It was also said that if they would attract prison sentences elsewhere, then Pitcairn should be no exception.'

Only one person dissented, and that was Len Brown. Len was concerned because, as he saw it, women were hopeless in the longboats. In his quaintly accented English, he told Moore, 'The island will be doomed, Si-*mon*.'

Never before in his long career had Moore had 'a more profound feeling of the difficulty and significance of the decision we had to take'. It was not until February 2002 that he finally made up his mind. The prosecution would go ahead. He informed the community in a videotaped message that reached the island in May. Moore said he would not be laying charges, however, until the vexed issue of a trials venue had been resolved.

Faced with an indefinite period of limbo, the Pitcairners decided it was time to fight back.

In August 2002 the *New Zealand Herald* ran an article across two pages, quoting three 'former Pitcairn Islanders' living in Auckland. The three said that their cousins on the island were frustrated by the media coverage, which in their opinion was based exclusively on information from the British. One of the interviewees, 'Alex', who revealed that he had been questioned by police, suggested that Britain was trying to rid itself of its financial obligations. He also told the *Herald* that, on Pitcairn, teenage sex was common and even some ten-year-olds were sexually active. His companion, 'Sarah', said that Britain was partly to blame for this, as it had failed to provide the Pitcairners with guidance. The third interviewee, 'Mary', claimed the islanders could not be judged as if they lived in New Zealand. 'Different countries have their own way of life,' she explained.

This article, presenting the child abuse case as a David and Goliath contest, set the tone for the way it was reported until the trials two years later. Almost every news report reproduced the Pitcairners' claims of a culture of under-age sex, and a plot by Britain to shut down the island. It was the mutineers' descendants versus the big bad colonial power — and the fact that the alleged victims were Pitcairners too, with an equally impeccable lineage, was rarely mentioned.

From mid-2002 the islanders were able to use email, and they joined the propaganda campaign, corresponding regularly with their supporters and with journalists whom they believed to be sympathetic. They also bombarded Richard Fell, who had replaced Martin Williams as the British Governor, with angry emails.

Meanwhile, the other parties were quiet. Simon Moore was unwilling to comment until charges were laid, British officials were cautious, and police were not talking. Neither were the complainants, of course. As for those Pitcairners who, as it later turned out, were horrified by the men's alleged behaviour, such as Pawl Warren and Brenda Christian, they were keeping their own counsel.

That left the accused men and their families in a position to monopolise the debate, and to assert, without fear of contradiction, that Britain was getting itself into a lather about youthful canoodling behind the coconut palms. The men, who had not yet been named, made public statements about the case, with few outsiders aware that they had their own agenda. 'Alex', for instance, was Brian Young, later to be charged with serious sexual offences. 'Sarah' was his Norwegian-born wife, Kari, who had lived with him for 15 years on Pitcairn.

Steve Christian did not bother with pseudonyms. Instead, he exploited his position as mayor to attack the British government and the prosecution. He did not disclose — and few people outside the island realised — that he was himself directly affected by the legal action. Another man in his situation might have stepped down. Not Steve. Already in October 2000, shortly after being interviewed by police, he had flown to London for a gathering of leaders of the British Overseas Territories. Baroness Scotland was among seven British ministers who attended the meeting, which included drinks parties and official receptions. Steve also travelled to Chicago in his official capacity, and in May 2002, soon after Simon Moore's announcement that he planned to lay charges, gave a speech to a United Nations seminar in Fiji on decolonisation. Steve inveighed against the delays in the criminal case, calling them 'an abuse of process', and criticised Britain for neglecting the island and its infrastructure. 'Must we hijack a yacht, or be invaded like the Falklands, to get attention?' he inquired theatrically.

On his way home via New Zealand, Steve was due to see Richard Fell, a courteous, unflappable man who had become the islanders' principal *bête noire*. When Fell refused to allow him to bring a lawyer, the meeting was cancelled. Steve called it 'yet another example of the pattern of high-handed behaviour exhibited by the Governor's office'.

He did not seem worried about the impending prosecution. 'I think Steve thought that nothing was going to touch him,' says one British official.

A key figure behind the scenes was Leon Salt. In theory, the Commissioner was just a British employee; in practice, he was enormously powerful. He ordered supplies for the islanders, and arranged for them to be delivered. He organised passenger berths on container ships. All mail to and from Pitcairn passed through Salt's hands, as did email messages, via a central server in his Auckland office.

Salt — tall and rangy, with long, curly hair and a big moustache — had Pitcairn blood; he was well educated, somewhat alternative in his lifestyle. He owned a smallholding north of Auckland and had a passion for vintage cars. He was fiercely attached to the island and its inhabitants, having spent three years teaching on Pitcairn before becoming Commissioner in 1995. He knew the individuals, their relationships, their feuds and affairs. He knew precisely how the tiny, squabbling community functioned.

While some locals saw the softly spoken Salt as their champion, others claim that he favoured certain families, particularly Steve Christian's. If Steve wanted an item loaded onto the next ship leaving Auckland, it would get on, some islanders say, at the expense of goods belonging to others. Leon Salt was good friends with Steve, who called him 'Boss', and with Steve on Pitcairn and Salt in Auckland, it is said, the pair ran the island between them. In 2002 they deported an English journalist, Ben Fogle, who had arrived by yacht. Salt, who was visiting, spat at Fogle's feet and would not permit him beyond The Landing. 'We don't want your sort spying on us,' he told him.

When Operation Unique started, Salt was helpful. Police worked out of his office, at his invitation, and he unearthed documents from his archives for them. He was a fund of useful information, most of which he carried in his head. When police voyaged to Pitcairn to interview suspects, the Commissioner went too, and stayed with them at the Lodge. Salt, say British officials, was level-headed about the island and 'didn't buy into the myth'. Almost everyone, including Simon Moore, regarded him as a thoroughly good bloke.

Those who know him say he was revolted by the child abuse allegations. But he felt it was 'inappropriate to apply a UK solution to a Pitcairn problem', he told the Governor. Salt wrote, 'The UK has ignored law and order on Pitcairn for 200 years ... It would seem perhaps incongruous that UK justice is to be imposed in all its might after all this time, particularly given the fact that reported serious crime has escaped investigation in the past.'

Salt supported an amnesty and, astonishing as it seems, he even told police, according to Peter George, 'I'll get the men to plead guilty — provided there's an amnesty first.'

After that avenue was closed, his attitude changed. Detectives asked Salt to sign an affidavit releasing documents from his office; if the affair got to court, he would have to give evidence for the Crown. He refused, and withdrew all co-operation from the inquiry, telling prosecutors that if they proceeded as they intended, history would 'judge them very poorly'.

The men and their families, unwilling to see the case go to trial, pressed, instead, for a 'truth and reconciliation commission', based on the body that probed human rights abuses in apartheid-era South Africa. The idea of transposing truth and reconciliation to Pitcairn had initially appealed to major players, including Simon

Moore, but had to be abandoned once it was decreed by Baroness Scotland, Britain's Overseas Territories Minister, that the conventional legal process had to take its course. Still, Moore remained hopeful that the healing principles it embodied could be integrated into that process.

New Zealand is a pioneer of 'restorative justice', which offers criminals who plead guilty the opportunity to express remorse, apologise to their victims and make reparations; when they then go before a court to be sentenced, they can expect a significantly reduced penalty. Moore believed that this approach would enable most of the Pitcairn men to avoid prison. Christine Gordon, his deputy, consulted restorative justice experts, and researched a model employed in a Canadian–Indian community where generational child sexual abuse had been exposed.

But there was an obstacle. Steve Christian and the others were not prepared to plead guilty unless they received a guarantee that they would not be prosecuted. It was back to square one: trials.

Apparently confused, the Pitcairners continued to demand truth and reconciliation, which they sometimes referred to as restorative justice, as if the two were interchangeable. So Moore would declare that restorative justice had always been on the table, and the islanders would retort that they had asked for it in vain. Although the islanders did not acknowledge it, even truth and reconciliation would have required the men to admit their crimes. On Pitcairn, Meralda Warren explained to the media her understanding of the process: 'They [the men and their victims] face each other and get it over and done with, no big court, no media, nothing. And then we continue with our lives, put it all behind us.'

One British official says, 'They saw it as a brilliant idea that offered them a way out. You just say sorry, then everyone goes home and forgets all about it.'

★ ★ ★

Despite resistance by the islanders, and some misgivings on the part of lawyers and officials, Pitcairn was headed for the courts. The question was: where would a court sit? This was an issue that had been exercising Britain since 2001, for while Simon Moore had not yet decided whether to prosecute at that point, the practicalities were so daunting that it was obvious that officials needed to begin grappling with them right away.

Now that trials seemed a reality, the question was more pressing. Court cases, normally, are held where a crime was committed, often in an offender's own community. But could judges and leading silks be expected to travel across storm-tossed seas, and live, possibly for months, in a place where buildings were infested with termites, and the call of nature necessitated a trip along a muddy track to a malodorous pit toilet? Then there were the victims, most — if not all — of whom would decline to give evidence if they had to go back to the island to do so.

Alternative locations were discussed; New Zealand — where British diplomats were stationed and several defendants lived, along with many of the complainants — appeared to be the best option. First that country would have to pass special legislation, though. Britain opened negotiations on creating a 'Lockerbie-style' court to sit in New Zealand, following the example of the Scottish court established in the Netherlands to try two Libyans charged with bombing a Pan Am flight in 1988. The New Zealand government was receptive, and the Pitcairn Trials Bill was introduced into parliament in late 2001.

However, Britain had not given up on the idea of trying the defendants on home soil. A Pitcairn Logistics Team (PLT) was set up and, not surprisingly, reported that the logistical problems would be 'immense'. If trials took place on the island, said Tony Abbott, head of the PLT, a British warship might have to be anchored offshore to accommodate the judges.

For Martin Williams, the then Governor, the organisational aspect was only one of many challenges thrown up by the case. 'The whole thing bristled with complications and complexities and novelties,' he told me later. Williams warned officials in London that defence lawyers might argue, with success, 'that the facilities on Pitcairn were so primitive as to preclude the possibility of a fair trial; or that the law was so obscure that it could not reasonably be enforced; or that the widespread nature of the offences, and the total absence over many years of any attempt by HMG [Her Majesty's Government] to apply the law, meant that it could not reasonably be applied now without further warning'.

As he and others wrestled with such matters, further steps were taken to plug the holes in the Pitcairn legal machinery. Supreme Court judges, Appeal Court judges, a magistrate and a court registrar were appointed. The island already had a Public Prosecutor; in 2002 Paul Dacre, an Auckland criminal barrister, was appointed Pitcairn Public Defender, with Allan Roberts as his deputy. At their swearing-in ceremony, Dacre gave an ominous hint that he was preparing for a lengthy legal battle. According to Tony Abbott, Dacre indicated that 'every opportunity could be taken to proceed through every possible form of appeal, including the Privy Council and the European Court [and therefore] any custodial sentence could be delayed for many years'.

Like the prosecutors and judges, the defence lawyers were New Zealanders. But the men were being prosecuted under British law, which had traditionally been used to deal with serious crime on Pitcairn. The island's own laws covered relatively minor offences, such as letting one's chickens run amok and calling 'Sail ho' when no ship was in sight.

The Pitcairners' preference, if there had to be trials, was for them to be at home, and in August 2002 the island women, led by Betty Christian, launched a letter-writing campaign. They lobbied media outlets and influential figures such as Tony Blair, the British Prime Minister, and his New Zealand counterpart Helen Clark. Nadine Christian, Randy's wife, urged Clark, 'Please give Pitcairners the right to face their problems like any country — in their own homeland.'

Betty Christian wrote, 'To hold trials in a foreign country, to stand before judges who have never been to Pitcairn and have never experienced living on Pitcairn, would be more criminal than the cases they may be judging.' She added, 'We have been kept in the dark, been expected to get on with our lives as best we can with this cloud hanging over [us] ... not knowing what will happen to us, our families and our future here on Pitcairn. Our very existence is at stake.'

In the background, quietly applauding the women's new-found activism, was Pippa Foley, who had taught on the island a decade earlier, and had recently returned at the suggestion of Leon Salt. (One of his tasks was to recruit schoolteachers.) The Pitcairn teacher had the supplementary role of 'Government Adviser' — effectively, Britain's representative on the island. But Foley, like Salt, was a bitter critic of the legal process. In an email to friends, she reported excitedly that the locals had 'declared themselves the indigenous people of Pitcairn ... [with] a right to determine their own trial venue and their own form [of] justice'.

Steve Christian added his voice to the women's, writing to Helen Clark that the islanders had endured three years of 'sheer mental torture'. In late 2002, again in his official capacity, he addressed the New Zealand parliamentary committee that was examining the Pitcairn Trials Bill. Speaking by satellite phone, Steve claimed that the island would not survive if trials were staged in New Zealand. 'The community feels that the whole procedure has violated our human and civil rights,' he told committee members.

Just before Christmas 2002, the parliament in Wellington approved the Bill. That meant that, as far as Operation Unique was concerned, the Pitcairn courts could sit in New Zealand. Legal arguments and pre-trial hearings could take place in Auckland. The venue for the trials themselves had not yet been settled, however.

For the islanders, the passage of the Pitcairn Trials Act was a blow, representing concrete progress in the slow march towards judgement day. On the other hand, the Pitcairners had made substantial headway in their crusade to depict the affair as a miscarriage of justice. Many people, including journalists and academics, now believed that the accused men — and not the women poised to give evidence against them — were the real victims.

CHAPTER 7

Key witnesses evaporate

It was 2003; all the key personnel were in place, and prosecutors were preparing to lay charges. At the same time, the campaign of resistance by the Pitcairners was mounting, led by two figures of authority: the teacher and senior administrator.

Allen Cox had replaced Pippa Foley at the school early that year. Like Foley, he already knew Leon Salt. Cox was a British employee, and so was Salt; by this point, though, the Commissioner was actively seeking to undermine the prosecution. Confined, for the most part, to Auckland, he wanted a co-conspirator on Pitcairn, and a conduit to like-minded islanders. Cox, a tall, blunt New Zealander, 59 years old and nearing the end of his career, was the perfect candidate.

Having taught on Pitcairn in the early 1980s, Allen Cox was not surprised, two decades later, to learn about Operation Unique. 'I have no doubt the guys are guilty as sin,' he told his son, Andrew, in an email. 'The sexual abuse has been going on from the time of the Bounty. I guess that this is the unfortunate generation that got hit.'

As will be clear from that statement, Cox was firmly behind the men. When social workers suggested that they join forces to shore up the community, he and his wife, Judy, also a teacher, rebuffed them. 'Jude and I will support our friends (all=the accused) in our own way,' Cox told Salt in an email. In an article for the *Miscellany*, the local newspaper, he noted 'the millions of dollars this is costing and how the money could be better used'.

For him, the Pitcairn assignment meant, primarily, easy wages. As he wrote to friends in New Zealand, 'School is pretty cruisy here — if you have to teach this is the place.' He only had three pupils, and 'there are no curriculums, longterm plans, work books, tracking sheets, achievement objectives ... Favourite activity is video watching.'

In his other role of Government Adviser, Cox was supposed to be Britain's eyes and ears on Pitcairn. He performed that function for Leon Salt instead, with the two men working together to thwart the British government and the legal process.

As soon as the teacher arrived, Salt advised him to set up a private email account and send 'unofficial, off-the-record correspondence' to Salt's private address. 'This way, I can keep some things off the hard drive at work, where one day I'm sure, the Governor will send someone in to find out all he can,' he explained.

By this stage, it seems, the Commissioner felt only contempt for the British. They were 'arrogant beyond belief', he told Cox; Tony Abbott of the Pitcairn Logistics Team was a 'dickhead', while the Governor, Richard Fell, was a 'sad bastard' who 'thinks colonials are stupid and gullible', and was trying 'to bankrupt us so that ... they have another excuse to close the place down'. When Fell passed a new child protection law, overriding the island council, Salt proposed that the locals 'consider a ceremonial burning of it'.

His main concern, however, was the laying of charges, which — under the hotch-potch of legislation now governing Pitcairn — had to take place on the island. Salt told Allen Cox that he had heard it might happen in April, cautioning, 'Keep that completely confidential as at this stage there is still a possibility, remote though it may be, that we can engineer a change of decision.' Fate at first seemed to be with them, when a hitch arose with the boat that Britain had previously chartered for the Pitcairn run. But not long afterwards a deal was struck with Nigel Jolly, owner of the *Braveheart*.

Leon Salt was determined to be on the island for the court sitting, and he was furious when Fell informed him his presence would not be required. The islanders had to take a stand, he insisted. With Steve Christian away, Salt suggested that Cox tell Randy, the acting mayor, to call a public meeting. The locals 'could then decide that they would not go out [on the longboat] to meet the legal team arriving on the *Braveheart* unless I was with them', Salt said. The plan 'would take some engineering and it could easily fall over if anyone was to indicate to the [military police] that it was premeditated'. He added, 'The bottom line is ... that all of these tactics will help in the long run to keep these men from incarceration and to keep Pitcairn alive.'

This was strong stuff, and Salt — who constantly reminded Cox to delete private emails — was anxious about him 'blowing your cover, or mine'. The next day he warned, 'You will need to be confident that any of the suggestions made last night cannot be traced back to you ... Neither of us should be seen to be inciting civil disobedience.'

The two men exchanged 'private' emails throughout Allen Cox's stay on the island, one of which was discovered behind a filing cabinet after he left in late 2003. The rest were retrieved from his laptop, which was British government property, by Kent Police forensic experts.

★ ★ ★

Prosecutors, for now, were oblivious to the plots being hatched by the Commissioner and the Government Adviser. They faced a more serious problem. Their key witnesses were evaporating.

During the investigation in 2000, 31 people, including two women who had lived on the island as outsiders, had related their stories of childhood abuse to detectives. Twenty-six had given statements, with three making plain from the outset that they did not wish to testify; the rest, in theory, were willing. By April 2003, when charges were laid, more than half had dropped out, leaving the prosecution with only ten complainants.

Some women changed their minds within a year. The first to do so was Catherine, who had explained the island's sexual norms to police, triggering the wider investigation. While few Pitcairners were aware of her pivotal role, everyone knew that she was a complainant. In an effort to appease the islanders, particularly her mother, Catherine claimed that she had been tricked into making a statement. Her mother pressed her to retract it. Catherine resisted. Her mother kept chipping away at her. In 2001 Catherine and her partner decided to move back to Pitcairn. Aware that life there would be unbearable unless she distanced herself from Operation Unique, Catherine told detectives that she could not give evidence. According to a family member, this was 'a direct result of pressure from her mother', who, on hearing the news, said to her, 'Congratulations. You're a member of the family again.' However, like others who subsequently recanted, Catherine signed an affidavit confirming the truth of her original allegations.

The next witness to withdraw was Gillian, who from the age of two or three had been molested by her uncle on Pitcairn. By the time the investigation started, Gillian was in her teens and living with her family in Auckland. When police arrived at their house, Gillian's mother greeted them enthusiastically. 'Thank goodness something's finally being done about the sexual abuse on Pitcairn,' she said. Gillian gave a statement, and so did her mother, who clearly believed her daughter's allegations.

Two months after they spoke to detectives, Gillian's father was questioned. Several women had accused him of sexual abuse. That changed everything. Gillian had to stand by her family, her parents told her. When police asked her to sign a declaration that she was still prepared to go to court, her mother, according to Karen Vaughan, urged her to state that she would not testify under any circumstances. Gillian, normally an easygoing girl, snapped at her, saying she could make up her own mind.

In late 2002, with her mother threatening suicide and her parents' marriage disintegrating, Gillian announced that she could not continue. She apologised to Vaughan, who had received angry phone calls from both her parents. Vaughan suggested that they meet up and talk. Gillian replied, 'I want to see you, but my mother and father say no.'

A few months later, by chance, Vaughan bumped into Gillian in an Auckland medical centre. They arranged to meet in a café. Vaughan was accompanied by her English colleague, Peter George. Gillian told them, 'I want to go ahead with it, and I know I should, but my parents will kick me out of the house and disown me if I have anything to do with the investigation.' After discussing it further, Gillian agreed to reconsider. She gave George and Vaughan her new mobile number and departed with a friendly wave. Two hours later, police learnt that the family lawyer had telephoned to register a complaint 'about you two following [Gillian], spying on her, and bullying her to come back on board'.

A few days later, detectives opened a letter from Gillian's best friend, Susan, who had given them a lengthy statement in 2000, naming a number of men including Steve Christian. Susan, who informed police that she no longer wished to co-operate, lived in Australia, but had just been to stay with Gillian's family. The letter bore the postmark of their Auckland suburb. That was probably significant; so was the fact that Susan was about to visit Pitcairn.

During the months that followed, a succession of other women notified police that they were no longer willing to take part in the prosecution. Friend followed friend, and sister followed sister. One evening three members of the same family pulled out, one after another. This was, to some degree, foreseeable: victims of rape and sexual abuse often feel trepidation about going to court. With Pitcairn, though, additional factors were at play. Witnesses would have to give evidence against friends, relatives and former neighbours. Some were reluctant to see men whom they had grown up alongside go to jail. Others did not consider themselves victims. All were frustrated by the time that it was taking for the case to inch its way through uncharted legal waters.

However, as Catherine's and Gillian's experiences demonstrate, the main reason why complainants dropped out was pressure — from their relatives and from the Pitcairn community, that uniquely small, close-knit collection of families, as interlaced as a wisteria vine, and just as strangulating. Pressure had been applied since 2000, when the gravity of their predicament had started to dawn on the islanders. As the investigation gathered pace, they looked around for scapegoats — and rather than blame the men, they blamed the women for speaking out. The unforgivable crime, in the Pitcairners' eyes, was not sexually assaulting children, but betraying the island.

The men were not shunned, not even by parents living side-by-side with their daughters' alleged rapists. No outraged mobs surrounded their houses; there were no punch-ups, nor even harsh words traded. The vitriol was reserved for the victims who had broken the Pitcairn code of silence.

The locals deployed every conceivable weapon, including threats, cajolery and emotional blackmail, police claim. And the women were susceptible, for most of them still had relatives on the island and retained strong ties with the place. Now they were being warned that if they persisted with the case, they would never again be welcome there. They would lose their homeland, their culture, their identity — and, they were told, they would be the cause of the community's demise.

Women whose families occupied a lowly position in the island's pecking order were especially worried about the repercussions. One feared that her elderly mother might starve, denied access to supplies off the ships. Some complainants withdrew just before visiting Pitcairn; otherwise, they knew, their time on the island would be made intolerable. Others, brave enough to visit while still involved with the case, backed out on their return. One woman, Fiona, who had accused all three of Steve Christian's sons of assaulting her, lived for a year on the island, withstanding a daily onslaught from her own family as well as Steve's. It was not until her best friend, Tania Christian, the younger sister of the three men, came home to Pitcairn for Randy's wedding and refused to have anything to do with her that Fiona finally cracked. When she next saw police, she handed them three letters retracting the allegations, which her parents had helped her to type. She told Karen Vaughan, 'You don't know what it's like here. I have to live with these people and they're making my life hell.'

The victims had a choice. They could pursue their complaints and cut all links with the island, or they could opt for a peaceful life. Most chose the latter course — and in every case, claims Vaughan,

'there'd been intimidation, there'd been family pressure ...
There wasn't one where the complainant had just said "I don't want
to do this any more."' Peter George agrees. 'It was a nightmare to
keep the women on board all those years, particularly when the
drums of Pitcairn were beating.'

In early 2003 the story took another unexpected turn: several
women gave interviews to the New Zealand media, alleging that
they had been trapped or coerced into making statements. Some of
them claimed to have been offered tens of thousands of dollars to
fabricate allegations. A number of women had lodged complaints
with the British and New Zealand police. An Auckland lawyer,
Ron Mansfield, had been hired to represent them — 'to fight for
their right to withdraw their claims', as the *Dominion Post* phrased
it. Herb Ford, the Pitcairners' Californian advocate, was helping to
raise funds to pay for Mansfield's services, and Leon Salt was also
said to be involved.

While all the detectives were cited in the alleged skullduggery,
the name of Karen Vaughan, in charge of liaising with the victims,
came up most frequently. (All of them denied it.) Among their
accusers was Catherine, who said that the police 'have hurt us all
deeply in the way they have gone about this'. Vaughan, she claimed,
had 'tried to make me say and do things I did not want to and were
not even true'. Gillian, who had been threatened with eviction, told
the *Sunday Star-Times*, 'I did not realise I signed a complaint, as I
never at any time would be willing to go to court or want to
prosecute anyone on Pitcairn ... I only wanted the Pitcairn men to
learn how to treat girls.' Gillian also went on national television in
New Zealand with her mother, to relate her story of alleged
bribery.

Not only had they *not* been sexually abused, declared Gillian and
others who had recounted such compelling tales a few years earlier,

but nor, they were sure, had any other Pitcairn girl. From that point on, these women would be at the forefront of the campaign to discredit the prosecution, defending the very men whom they had previously accused of raping and assaulting them.

On 3 April 2003 the *Braveheart* dropped anchor off Pitcairn. On board were the Pitcairn magistrate, Gray Cameron, several police officers, and the two legal teams, headed by Simon Moore and Paul Dacre. Charges were about to be laid. Leon Salt was not among the passengers, but he was still pulling strings, instructing the islanders — through the teacher, Allen Cox — to 'delete anything [on their computers] that is not for the eyes of others'.

The *Braveheart*'s captain, Nigel Jolly, radioed the island. Steve Christian responded, and informed Jolly that 'the folks here', in the light of allegations about police misconduct, were not happy about fetching the detectives. Paul Dacre, who clearly wanted to get onto dry land, reassured Steve over the radio that 'our fight is only just beginning'. Steve replied that Pitcairn was 'united in its cause'. Everyone on the island could hear the conversation. Yet before it had concluded, quad bikes could be seen descending the Hill of Difficulty; the locals, it seemed, were more interested in meeting the boat, which was bringing goods from Mangareva, than playing along with Steve's games.

Out came the longboat, and Steve and Randy Christian ferried the prosecutors who were about to charge them to The Landing. The atmosphere on shore was subdued. Christine Gordon, Simon Moore's deputy, says, 'There was a real sense that something big was happening.' Moore noticed that certain islanders who had been welcoming on their previous trip were frosty. As for the accused, Dacre had told them to keep their distance this time. There would be no fraternising — although Dennis Christian, a friendly soul, still greeted the police and Crown lawyers with a cheery hello when he saw them around the island.

Some Pitcairners expressed the view that, beneath their bravado, the men facing court were afraid. They also said that Steve's family was planning a 'scorched earth policy' — determined that if he and his relatives went down, they would take the whole community with them.

On 9 April the defendants gathered in an anteroom at the back of the church before crossing the square and filing into court. Just two islanders were in the public gallery to watch this momentous event in Pitcairn's history, according to witnesses. Also present were Allen Cox and Lyle Burgoyne, a Seventh-day Adventist nurse and lay pastor who, like Cox, was close to the locals.

One by one, beginning with 77-year-old Len Brown, the men rose to their feet. Gray Cameron read out the charges, then remanded each of them on bail. Len was followed by his 48-year-old son, Dave, who was visibly shaking. Then came Dennis Christian, 48. Then Randy Christian, 29. Then Randy's father, 51-year-old Steve Christian. Steve affected an air of disdain as the magistrate listed the allegations against him. As he left court, he muttered audibly, 'What a load of shit.' Terry Young, 44, was the last to stand up. The seventh defendant, 46-year-old Jay Warren, was away with the court's consent and was charged in his absence. Also charged, although not present, were Shawn Christian, 27, and Trent Christian, 30, Steve's youngest and eldest sons.

Court adjourned for lunch, and during the break Steve and Lyle Burgoyne pinned a notice up on the board outside the courthouse. It was a press statement from Herb Ford in California, condemning the prosecution as 'tainted'. Steve then made a public announcement over the VHF radio, urging every islander to go down and see it.

Steve's actions struck Simon Moore as 'quite remarkable and brazen', he says. Moore had not been intending to contest a court order prohibiting publication of the accused's identities. Now he changed his mind. An email from Nadine Christian to a television journalist in New Zealand had also come to Moore's attention. Nadine had written earlier that day, 'Nine men being charged? That's what you get for reporting from so far away. I live here and KNOW 9 men were NOT charged.'

When court reassembled, Gray Cameron agreed with Moore that the email was 'not only misleading but mischievous' — and that suppressing names would leave Nadine and others with ample scope to continue sowing confusion. Nevertheless, he imposed an interim order, leaving the matter to be discussed more fully in Auckland. Paul Dacre, the Public Defender, had argued that the order would shield the defendants from 'an unwarranted and prolonged blaze of adverse international publicity'.

The magistrate also issued a memo, to be placed on the noticeboard and distributed to the media, containing details of the 64 charges. He stressed that they were 'extremely serious', comprising 21 counts of rape, 41 of indecent assault, and two of gross indecency with a child under 14. A few months earlier, Simon Moore had revealed that among them were the rape of girls aged seven and ten, as well as the indecent assault of a three-year-old. Some were 'specimen', or representative, charges, with one count encompassing multiple incidents. The alleged offences had been committed between 1964 and 1999; all the victims had been under 16.

Two months later, in an Auckland court, another 32 charges — including ten counts of rape — would be laid against four New Zealand-based men: Brian Young, 48; Kay Brown, 46; Ron Christian, 33; and 78-year-old Albert Reeves, the former teacher. In total, 13 men would be charged with 96 offences.

★ ★ ★

A now notorious incident took place following the proceedings on Pitcairn. During the return voyage to Mangareva, with the magistrate, police and prosecutors on board, the *Braveheart*'s crew decided to anchor overnight at Oeno Island, an uninhabited atoll in the Pitcairn group with beautiful white sand beaches. As the sun went down, Nigel Jolly, the *Braveheart*'s skipper, brought out a bottle of whisky; then his son, Matt, appeared wearing a red sparkly wig and a pair of plastic breasts. Nigel insisted that everyone try on the outfit, saying it was a ritual for charter passengers. First to comply was Gray Cameron, who had his photograph taken by a crew member. Then it was Simon Moore's turn to pose for the camera. Last up was Christine Gordon, who draped herself seductively over the prow. The pictures were downloaded onto a disk and presented to the lawyers at the end of their trip.

Three months later, the *Braveheart* passengers received some disturbing news: photographs of them wearing the tinsel wig and false breasts had appeared in the New Zealand papers. Served up cold, the pictures seemed shocking, suggesting unbecoming behaviour by senior lawyers and an apparent trivialisation of the offences they were prosecuting. Journalists and commentators questioned the lawyers' professional credibility.

Moore, who was on a family holiday at the time, was horrified. Gordon felt 'absolutely devastated', and feared that her whole career as a prosecutor was in jeopardy. 'We were quite clear in our own minds that we hadn't done anything wrong, but we were concerned about the spin that might be put upon it,' she says. 'We were very worried about the impact on the case and the complainants.'

In an interview with New Zealand television, Moore emphasised that the photographs reflected 'a couple of minutes of lightheartedness in the middle of the ocean'. He and the others had, 'in the spirit of the moment', simply gone along with what they had assumed to be a shipboard tradition. The media interest died down, but the prosecutors still had to pacify their bosses: Pitcairn's British Governor, the Pitcairn Chief Justice, the New Zealand Solicitor-General, the New Zealand Attorney-General and the New Zealand Chief Justice. None of those distinguished figures was fazed by the pictures, says Simon Moore; nor were the complainants, who found them quite amusing. Out of 300 letters and emails that Moore was sent by friends, colleagues and members of the public, just one was critical.

The only people who appeared to be affronted were those Pitcairners who were already opposed to the prosecution. Meralda Warren was widely quoted. The photographs, she said, were 'degrading — to women, to everyone, to what the prosecutors represent'.

Someone had leaked the pictures to the media, and Nigel Jolly was determined to find out who. The crew denied it. Then Jolly remembered that an islander had travelled on his boat soon after it carried the lawyers to Mangareva. Had that person, perhaps, gone snooping around and discovered the digital images on the boat's computer?

By July 2003, it was later established, the photographs were circulating on Pitcairn. In an email to Leon Salt, retrieved from Allen Cox's laptop, the teacher wrote, 'Saw some of the photos from the disc — wow — how compromising can you get? Steve is not sure how to use them. Defence are urging caution.' Shortly afterwards, the pictures were published in New Zealand, and subsequently in Britain. A British Sunday tabloid, *The People*, ran an additional shot of Peter George and Robert Vinson, the English detectives, drinking beer on the *Braveheart*'s deck, under the headline 'Cop Parties on Paradise Island'.

Meralda, like quite a number of women on Pitcairn, had vacillated dramatically in her attitude to the sexual offending. In 1999 she had allegedly obstructed Gail Cox's efforts to bring Ricky Quinn to justice. Nevertheless, when Operation Unique started, she had strongly supported it, and so had her mother, Mavis. Now Meralda appeared to have switched back.

The reasons for this see-sawing may be complex. What is certain is that by 2003 Meralda, in common with other islanders, was feeling the strain of having lived with the case for three years. She told Sue Ingram of Radio New Zealand that it was 'like the bottom had fallen out of our world ... We lost our trust for each other.'

The community was split into two hostile camps: a minority who deplored the men's alleged behaviour and a majority who denied or excused it. The latter called the former traitors. Mike Lupton-Christian says, 'I tried not to take sides, but that was interpreted as being on the other side.' Community events — cricket matches, fishing trips, holidays on Oeno Island — virtually ceased, thanks to a go-slow by the men. One islander recalls, 'It was stated that while all this was going on, we were not doing that stuff — more or less making the community feel guilty for their actions.'

Tensions rose further after charges were laid. One woman was branded the architect of Pitcairn's woes because she had, supposedly, 'snitched' to police. Her husband, among a handful of local men not charged, received threatening emails from a female islander overseas, alluding to skeletons in his past. Like his wife, he was seen as being in the 'British camp'. Stories, meanwhile, were spread about the military police, or MDPs, who, it was claimed, were drinking to excess and staying out all night. One officer was even said to be sleeping with a 15-year-old girl — a rumour that led to Richard Fell's memo, which we later saw on the Pitcairn noticeboard, reminding the locals that malicious gossip was against the law.

From early 2003 the islanders had yet another outsider living in their midst: Pitcairn's first resident diplomat, a Governor's Representative. The first incumbent was a plain-spoken Englishwoman, Jenny Lock, who presided over a string of unpopular projects, undertaken in the event that trials were held on Pitcairn. The white weatherboard courthouse was painted and a carpet was laid over the wooden floor to improve acoustics. Curtains were draped over the shipping insignia on the walls; a dock was built, and a witness stand. The islanders grumbled that the courthouse, now the object of so much attention, had been condemned some years back. Outside, Bill Haigh, the New Zealand-based communications expert, on one of his many assignments to the island, set up satellite dishes for a video link. Lastly, construction of the jail was completed.

In August 2003 the judges visited Pitcairn and decided that it was, after all, a realistic trials venue. The case could have gone ahead within weeks. In September, though, defence lawyers mounted the first of a series of legal challenges to the validity of the prosecution. Their arguments, which were considered in Auckland, were all rejected, but by then another year had elapsed.

Although it is something very rare in British criminal cases, the defendants continued to enjoy anonymity. That meant that Steve Christian, speaking as the island's mayor, could carry on lambasting the British government with the apparent mandate of the community, secure in the knowledge that no one could link him personally with the case. Likewise Kari Boye Young, the wife of Brian Young, one of the New Zealand-based defendants, could maintain her blistering public attacks, with few outsiders aware she had a direct interest. Kari had become one of the prosecution's most vociferous critics; she was also among several people given a warning by detectives for contacting victims and attempting to pressure them.

While the men's identities were not generally known, anyone with an understanding of the island's power dynamics could have made a reasonable guess. 'If you want to know who's been charged,' one official remarked, 'just take a look in the back of the longboat.'

By 2003 Leon Salt had been Commissioner for eight years. He was 'totally dedicated to the island', according to Bill Haigh, who knew Salt well and believes that he thought he had a job for life. But Salt's relationship with his British bosses was deteriorating. In February he told the Deputy Governor, Matthew Forbes, that in future he was only prepared to communicate with him in writing.

British diplomats were in a delicate position. All documents relating to the criminal inquiry were stored in Salt's office. An attempt at mediation failed. In September, Governor Fell sacked Salt, citing 'a breakdown of trust and confidence'.

Steve Christian was livid. He called a public meeting, at which he expected to hear demands for Salt's reinstatement. He was disappointed. Claiming that people had been afraid to speak up, Steve held a second meeting a few days later. The minutes, written up by him, record that the islanders were again 'too timid to state true feelings'.

Leon Salt sued the British government for unfair dismissal, and, although stripped of his power, remained a central figure in the Pitcairners' struggle to avoid going to jail.

★ ★ ★

At a court hearing in Auckland in July 2004, it was determined that the trials of the seven Pitcairn-based men would begin on the island on 29 September, with the complainants giving evidence from Auckland by satellite link.

Grant Pritchard, Jenny Lock's successor as Governor's Representative, now had to implement one of Richard Fell's most controversial decisions, obliging the islanders to surrender their guns to military police for the duration of the trials — or have them confiscated. Gail Cox had compiled a firearms register in 1999, ascertaining that the locals between them owned 31 rifles, shotguns and pistols. The guns were used to shoot sharks and goats, and to blast breadfruit out of the trees.

The Harry Christian murders in 1897 had been the only recorded killings on Pitcairn since the mutineers' time. However, British officials felt it prudent that this armoury of weapons be kept under lock and key, given the worsening frictions. They also believed there was a suicide risk. The Pitcairners were incensed. 'We are being treated as if we are a murdering, suicidal bunch of no good, good-for-nothing, sex crazed cowboys', wrote Mike 'Cookie' Warren, in one of many emails flying between the islanders and their supporters at that time.

During a video conference between Adamstown and Wellington, Steve Christian pointed to Grant Pritchard, who was sitting beside him. 'Listen,' he said to Richard Fell and Matthew Forbes, 'if I wanted to kill Grant, I wouldn't shoot him. I'd just push him off a cliff.' Pritchard, a laconic young diplomat in his mid-30s, blanched.

Two days before the lawyers, judges and diplomats left New Zealand for Pitcairn, more drama struck. Fell received a letter from an Auckland criminal barrister, Christopher Harder, a colourful character who had recently been fined for punching another lawyer in court. Harder informed him that he had come into possession of thousands of pages of documents relating to the Pitcairn affair, including confidential Foreign Office correspondence, and private letters and emails between lawyers, officials and government ministers. According to the barrister, they revealed a high-level 'conspiracy' to pursue the men through the courts and deny them restorative justice.

Harder urged the Governor to halt the legal process, which 'would not only allow for justice to be done, it would also prevent considerable embarrassment to Her Majesty's Government by keeping these documents closeted from media scrutiny'. Otherwise, he said, he would release the papers to the press.

Government lawyers immediately sought an injunction to stop Harder from publishing the documents or passing them on. One other person was named in the court order: Leon Salt. Salt must have copied the files while clearing his desk. Then, it seems, he gave them to the maverick lawyer in the hope of causing maximum trouble.

I found out about the Harder papers in Mangareva, while waiting to board the *Braveheart* for our voyage to Pitcairn. They were to be a headache for Britain for a long while yet. But for now everyone's focus was on the trials, which were finally about to begin.

CHAPTER 8

The trials begin

On the morning of 29 September 2004, a curious sight greeted the people of Adamstown.

It was early spring, and the day had dawned sunny and bright. Sometime after 9 a.m., groups of strangers emerged. They strode purposefully along the rutted main track, dressed in dark suits and polished shoes — and, in some cases, long black gowns that almost trailed in the red Pitcairn dust.

Among these figures was the Pitcairn Chief Justice, Charles Blackie, climbing the winding back lane from the Mission House, where the judges were billeted, up to the square. Graham Ford, the registrar, escorted him into the small museum adjoining the dilapidated wooden courthouse, which had been commandeered as the judges' retiring room. Minutes later, Ford entered court through a connecting door and ordered that 'all be upstanding for the Chief Justice of the Pitcairn Supreme Court'. Blackie appeared, bowed briefly and sat down. And so began one of the most unusual trials in British criminal history.

Looking around, the judge would have seen that the paintwork in the courtroom was peeling. A dock had been built, but was not being used because of limited space. Instead, the defendant stood in the front row of the public gallery, wearing shorts, rubber thongs and a blue T-shirt with a *Bounty* logo. Stevens Raymond Christian, the island's 53-year-old mayor, was scowling, perhaps because the long-standing suppression order had just been lifted. He and the other six men about to go on trial could be named, for the first time, in media reports.

Blackie would be officiating at the first of the seven trials, each of which was to be heard by one judge, sitting alone; three judges were to share the trials between them. There was no legal provision for trial by jury on Pitcairn, and besides, the chances of assembling an impartial panel were slim. The trials were to run simultaneously so that each witness could testify against a number of men, back to back, and then go home. Six weeks had been set aside for the whole case.

The Chief Justice was a former navy reservist, as was his fellow judge, Russell Johnson; now they were to lay down the law in a community founded by fugitives from the British Royal Navy. The third judge, Jane Lovell-Smith, was cut from different cloth. She had been seasick all the way to Pitcairn, and was to spend her entire stay dreading the return voyage to Mangareva. All three were district court judges in New Zealand, with a weekly diet that consisted of rape, murder, drugs and armed robbery. The *Braveheart's* inflatable had brought them to shore; when they stepped onto dry land, one of the accused, Dave Brown, had spat at their feet.

Steve's sister, Brenda Christian, who had replaced Meralda Warren as police officer in 2001, stood guard at the main door of the court. The only other locals present were Tom and Betty Christian, Cookie Warren, and his mother, Royal, watching from the public gallery. It was Cookie who had warned me in an email that journalists were not welcome on Pitcairn. Now we were seated right in front of him, the six members of the media pool, whispering as we identified those around us.

It was time for proceedings to start. Simon Moore, the Public Prosecutor, got up, looking uncomfortable in his buttoned-up bar jacket and stiff wing collar. The lawyers were in full English court regalia, apart from horsehair wigs — the sole concession to the tropical heat. Fans pushed hot air from one corner of the low-ceilinged room to another; thin green curtains fluttered at the windows. Through a chink, palm trees could be glimpsed, swaying gently. Brenda closed the door and took a seat beside her brother.

Steve faced six counts of rape and four of indecent assault. He leant back, arms folded, as the court heard that the offences dated from 1964 to 1975, when he was aged between 14 and 25. Even as a teenager, Simon Moore declared, Steve had been 'a prominent influential figure within his peer group'.

I glanced over at Steve, sitting a few feet away. He gave off an impression of compact strength. A secretive half-smile curled around his lips. He seemed a man at ease with himself, self-contained. But I also detected a coiled tension. This was not someone accustomed to being crossed.

After a short interval for the satellite link to be set up, a female figure appeared on a television monitor at the front of the room. She was middle-aged, with red hair, and wore a black jacket. She looked absolutely terrified. Steve shifted in his chair.

Jennifer, allegedly, had been Steve's first victim. She had flown from England to tell her story and was in a video-link studio in Auckland, together with a counsellor and court registrar. Simon Moore switched to a seat facing the monitor and began to question her gently. Taking herself back 40 years, Jennifer recalled a frightened girl who was bullied and picked on, especially by Steve, who 'seemed to be the leader of the pack,' she said.

As the adult Steve gazed at the screen, Jennifer described an incident that had occurred in about 1964, when she was 11 or 12.

It was a Sunday or public holiday, and she was one of a crowd of young people walking up to a scenic spot, Jack Williams Valley, for a picnic. Falling behind, she noticed Steve and two other boys waiting for her in a grove of banyan trees. Steve, who was two years older than her, grabbed hold of her, pushed her to the ground and pulled down her shorts; then, as the other two pinned her down, he raped her. Jennifer, who was a virgin, struggled to break free, 'twisting and turning'. When Steve had finished, he told his friends, 'Your turn if you want.' They declined, and the three of them ran off laughing.

That evening Jennifer's mother found her bloodstained underwear, and Jennifer explained, 'It was Steve and them again.' She said nothing more, 'scared that ... she wouldn't believe me'. Steve and the other boys, when Jennifer saw them, acted 'as if nothing had happened'.

All this Jennifer related in a steady tone. But she became upset as she recounted how her parents — both regular churchgoers — had fought constantly, trading accusations of infidelity. From a young age, Jennifer said, her voice now shaky, she had watched her father pour water over her mother after beating her unconscious. As a result, she came to associate sex with violence — and that, she told the court, was why she complied when Steve drew up outside the church one evening and ordered her to get on his motorbike.

It was a year or two after the attack under the banyans. Steve drove her up to Aute Valley, where many of the islanders have gardens, and raped her in a shed, on a bed of banana leaves. He was rough and it was painful, Jennifer still remembered four decades later. That night her father thrashed her with a razor strop for missing prayers. She did not tell him why she had been absent. 'Don't say anything,' Steve had warned her. 'Nobody's going to believe you.'

115

Steve raped her twice more, Jennifer claimed, accosting her while she was chopping firewood and taking her to a forested area, Doodwi Ground. 'Did you resist in any way?' asked Simon Moore.

'What's the point?' she replied. 'Just let him get on with it. He's going to do it anyway.'

When she arrived home, her father was angry again. 'I didn't bring enough firewood,' she said. 'I can recall Dad being annoyed at me for that.' Jennifer started to weep. Head in hands, she covered her face with a tissue. 'It's my fault,' she sobbed. 'My fault.'

Steve shuffled his feet, and stared down at the cheap blue carpet.

Moore asked Jennifer why she had kept these events to herself for so long, telling no one, not even her husband, until she was contacted by Kent detectives.

'Out of shame, out of guilt, out of nobody would believe me,' she responded. 'It just seemed to be ... how the girls are treated, as though they're a sex thing. Men could do what they want with them. They seemed to be a rule unto themselves.'

During four hours of cross-examination, Paul Dacre, the Public Defender, pressed Jennifer on why she did not inform her parents. Surely they would have believed her, he insisted. 'They probably [would have] believed me, but ... they couldn't do anything about it,' she said. 'There's nobody on the island that you could turn to for anything like this ... That's the way of life on Pitcairn. You get abused, you get raped. It's the normal way of life on Pitcairn when I was growing up.'

Dacre reminded her that two of her peers had been brought before the magistrate for deliberately setting a fire. 'So the situation on Pitcairn wasn't that it was a lawless country, was it?'

Jennifer interjected, 'But could I just please point out that that incident is visual. You could see the damage. You can't see the damage of a rape.'

Moore then returned to the chair and asked Jennifer about her interview with detectives, which had occupied an entire day in late 2000. She explained, 'They asked one question and everything ... just came flooding out ... from the very first incident that happened to me when I was three, right through up until I left home ... and I had to stop because they couldn't keep up with me ... with writing.'

Jennifer moved to England at 19 to get married. Simon Moore asked her again why she had never spoken to her husband about the abuse. Jennifer said she had blamed herself for what happened, and anyway, she had not wished to disillusion him about the island. 'Everybody in the outside world thinks Pitcairn Island is a paradise,' she cried. 'But it was sheer hell back home when I was growing up. Pitcairn isn't a paradise at all. It's hell.'

The next morning the judges and lawyers descended on the square again, like a flock of oversized bats. Steve Christian was still mid-trial, but with the hearings arranged around the witnesses, Dave Brown's was about to begin.

Dave, the island's works manager, took his brother-in-law's place at the front of the public gallery. He was barefoot. Like Steve, he wore a *Bounty* T-shirt; Dave's was red. While the shirts were produced for sale to tourists, they appeared to have become a kind of uniform. Dave, 49, slouched in his chair, affecting insolence but looking frightened.

Christine Gordon told the judge, Jane Lovell-Smith, that Dave was charged with 13 indecent assaults and two counts of gross indecency. (A 16th charge had been dismissed.) The alleged crimes spanned two decades, from 1970 to 1991, and involved five victims. Gordon spent a considerable time reading out the background to all the charges.

The mother of one victim was in court, and I was astonished, before proceedings started, to see her walk over to Dave and warmly embrace him. Then she sat, head bowed, as Gordon, in dry, lawyerly language, related what Dave did to her 15-year-old daughter 20 years earlier. Her husband was outside on the verandah, listening through the open door with an absent expression.

According to the Deputy Public Prosecutor, Dave's attitude to young girls was that they were 'available for him as and when he chose'. He began offending in his teens, then moved to New Zealand, where he lived for 11 years; on returning to Pitcairn with a wife and child, he 'resumed his old habits'. As Christine Gordon outlined the evidence against him, Dave cradled his head in his hands.

The first witness to appear on the screen was Isobel, a dark-haired woman in her late 30s, and the younger sister of the first complainant, Jennifer.

Isobel was questioned about a birthday party held at a place called Flatland when she was five. The children were playing hide and seek, Isobel recounted in a small voice, with frequent pauses, and she found a cave-like area among the shrubs that seemed 'a real good place to hide'. Dave, who was in his late teens, followed her in. 'I thought he was going to hide too,' Isobel said. Dave knelt down beside the little girl. 'He put his hand over my mouth and said to be quiet … Then he told me to open my mouth, and he put his penis into my mouth.' After a little while, they heard people approaching. Dave 'pulled his pants up and just left me there', Isobel recollected.

On another occasion, Isobel said, Dave turned up while she was playing in the village square with a friend, Marion. He steered them into the church, into a back room where Sabbath school was taught, and instructed the girls, both aged about seven, to take down their knickers. Then he lay on top of Marion and stuck his penis between her legs. Afterwards, Dave made them 'promise not to say anything'.

At the end of Isobel's evidence, the court took a break. The lawyers and spectators popped out for some air; Dave popped out too. Claire Harvey, the journalist for *The Australian*, snapped a photograph of him. 'You people have no shame,' he growled. We looked at each other, trying not to laugh at the absurdity of the situation.

Next, Jennifer reappeared to testify that Isobel had told her about the episode in the bushes while she was giving her little sister a bath before bedtime that same evening.

Jennifer confessed that she did not take any action — and years later, she said, Isobel and her partner berated her about it over dinner. 'They were blaming me that I didn't do anything to help ... or sort it out. They expected that I should have done something, and I didn't. I couldn't do a thing to protect her because I knew what had happened to me. I couldn't protect my own sister.'

Tears rolled down Jennifer's face.

A day or two later, Dave Brown buttonholed me in the island store. 'I'm not a tractor driver,' he said crossly. 'I'm the works supervisor.'

Dave had been reading our stories online, and was peeved to see that I had (by mistake) demoted him. He also castigated me for a piece in which I had described encounters with various locals in the shop. Why had I only mentioned him and Steve and Randy, Dave demanded to know; why not other islanders?

'Well,' I said lamely, 'you're the ones who are interesting. I mean, you're the ones who're on trial.' I was not used to being challenged so directly. But then I was not normally surrounded by the people I was reporting on. We were living at the heart of the Pitcairn community, and the usual distance between journalist and subject was non-existent.

The islanders, avid consumers of the internet, were monitoring every word we wrote or broadcast, and Dave was not the only one who was quick to tell us if he didn't like something. Carol Warren showed up on our doorstep, indignant about being misquoted, she said, in an article about the meeting at Big Fence. Many of the women had been chatty and accessible that day. Once they read our first court reports, they turned glacial. From then on, apart from giving us baleful stares, and the occasional dressing-down, most of them ignored us.

British diplomats, too, were scrutinising our output. Matthew Forbes, the Deputy Governor, would wander over from next door, waving a printout of a story. He was keen to get a good press — after all, hadn't Britain acted promptly once it found out about the alleged child abuse? He seemed less keen to talk about preceding decades.

We received feedback from the locals in emails as well as face to face. Cookie Warren, who had attended court on the first day, wrote to tell me that I was clearly 'prejudiced towards conviction'. Meralda Warren fumed, 'Our men are not rapists or child molesters. The media including you, Kathy, have been getting things printed well out of proportion.'

At the same time as our relations with the islanders declined, we journalists were getting to know each other better. Ewart Barnsley was a personable, somewhat reserved man with a reassuring air of having seen it all before; his cameraman, Zane Willis, a bluff, sunburnt Kiwi, was a technology whizz who rigged up the house so that we could all surf the internet and make the most of the limited electricity. Sue Ingram, a brisk, hard-working Englishwoman, had been on a journalism course with me 20 years earlier, and I also knew Neil Tweedie slightly from my days in London. Neil played the cynical 'Fleet Street hack', but was a thoughtful, intelligent person who balanced his occasional black moods with searingly funny observations. Claire Harvey, an Australian journalist based in Wellington, was young, keen and extremely bright; Claire and I hit it off straight away. Claire was 28, Ewart was 58, and the rest of us were in our early 40s.

Len Brown's trial was supposed to begin on Friday, 1 October, but Jennifer — who would be giving evidence again — had a migraine, so it was adjourned until Sunday. My media colleagues and I decided to hold a cheese and wine party in the evening — even though there was only one variety of cheese available on Pitcairn. Most of the outsiders on the island accepted our invitation, but not the defence lawyers: Paul Dacre, Allan Roberts and Charles Cato, who had joined the team just before the trials. Roberts explained quietly that they couldn't be seen to be socialising with us: their clients would be furious.

The next day was Saturday, the Seventh-day Adventist Sabbath. Still in reporting mode, the six of us went to church. The service was led by Pastor Ray Coombe, who had travelled with us on the *Braveheart*; Coombe and his wife, Daphne, were an engaging couple.

Aware that only a handful of locals still practised the religion, I was surprised to see the pews almost full. Many of the worshippers were outsiders, I soon realised; however, there were also islanders present who — it was said — never usually stepped inside the brick building. Coombe read from the Book of Daniel. Then he proclaimed, 'There'll be stresses and trials in our life too, just as there were for Daniel ... This week has been a historical but difficult time for Pitcairn Island. The peaceful, unhurried and carefree atmosphere has been interrupted.'

Afterwards Claire Harvey and I, together with Neil Tweedie and Sue Ingram, spoke to Coombe in the pews. He said it had been a 'rough week' for the islanders. 'They feel threatened and under attack,' he told us. 'They feel a sense of inadequacy that they can't do anything except submit to the process. Others want to fight what's happening. Apprehension is the prevailing mood.'

I wondered if Coombe appreciated how serious the charges were. He had not been into court, apart from poking his head into Steve's trial. 'I'm here to help the community at a difficult time, and I can only do that if I'm seen as totally neutral,' he explained. At the end of the interview, Coombe handed us his business card. Far from being a humble pastor, he was a senior member of the Church's communications staff.

That afternoon, I made the gruelling climb up to Christian's Cave, curious to view from close up the place with an irresistible draw for Fletcher Christian. I had already seen it from afar. In fact, the cave, which overlooked Adamstown, was like a perpetual brooding presence — visible from everywhere in the village and particularly conspicuous, in an unsettling way, from outside our front door.

My fellow walkers were Robert Vinson, one of the detectives, another Kent officer, Max Davidson, and Fletcher Pilditch, the serendipitously named third Crown prosecutor. Picking up the path just beyond the pink timber school, we followed it up through a forest of roseapple and candlenut, passing a large boulder beneath which William McCoy, the mutineer, is thought to have built his infamous still. Emerging into the open, we admired the wild and beautiful ocean, dashing itself to bits against Pitcairn's rocky shoreline. Then came a long and increasingly steep ascent up a gravelly slope, at the top of which you had to sidle along a narrow ledge and jump across a hair-raising gap. There was no trace of

Fletcher inside the cave — not even a tell-tale scratching on the wall.

Later that day, a few of us walked down to Bounty Bay for a swim. The bay was churning like a washing machine, although the ocean itself was relatively calm. Thrashing around, I thought the breakers might pick me up and fling me onto the rocks or the concrete slipway.

At The Landing, Meralda Warren marched up to Claire and me. 'Congratulations,' she said, 'you two are the new Dea Birketts.' Her eyes were flashing. We knew how much the Pitcairners hated Birkett's book. 'The truth will out,' Meralda declared. 'You'll see.' Then she shot us another look of loathing and stalked off.

The following morning, Len Brown's trial got under way. Len, the father of Dave Brown and Olive Christian, had allegedly raped Jennifer twice, when he was in his mid-40s and she was in her teens.

In his youth, Len had been famous for scaling every cliff face on Pitcairn, and also for swimming the circumference of the island. He was still reputedly the best fisherman on Pitcairn, and the best wood carver. For court, Len wore a dirty cream shirt and old grey trousers. I noticed his broad, splayed feet, the legacy of a life lived almost permanently barefoot.

Every morning before school, Jennifer would visit her father's three watermelon patches, situated in scattered parts of the island. To encourage the seeds to grow, she would pick the male flowers and insert them into the females, together with their pollen. This had to be done in direct sunlight, so she would follow the sun as it reached each garden.

One day, while Jennifer was bent over the plants in a location called The Hollow, she looked up and saw Len approaching. He was 'very tall, very strong, very fit'. After a cursory chat about gardening, 'all of a sudden he just grabbed me and started pulling me'.

Len informed her, 'I'm going to do it.'

'What?' asked Jennifer.

'Sex,' he replied.

Len drove Jennifer to a secluded spot, Garnets Ridge. He tripped her up, and 'I went down with a bang onto some stones,' Jennifer told the court. Then he raped her.

'When he'd finished, what happened?' asked Fletcher Pilditch, the prosecutor.

'The bastard just got on his bike and left me there on the ground.'

And did she tell anyone about it?

'No, I didn't. There wasn't any point.'

The next morning, at The Hollow, the same thing happened — except this time Len dispensed with the small talk, and did not whisk Jennifer off somewhere quieter. 'He just did what he did before, hooked my legs underneath me, banged me down to the ground and he raped me.' Jennifer began to cry. 'He raped me in my father's garden,' she wept. And then Len left, without having said a thing.

After that, Jennifer changed her routine, inspecting the gardens in a different sequence. That meant the sun was not on the flowers, and she had to force open the buds to thrust in the stamen. The plants did not develop, and her father was again irate. For Jennifer, that was preferable to risking another attack by Len.

I was so gripped by this story of wordless violation that it was only later that I was struck by the grimly ironic parallel between Len's actions and Jennifer's.

Allan Roberts, the Deputy Public Defender, observed that Jennifer's account was more vivid than the one she had given to police in 2000. Was her memory more accurate now, he inquired. The question was clearly intended to needle, yet even Roberts may not have anticipated its effect.

'I lived my entire life that day, as best I could recall,' Jennifer cried, referring to the police interview. 'It's like a film going round and round on a never-ending reel in my head. Every single thing that happened to me on Pitcairn, I'm reliving, which I've pushed to the back of my mind for a long, long time. And things are coming out that I didn't realise I'd buried so deep, so long ago ... You bury things that you don't want to remember ... You don't want to admit what happened to you. You don't want to admit that they just do what they want to you, get up and sod off, and leave you lying there. And all those memories, God, I don't need anybody to tell me what they are, because I lived them. And I've been living them since I was three years old, right up until I left that godforsaken island to come and live in England, where I was saved from that lot on Pitcairn ... And I dare anybody to stand there in that court and tell me that I'm a liar. Because it bloody well happened to me, exactly as I said it.'

Roberts calmly repeated the question. Jennifer exploded. 'When you're having that nightmare ... it all comes back as though it happened to you yesterday ... So you can dress it up as you like, say what you want, but I know the truth. I was there, you weren't. If you were, then my God, you wouldn't be sitting there saying what you're trying to say to me ... Or I'll be putting you in jail alongside Len Brown, give me a chance, if you were actually there when it happened.' Jennifer was shouting.

The judge, Russell Johnson, suggested a break. I got up. I was shaking. I felt as if I had just witnessed an exorcism. I walked outside and inhaled mouthfuls of air. Steve rattled past with a bundle of sugarcane on the back of his bike. Len was still sitting in the public gallery, impassive. Being quite deaf, he had most likely not heard a word.

Steve was back in court that afternoon for the evidence of his second victim, Charlotte, who had flown into Auckland from Australia. On touching down, Charlotte had almost pulled out her mobile phone to tell police she could not go through with it. However, by the time she reached the witness box, this slightly built woman in her early 40s was composed and quietly resolute.

Charlotte had left the island in the 1970s and returned for only two short visits, one following her father's death. Questioned by Christine Gordon, she transported herself back a quarter of a century to a day when she was playing with friends at Taro Ground, the site of the radio communications station. Steve drew up on his motorbike and invited her to 'go for a ride'. On Pitcairn, 'go ride' is slang for sex, but Charlotte only understood the literal meaning. She was 12 years old, and a virgin with 'very minimal' sexual knowledge.

Steve, who was 21, drove her up to Highest Point, the summit of the island, and led her into some bushes. She still had no idea what was happening. He ordered her to lie down in the grass, and then he removed her underwear and raped her. 'I remember it really hurt,' she said.

In court, Steve sat straight-backed, his gaze fixed on a spot on the wall, as Charlotte recalled a second assault. It was a few months later, and she was at The Landing, swimming in the bay and playing among the rocks. Steve spirited her off and raped her in a boat inside the shed, she alleged.

Paul Dacre suggested to Charlotte that she had consented on both occasions. On the monitor screen, Charlotte looked incredulous. 'What 12-year-old would give consensual sex?'

Steve had already had sex with the other girls her age, she

The surf-lashed cliffs of Pitcairn Island rise up to 337 metres above sea level.

Pitcairn Island seen from the deck of the *Braveheart*, which transported journalists and other visitors to the island for the 2004 trials.

(Top, left) Deputy Public Defender Allan Roberts approaching the Adamstown square, where the courthouse is located, during the Pitcairn trials.
(Top, right) Steve Christian walking towards the courthouse with Charles Cato, one of the defence lawyers, during Steve's trial.

The women's meeting at Big Fence: (left to right) Vula Young, Betty Christian, Meralda Warren and Carol Warren.

Looking down on Bounty Bay and the boatsheds from mid-way up the Hill of Difficulty.
(Below, left) Steve Christian presiding over the giving of presents during Christmas celebrations in the Pitcairn square.

(Top, right) A model *Bounty* is set alight in Bounty Bay on the anniversary of the torching of the ship by the mutineers in 1790.

Brenda Christian feeding Ms T, sole survivor of five Galapagos turtles brought to Pitcairn by an American sailor in the mid-20th century.

Pitcairn Commissioner Leon Salt (left), with Detective Superintendent Dennis McGookin, who headed Operation Unique and investigated the first sexual misconduct allegation in 1996.

Charlene Warren, one of the Pitcairn women who withdrew their police statements, on the island with her daughter, Torika.

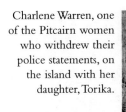

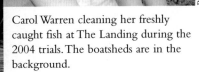

Carol Warren cleaning her freshly caught fish at The Landing during the 2004 trials. The boatsheds are in the background.

Defendants Terry Young (left) and Dave Brown in the square, packing locally produced Pitcairn honey to dispatch on an imminently expected container ship.

(Top) During the Pitcairn trials, passengers from the *Clipper Odyssey* cruise ship visited the island. Here, lawyers browse the souvenir stalls. Mike Lupton-Christian is far left; Len Brown is seated in the background.

(Right) Albert Reeves, the former teacher, tows a Pitcairn Islander during a lighthearted moment in the late 1950s.

(Left) Rowing one of the old wooden longboats, 1964. Nowadays the boats are made of aluminium, and have a powerful diesel engine.

PHOTO COURTESY OF KATHY MARKS

Len Brown and Brenda
Christian gutting their catch
after a day's fishing off the
rocks at Tedside.

PHOTO COURTESY OF CLAIRE HARVEY

Pitcairn's longboat, with Pawl
Warren on prow, coming
out to the *Braveheart* to
fetch visitors arriving for
the 2004 trials.

Pawl Warren, outside his house
on the island during the
Pitcairn trials, displaying some
of his multiple piercings.

PHOTO COURTESY OF KATHY MARKS

Jubilant after raising the *Bounty*'s cannon: (top, left to right) Dave Brown, Shawn Christian, Jay Warren, Terry Young, Dennis Christian, Steve Christian and Nigel Erskine, marine archaeologist from James Cook University; (bottom, left to right) Randy Christian and Pawl Warren.

English-born couple Bill and Catherine Haigh on their quad bike. Bill is a communications expert, and they have spent long periods living on Pitcairn.

observed. 'As kids, we all knew what was going on. He seemed to take it upon himself to initiate all the girls, and it was like we were his harem.'

Why didn't she tell her parents about the rapes, Dacre asked.

Charlotte sighed. She said it was 'generally known' that such things happened. But 'nothing was done about it, it was shoved under the carpet ... It's an act that everybody on the island knew was happening, and nobody wanted to say it was wrong and deal with it or do anything about it.'

Charlotte's parents had been respected figures in the community and leading members of the Church, Paul Dacre pointed out. Surely 'if they'd heard that something bad had happened to their daughter, both of them would have done something about it?'

Charlotte replied, simply, 'I don't know whether they would have done something about it.'

After court finished for the day, Brenda Christian made an announcement over the VHF radio system, appealing to everyone to drive slowly because of the dust. Quad bikes should reduce speed to 10kph (6mph) in Adamstown, she said, and preferably 5kph (3mph).

It had not rained for weeks — the level in our rainwater tank was worryingly low — and the dust was atrocious. Bright red and clingy, it rose off the dirt tracks and embedded itself in your skin, hair and clothes; by evening a coating had formed that was difficult to dislodge, even with determined scrubbing. The dust had also invaded every corner of our house, leaving floors and furniture sporting an unattractive red-brown sheen.

Simon Moore had arrived on Pitcairn still entertaining the hope that some, if not all, of the men might plead guilty. It soon became obvious that, with Steve Christian setting the tone, it was all for one and one for all — and no one was owning up to anything.

On Monday, 4 October, nearly a week into the trials, that united front suddenly cracked. Dennis Christian stood in court, looking self-conscious, as his lawyer, Allan Roberts, announced that Dennis was admitting to three charges of assaulting two girls. Moreover, he had emailed his main victim, Carla, apologising for his conduct of several decades earlier and expressing remorse.

Dennis's conversion on the dirt road to Adamstown provoked a minor media frenzy. Did he think others would follow Dennis's example, we demanded of Simon Moore. Moore dubbed it a 'psychological landmark', but was cautious about the implications.

It was speculated that gentle, mild-mannered Dennis had done the honourable thing to spare his mother, Irma, the ordeal of a trial. Dennis's courage in breaking ranks was praised, as was the fact that he had saved two women from giving evidence. All was not quite as it appeared, though. Aware that Carla, in particular, was a reluctant witness, Dennis had waited to see whether she turned up at the video-link studios to testify, as scheduled, that morning. She did, but was still hesitant about going ahead; detectives at her end urged her to call Dennis's bluff. It was only when he was convinced that Carla was about to take the stand that Dennis presented his guilty pleas.

Russell Johnson, the judge, remanded the 49-year-old post-master on bail until the conclusion of all seven trials, when verdicts and sentences would be delivered together.

That afternoon Sue Ingram called at Dennis's house to request an interview. He was not in, so Sue had a brief word with Irma. The next day Paul Dacre stood up in court and claimed the media were 'hounding elderly relatives'.

* * *

The day after Dennis's guilty plea, we had an early morning appointment at the prison. Pawl Warren was going out hunting, and we journalists had arranged to tag along. First, however, Pawl had to collect his .22 Remington rifle, which — like all of the islanders' firearms — was in the custody of military police at the jail.

During the trials, guns could only be used under supervision, so the senior MDP officer, Sergeant Vinny Reid, accompanied us. As Pawl and Reid strode through the undergrowth, which danced with fragments of sunlight, Claire, Neil, Ewart, Zane and I hurried to keep up. 'There's going to be holes in the sky today, mate,' joked Pawl, said to be one of Pitcairn's sharpest shooters.

Reid paused in a banyan grove and unclipped his hand-held radio. 'This is a public announcement,' he barked in his broad Scottish accent. 'There will be a shooting at Tom and Betty's at 9 a.m. Repeat. There will be a shooting at Tom and Betty's at 9 a.m.'

Once in Tom and Betty Christian's garden, Pawl took a little while to locate his quarry. Spying it high up in a tree, he raised his rifle to his shoulder, took aim and fired. A large breadfruit thudded to the ground, ripe and ready for the cooking pot.

Although breadfruit had been the indirect cause of their woes, the mutineers and their descendants took to it. There were breadfruit trees growing on Pitcairn when Fletcher Christian's band landed, and nowadays it is a staple food. The melon-sized fruit — Betty calls them 'mutiny fruit' — are similar to potato, but creamier and more flavoursome. Pawl said, 'You can mash 'em, boil 'em, stew 'em, bake 'em. They make beautiful chips, to eat with fish or corned beef.'

In Betty's kitchen, she and Tom recalled once finding their tree so heavily laden that they picked all the fruit, and everyone on the island prepared a dish for a communal banquet. There was boiled breadfruit, breadfruit stew, breadfruit salad, breadfruit puffs, breadfruit patties and breadfruit fritters. There was breadfruit pilhi, a paste baked in a banana leaf, after a Tahitian recipe, and shepherd's pie with mashed breadfruit on top. Meralda Warren baked breadfruit scones.

As we talked, Tom snipped away at a pile of dried bananas. Some of the Pitcairners had begun exporting dehydrated fruit to New Zealand, where it was highly prized as organic produce. Since stamps were no longer lucrative, they were trying to find new sources of income.

Conversation turned to the trials. Tom was scathing. 'Why dig up all these things from the past?' he snorted. 'It's like archaeology. Anyway, the wounds heal over time.' Betty said, 'These guys were for the most part quite young. It seems like there was a phase when everybody went crazy. I think they've matured now.'

The bottom line, for both of them, was that the men were needed, especially on the longboats. 'These guys, all their lives they've been operating the boats,' said Betty. 'They drive the machinery, they maintain the roads, they go out to supply the firewood. They are the workforce, exactly. They're the key people here that keep the community going.'

Later that morning, the video of Steve Christian's hour-long interview by police in 2000 was played back to the court. It had been conducted in Auckland, where Steve had just stepped off a ship from Pitcairn, and he told detectives that the allegations had 'struck us out of the blue'.

On the video, Robert Vinson interrogated Steve about four Pitcairn women: Charlotte, Sophie, Joanne and Heather. (Jennifer had not yet spoken to police.) All four had said that they were virgins when Steve had sex with them, mostly at the age of 12 or 13. Steve claimed in the interview that each girl had consented.

However, he could not bring to mind any specific incidents. So how could he be sure they had consented, asked Vinson. 'Well, it's just ... I've never taken anyone against their wish,' Steve replied. 'To me, rape would be to grab someone and force them.' He also disagreed that Charlotte had been a virgin. 'These girls were fooling around with everybody else,' he said coolly.

Turning to the subject of Sophie, Vinson said she had given a statement saying that Steve had led her into a grove of trees near Big Fence and told her 'she could be like all the other girls you had broken in'. He then proceeded to rape her, 'and she was crying out in pain'.

'No comment,' said Steve.

On a subsequent occasion, according to Sophie, Steve had forced her to perform oral sex and masturbate him. Then he had raped her again, telling her 'it wouldn't be as bad as the first time', and 'the more you do it, the better it gets'. He also attempted to rape her anally, despite her protests.

'No comment,' replied Steve, for the umpteenth time.

By this stage, Steve seemed weary and mildly exasperated. Yet never once during the interview did he appear seriously rattled. He sat calmly under the fluorescent lights, hands clasped on the table before him.

In court, Steve looked bored as the video was running.

During a lull in the evidence, I saw Steve locked in conversation with Matthew Forbes in the square. I later discovered that they had been discussing development plans for Pitcairn and an application to visit by a television team. Regardless of what was going on in court, it was plain that Steve was still the boss.

The following day, Jay Warren's trial opened. The prosecutors made a theatrical entrance on a borrowed quad bike, gowns flying, a crate of documents perched on the front.

Jay, 47, was Pitcairn's director of biosecurity. He was charged with one relatively minor offence. It could have been heard by a magistrate, but he had chosen to be tried by the Supreme Court, in order to participate in a legal challenge that would be questioning the fairness of the prosecution.

Jay seemed different from the other accused. He was quieter, diffident even, and did not join in the men's giggling and banter. He was said to be a decent person, although thoroughly dominated by his wife, Carol: a fact remarked on by most visitors to the island. Carol, a more forceful character, usually spoke on behalf of the Warren clan, and Jay, it was said, consulted her before making any decision of importance. In court, as around the island, Jay gave little away.

Jay's alleged victim, Suzie, told Chief Justice Blackie that he had molested her in the water at Bounty Bay when she was 12 and he was 27. A group of islanders, mainly young people, had gone body surfing after school; Jay swam up behind Suzie and stuck his hand down her bikini bottom. 'I was wearing flippers, so I just struggled to kick and swim away,' she said.

Paul Dacre, Jay's lawyer, asked Suzie whether there had been any further episodes involving Jay. 'No,' she said, adding, 'I was getting smarter at making sure I was away from anyone.'

Jay then gave evidence, the first defendant to do so. Dacre seized the opportunity to quiz him about the Pitcairners' knowledge of British law, which was to be a central component of the legal challenge. Jay had been magistrate until just after the Ricky Quinn affair in 1999, when Lea Brown, Dave's wife, had replaced him. Dacre asked him what law he had believed applied on the island when he was in office. 'Pitcairn law,' Jay replied. 'We didn't know anything about English law until Gail Cox arrived.'

Cross-examined by Fletcher Pilditch, Jay agreed that he had been aware that serious crimes such as rape and murder would be handled by 'higher authorities', not the local court. He also conceded that Pitcairn was 'not a lawless island', and that if a crime was committed, 'the people of this community would expect something to be done about it'.

Another day, another defendant. Rain beat down on the tin roof of the courthouse, almost drowning out the sound of more guilty pleas. The big dry had finally ended, and Dave Brown had had a change of heart — a small one: he now admitted assaulting two of the five women named in his voluminous charge sheet. One was Janet, whom Dave had molested after a spearfishing trip, while still wearing his mask and snorkel. Janet had been 15, Dave 31. Dave had also assaulted 14-year-old Linda while she was driving his quad bike.

As his lawyer, Charles Cato, conveyed his guilty pleas to Jane Lovell-Smith, Dave stood up straight, in jeans and red *Bounty* polo-shirt, arms by his sides. Cato was a sharp, erudite lawyer, although he was to cause a few comic moments, once referring to his client as Dave Moore, and on another occasion calling the Hill of Difficulty the Hill of Deliverance.

The tape of Dave's police interview was shown, and we saw a very different Dave from the one who swaggered around Adamstown, full of bluster. This Dave was meek and almost reflective. He was questioned about Darralyn Griffiths, who, as we knew, had given a statement to police but long since withdrawn from the case. Dave acknowledged having had a 'relationship' with Darralyn that began when she was 'borderline 12 or 13'.

'Were you in love with Darralyn?' Robert Vinson asked.

'Yes, I think I was,' Dave mumbled.

Vinson: 'Do you think it's wrong for a man in his 30s to be having sex with a 12- or 13-year-old?'

Dave: 'Yes, when I look back on it now.'

Vinson: 'Is it a fairly normal part of Pitcairn life?'

Dave: 'It seems to be something that's been done right down through the ages ... Someone following on from someone else ... It didn't seem wrong ... Everyone was doing that sort of thing at that age.'

Police then asked Dave about seven other women, not including Linda, who had accused him of sexual abuse. He denied most of the allegations. Why would so many women make things up, wondered Peter George. 'Those girls hated my guts,' said Dave on the tape.

In the public gallery, Dave fidgeted.

A day or two later, Janet's mother thanked Dave for pleading guilty, thereby sparing Janet from having to testify. He had done the right thing, she said. 'I only did it because your bloody daughter blackmailed me,' Dave spat in response.

With several trials running at once, the proceedings took on a disjointed air. Trials would open, adjourn, resume and adjourn again. In between going to court, the defendants, apparently seamlessly, carried on with their normal lives: fishing, gardening, making carvings, repairing machinery, driving the tractor.

It struck me how peculiar it must all seem from their perspective. The courthouse had not been used as such for decades. (Ricky Quinn's trial had been held at the schoolhouse.) It was the Pitcairners' council chamber, their meeting room, their community centre. It was *theirs*. Now it had been taken over by strangers — strangers sitting in judgement over them.

The Adamstown square, meanwhile, was full of pesky reporters trying to photograph the accused as they went in and out of court.

The men did their best to wrongfoot us. There were two tracks leading up to the square, and the public hall itself had two doors. They could arrive on foot or by quad bike. Each day brought some new variation on this game of cat and mouse.

Meralda Warren lived behind the hall with her parents, Mavis and Jacob. The defendants sometimes retreated there before or after court. Once we pursued Dave in that direction, only to be met by an enraged Meralda, waving her arms. 'Get off, get off, it's private property!' she yelled.

Steve Christian was the exception. He would walk unhurriedly across the square, with his rolling gait, and the aura of a man whose birthright was power. Steve always entered and left court through the main door. He did not dodge the cameras. But he never met our eye.

The public benches remained deserted, but not for lack of curiosity: the locals, we had heard, were desperately keen to know what was going on. Had they attended, though, it would have been held against them; they had to stay away, signalling contempt for the process. Wives showed their loyalty not by being there, but by *not* being there.

There was another reason for the islanders' absence: if they pretended nothing was happening, maybe the judges and everyone else would pack up and leave.

The word around Pitcairn was that the trials were going extremely badly — for the prosecution. Indeed, it was being confidently predicted that the entire case was about to collapse.

CHAPTER 9

Let's make-believe

When the rain finally came, it seemed like it would never stop. It was as if the clouds were sucking up huge mouthfuls of the Pacific Ocean and dumping them onto our little patch of rock. Pitcairn's dirt tracks turned into mudslides, and walking even a short distance became a battle. The mud was deep and sticky; no sooner had you staggered a few paces, releasing each foot from its treacly trap, than you were liable to slither onto your backside. Boots acquired a layer of red goo, like a platform sole that grew heavier with every step. It was easier to do as the islanders did — go barefoot.

Our water tank was overflowing, but our clean washing had been hanging bedraggled on the line for days, and a backlog of mud-stained laundry was piling up. It was cold, too; I had to beg some extra blankets. Going out was such a struggle that I tried to stay close to home, where I moped around, feeling confined. As if Pitcairn was not already small enough, my world had shrunk to the four walls of the Lodge.

The roads were still rivers of mud when the sleek white shape of the *Clipper Odyssey* hove into view on Saturday, 9 October. I had been on Pitcairn for nearly two weeks and several trials were in mid-flow; now the island was preparing to welcome some new visitors. High winds and a big swell greeted the cruise liner, which was on its way from Tahiti to Easter Island, carrying a hundred or so passengers, mainly elderly Americans.

Weather aside, I felt bemused by the idea of tourists arriving at this particular time. I knew that, for many outsiders, the prospect of meeting Fletcher Christian's descendants was beguiling; however, seven of those men with romantic antecedents were on trial for raping and assaulting young girls. Did the *Clipper Odyssey*'s passengers really want to come here and mingle with the accused and their families? Wasn't the whole child abuse business just a little, you know, offputting?

It was a strange day, and it began with a stranger taking a photograph of me as I folded a pile of clothes in my bedroom. Stepping outside, I discovered that Adamstown — where the pace of life is usually languid, to say the least — was a hubbub of activity. Stalls had been set up in the square and along the main road, with souvenirs laid out under waterproof tarpaulins. There were Pitcairn stamps, postcards, T-shirts, cookbooks, woven baskets, local honey and the ubiquitous wooden carvings.

From the crest of the Hill of Difficulty, I could see the *Clipper Odyssey* pitching quite briskly about half a mile offshore. The two longboats were ferrying people to and fro, with the swell lifting their prows right out of the water and dashing them down again. Visitors with backpacks and sunhats and cameras were squelching their way along Pitcairn's muddy trails, while others were being shown around the island on quad bikes. A stout-hearted group was hiking up to Christian's Cave.

I browsed the souvenir stalls and bought a T-shirt from Carol Warren, who was all smiles as she hunted out the right size and colour for me. Terry Young, who was scheduled to appear in court on the Monday, sold me a wooden shark with teeth fashioned from real shark's teeth. I had a fascinating discussion with Terry about woodcarving. I was pleased that the locals were being so friendly today. Perhaps they didn't dislike us that much. Perhaps they just needed a while to thaw.

Terry was short of change, and said he would give me mine later. I thought he might slip me the dollar bills in court. But he sought me out at The Landing, where yet more stalls had been put up and tourists were milling around, chatting excitedly with the locals.

'What generation Pitcairner are *you*?' a middle-aged woman inquired as I stood on the jetty, surveying the scene.

'I'm not a Pitcairner,' I replied.

'But you work on the boats?'

'No,' I said. 'I'm a journalist.'

'Oh . . . so what are you doing on Pitcairn, then?'

'I'm covering the trials — you know, the child sexual abuse trials.'

'I see [backing off] . . . That must be interesting.'

At midday the visitors converged on Big Fence for fish and chips, provided (for a fee) by Steve and Olive Christian. No one found the choice of lunch venue untoward, it seems, including the American tour company chartering the *Clipper Odyssey*. It was as if reality had been suspended and everyone was engaged in a game of make-believe. Let's make believe that everything is rosy on the legendary island of *Bounty* fame. Let's make believe that the Pitcairn Islanders are all fine, upstanding citizens. Let's make believe that half of the mutineers' male heirs, including our lunch host, aren't accused of sex crimes.

More chips, anyone?

Some of the ship's passengers quizzed us in hushed tones about the case; they appeared to be enjoying the extra *frisson*. One Belgian woman said, 'We have exactly the same trials in our country not so long ago, so you can understand that happens everywhere.'

True, but it's not everywhere that crowds of tourists happily rub shoulders with alleged paedophiles, visit them in their homes, buy their souvenirs, pose for photographs with them, and treat them like nobility.

An American in his early 60s told me that he had been longing to visit Pitcairn since he was a boy. So how did it feel to be here at last? 'Awesome,' he replied.

The *Clipper Odyssey* was not the only vessel to arrive that morning: the *Braveheart* had returned, and would be transporting Ray Coombe, the pastor, and his wife, Daphne, to Mangareva, along with Sue Ingram. Like some of the other journalists, I had originally planned to leave after a fortnight too, but had changed my mind. In the late afternoon, after depositing the last visitors at the *Clipper Odyssey*, one of the longboats came back to fetch the departing passengers. A dozen outsiders, including media, lawyers and police, climbed in to see Sue and the Coombes off on the *Braveheart*.

As the longboat slammed into the breakers, I noticed Dave Brown observing us with an amused expression; perhaps he hoped we were going to be seasick. We drew up alongside the *Braveheart*, where it proved exceedingly difficult to transfer people and luggage. One minute the swell smashed the two boats together; the next we were way apart, with the *Braveheart* perhaps ten feet above our heads. The islanders scooped up Sue, Ray and Daphne, and flung them across the wildly fluctuating gap into the arms of the *Braveheart*'s crew.

The longboat set off, but rather than return to shore it made for the *Clipper Odyssey*, where it stopped by an open hatch. Most of the locals disembarked. Somewhat disoriented, we followed them, and found ourselves in an unfamiliar realm of teak furniture and gleaming interiors — all very different from our own living environment, defined by mud and mosquitoes and long-drop toilets. Claire Harvey and I looked at each other, flushed with excitement, as our feet sank into the carpeted staircase. 'There's a shop that sells perfume,' she whispered. 'And flushing loos!'

More exotic pleasures awaited us on the rear deck, which had a swimming pool and a poolside bar. We had not set eyes on an establishment serving alcohol since leaving Tahiti three weeks earlier. Neil Tweedie, the *Daily Telegraph* reporter, was already ensconced there, on first-name terms with the white-jacketed barman and looking considerably more cheerful than he had for some time. Brandishing his company credit card, Neil ordered a round of piña coladas.

Clad in mud-spattered boots and shorts, I sipped my cocktail and gazed at the opulent surroundings, wondering if I was dreaming. Steve Christian was standing a few feet away by the pool, beer in hand, in conversation with one of the ship's officers. Steve wore his usual enigmatic expression, but I had the feeling that he was not pleased to see us.

Pawl Warren was also at the bar, besieged by admirers. I realised why he cultivated the pirate image. The tourists loved it. They were practically queueing up to have their photograph taken with him.

After one drink, sadly, it was time to go; the longboat was waiting to take us all back to the island. On my way downstairs I spotted a plate of fruit sitting on a table. Despite Pitcairn's reputation as a Garden of Eden, we had hardly come across any fresh produce. I hesitated, then grabbed a couple of shiny apples.

A throng of islanders were assembled below; they must have spent most of the day on the ship, selling their souvenirs. The longboat was lurching around, and as we flung ourselves on board

Neil slipped on the wet floor and fell headlong. Dave and Steve burst out laughing. Just to annoy them, I pulled out my camera and started taking pictures of them. Waves of antipathy radiated towards us from the back of the boat. Not for the first time, I reflected that the men could shove us overboard if they wanted to.

The moment passed, and as we motored home with the sun going down I felt something quite perverse: a sense of belonging. Just for a few seconds, carried away by the beauty of Pitcairn at dusk and the camaraderie of those in the longboat, I imagined I was one of them — or yearned to be. Then I snapped out of it. What on earth was I thinking?

The following day, a Sunday, Pawl Warren took me on a tour of the island on his quad bike; Christian's Cave aside, I hadn't seen much beyond the Lodge and the courtroom. Notwithstanding Pitcairn's compact size, barely 2 miles long by 1 mile wide, it can take hours to circumnavigate because of the numerous hills and valleys. That weekend certain roads were still impassable as a result of the recent rains.

As Pawl negotiated a maze of tracks, some of which wove right along the cliff edge, I was struck by a sense of history reaching back far beyond the mutineers. At one site, Down Rope, there are ancient petroglyphs carved into a cliff face by Polynesians who inhabited the island, it is believed, from about 800 to 1400 AD. A few decades ago, the islanders hacked some of the carvings out of the rock and sold them to collectors, along with *Bounty* relics such as the ship's chronometer. In spite of history meaning so much to the Pitcairners, they did not appear protective of it: the oldest house on the island, built by Fletcher Christian's grandson, had recently been demolished.

Pawl and I travelled further along the muddy trails, shaded in places by awnings of giant tree ferns, and emerged in a lunar landscape of red earth peppered with enormous rocks. Below was St Paul's, an Olympic-sized natural pool, fed by waves pouring in between two basalt pillars. The surf was crashing into the pool with such energy that the spray almost obscured the towering outcrops. It stung my face as I stood at the top of the cliff, 260 feet up.

People have died at St Paul's and other locations around the coast, mostly swept out to sea by freak waves while swimming or fishing off rocks. The Pitcairn map is dotted with laconic place names: Where Dan Fall, Where Dick Die, Break Im Hip, Oh Dear, Minnie Off. As was reinforced to me during my excursion with Pawl, Pitcairn is quite unlike picture-postcard images of the South Pacific, and not only because it has no sparkling white beaches — in fact, no beaches at all. The island is all precipitous slopes and rocky escarpments, plunging ravines and windswept ridges. The rugged scenery is awe-inspiring, yet somehow oppressive. Nature's physical presence is almost overpowering.

At Highest Point, a desolate plateau with 360-degree views extending to an empty horizon in every direction, I was reminded just how isolated Pitcairn is. Adamstown was visible below, yet I felt far removed from the modicum of civilisation it represented. This was where Charlotte had been raped by Steve Christian, allegedly, and I could imagine how petrified that 12-year-old girl must have felt. Highest Point, 1,106 feet above the ocean, was the loneliest spot on a lonely island in the middle of nowhere.

When we arrived back at the village, I thanked Pawl and then headed straight to the square. A supply ship was due in two days, and the locals would be packaging their honey for export. Pitcairn honey, said to be among the world's purest, is a new industry, like the dried fruit. Trestle tables had been set up outside the post office, and a couple of dozen people were seated around them, hard at work.

I started taking photographs. Claire was already there, as were Neil and the TVNZ team, Zane Willis and Ewart Barnsley. Some of the islanders began to mutter. One was Lea Brown, Dave's wife. The muttering grew louder. Suddenly Dave stood up, came over to me and told me he was fed up with the 'lies' I had been writing. Cookie Warren walked up and joined in the attack, and Carol Warren, no longer the affable T-shirt saleswoman, added her voice to theirs. I attempted to defend myself, and then sloped off home, feeling bruised.

Later that day Betty Christian, who had been in the square, commiserated with me. 'They turned on you like a pack of wolves,' she exclaimed. Betty had felt bad for me, she told me. But she hadn't said anything at the time.

Monday, 11 October; Terry Young was due in court. His trial had already opened, but the principal witness had yet to give evidence. As he entered the square, he pushed my camera aside — rather different from the genial Terry who had sold me a shark carving 48 hours earlier.

In court, the carpet had a new reddish-brown pattern, thanks to the mud trampled across it; the carpet in our house was the same. The prosecutors, always well kitted out, arrived in gumboots, raincoats and waterproof leggings. Peeling off their wet-weather gear on the verandah, they emerged incongruously spic and span in their suits and gowns.

Terry was in the public gallery, a morose figure in a dark blue T-shirt, scruffy blue trousers and dirty trainers. The court had already been told that he offended for nearly two decades, focusing on four girls and resuming that behaviour after a year in New Zealand. Terry, a 45-year-old electrician, was charged with seven indecent assaults and one representative count of rape.

The first witness, Janet, alleged that Terry lay in wait for her outside the girls' lavatories one evening, during a community event at the school. She was ten. Terry unzipped her trousers and assaulted her. Janet did not tell anyone. 'It was just not something you talked about,' she explained. 'You didn't know who to talk to.'

Terry's main victim was Marion, a neighbour whom he allegedly abused for almost a decade. She was also the girl molested by Dave Brown in the church, according to Isobel, her friend.

Marion appeared on the video link. She looked sick with apprehension.

In a soft voice, she told the court that she had a clear memory of Terry raping her when she was 12. However, Marion said haltingly, he had indecently assaulted her for many years before that, perhaps since she was six. The attacks took place almost every week, sometimes in his bedroom or in a hut near Taro Ground, but mainly in the bushes, when they went out collecting firewood together.

As a baby, Marion had been so tiny, her grandmother told her, that 'they had to put me in a doll's bathtub inside a normal bathtub so the ants wouldn't eat me'. As she grew up, she remained small for her age. Terry, who was eight years older, was 'very stocky and quite strong, very well built'. When he started assaulting her, Marion protested, but 'he would ignore me or just carry on what he was doing ... After a while I stopped saying no. There was no point ... I would just lay there and let him get it over and done with ... The quicker he did it, the quicker I was able to go.'

Terry sat brooding in court, hands clasped over his belly, as Marion recalled that he spoke to her only to give her instructions — 'to go with him into the bushes ... to take my underwear off, put my underwear on, then tell me to go'. Afterwards he always warned her, 'Don't tell anybody.' He was bad-tempered, and

Marion was scared of him. Terry would insult her in front of his friends.

Marion's home life was wretched. Her parents were very strict and treated her like a servant; she was frequently thrashed with a 'jandal' (flip-flop) or coconut-frond broom. On the monitor screen, Marion removed her glasses and wiped her eyes. 'In our family, no affection was shown to anybody,' she stated in a wobbly voice. 'For most of my childhood I felt that I was in the way.' Her only escape was books, of which she became enamoured at an early age — and from reading Marion learnt that what Terry was doing to her was wrong. She could not refuse to help him fetch firewood, though; her mother would have beaten her for shirking a chore. There was no respite until she went to New Zealand at the age of 15 to finish her schooling.

Allan Roberts asked Marion why she had not reported Terry's conduct, not even to the schoolteacher, a New Zealander. 'It was too shameful to tell anyone, let alone tell someone that wasn't from Pitcairn,' she replied. When Roberts repeated the question, Marion began to weep. Jane Lovell-Smith adjourned the proceedings. But no one thought to switch off the video monitor, so as the lawyers debated what time to reconvene, Marion sobbed away on the screen, a handkerchief pressed to her face.

Later, Terry's police interview was played to the court. Questioned about four girls, Terry admitted molesting Catherine on his quad bike when she was 13 or 14; he said he also touched ten-year-old Sarah during a game of tag but claimed it was accidental. As for Marion, she 'asked me to rub her down ... her whole body' at the age of seven, Terry told detectives.

Asked how often he had been off the island, Terry mentioned a trip to Mangareva in 1987. 'We went in a longboat,' he said casually.

'To Mangareva?' asked Robert Vinson.

'Yes,' Terry replied.

I glanced at Judge Lovell-Smith, at the front of the court. Her face was frozen in horror and disbelief.

Vinson suggested there was a pattern of Terry targeting young girls, in some cases while teaching them to drive his quad bike. Terry retorted huffily, 'Nowadays if I see any girls walking, I won't even offer to take them on my bike.' He added, 'Sometimes they want . . . us to touch it [their genitals], they keeping coming and want us to touch them, the girls.'

The rain had recommenced, and was making such a racket that I could barely hear what was being said. When court broke for lunch, Lovell-Smith's colleague, Russell Johnson, arrived in shorts and gumboots, clutching a second pair of boots. They were for Her Ladyship, who was stranded at the square without suitable footwear. The pair exited together, Johnson chivalrously shielding Lovell-Smith with a big umbrella.

Steve Christian's trial reopened at the beginning of the third week, with Paul Dacre announcing that while Steve did not intend to testify himself, he would be calling three women to speak up for him.

First to enter the witness box was 76-year-old Royal Warren, Cookie's mother and the aunt of Steve's wife, Olive Christian. Royal was barefoot; she had white curly hair, and was dressed in a blue checked shirt and red shorts. She stood in the box, hands in pockets.

One of Steve's victims, Jennifer, had claimed that he propositioned her while Olive was at home giving birth to their eldest son. Royal had assisted Olive during her long labour, and she now asserted that Steve had been present throughout. Simon Moore inquired whether Steve had left the room at all.

'No,' said Royal.

'Not even to go to the lavatory?'

'Of course,' said Royal.

'How many times?'

Impatient, Royal rejoined, 'I don't know ... I wasn't watching him. But I know he never left the room to go and do anything harmful.'

Moore smiled. 'That's all the questions I wanted to ask you.'

Royal was followed by Brenda Christian. Brenda, a contemporary of Jennifer's, was asked about a childhood fight that Jennifer had described; Brenda could not remember it. This seemed peripheral, but was aimed at undermining Jennifer's credibility.

Despite Brenda testifying in her brother's defence, their relationship was said to be poor. Brenda told Claire and me, 'Steve gets on with his life, I get on with mine. If he's found guilty, I'll be there for his family. But if his family don't want me anywhere near them, that's their choice.'

Lastly, it was Carol Warren's turn. I had only ever seen 54-year-old Carol in old, work-stained clothes. Today she was scrubbed and fresh. She wore a pretty floral shirt, and had a sprig of frangipani tucked behind one ear. Carol, it seemed clear, was looking forward to the attention. Simon Moore adopted a honeyed tone. Carol simpered and fluttered her eyelashes. She flung the Crown prosecutor coquettish smiles.

Moore reminded her about the women's meeting at Big Fence. Wasn't it Carol who had told the media that it was normal for Pitcairn girls to have sex at 12?

Carol agreed, a little suspicious.

What about her own daughters, Moore asked. Didn't she disapprove when one of them, at the age of 12 or 13, started going out with a much older man? Didn't she tell his wife during a confrontation that her daughter was 'only a child'? Wasn't she livid when she caught the man up a ladder, trying to sneak in through her daughter's window? Didn't she bellow, 'You short married bastard, get the fuck out of here,' at which he lost his footing and fell into the shrubbery?

Carol paused. 'Let's just say I disapproved.'

Moore: 'And did you disapprove because of the age discrepancy or because your standards are different when it involves your daughter?'

Carol: 'Simply because he was a married man and there was no future in the relationship for her.'

I had the impression that Carol's day in court had not gone quite as she had hoped. Steve, who was in the public gallery, looked as if he wanted to kill Moore.

Turi and Darralyn Griffiths, a young married couple, were planning to build a house on Pitcairn. They had been waiting patiently for materials, which a supply ship, the *Buzzard Bay*, had attempted to deliver two months earlier. The seas had been too rough, and so the vessel had continued on, ending up in the Belgian port of Antwerp, where another ship, the *Condor Bay*, had collected the materials. Now the *Condor Bay* was making a special diversion to the island, at substantial cost, and was due on Tuesday, 12 October, the day after Steve Christian's witnesses — among them Darralyn's mother, Carol — had given evidence.

The ship approached just before dawn. It was blowing a gale, and there were swells of up to 23 feet; the *Condor Bay*, a massive vessel with decks piled high with containers, was tossed around like a twig. Once again, efforts to unload proved fruitless, and after removing a few pieces of light cargo the men called a halt. The ship, which was working to a tight schedule, departed for Auckland, with the building materials still on board. A week later they would be back where they had started, having gone halfway around the world, twice.

All that Turi and Darralyn got out of it was a few nails and plumbing bits. Darralyn remarked, 'It's a bummer that it's gone past again. Hopefully we'll be third time lucky.'

The next morning, before court, Simon Moore dropped round to the Lodge. He wanted to warn us that Steve Christian was in a fury. At a council meeting the previous night, Moore had heard, Steve had accused the journalists and prosecutors of behaving disgracefully on the *Clipper Odyssey*. According to Steve, we had all got riotously drunk; we had brought shame on the island, and upset the ship's officers and crew. Neil Tweedie had been so intoxicated that he could barely stand up, and when he toppled over while boarding the longboat, he had displayed his genitals.

Steve claimed we should never have been on the *Clipper Odyssey* in the first place. Only locals were allowed on the cruise ships.

None of this was true, and Neil was particularly unhappy with Steve's version of events. Simon Moore said that Steve was threatening to turn the incident into 'another tits and wig affair'.

Not all callers brought bad tidings. Early in our stay, Pawl Warren came round to lend us a ghetto blaster and some CDs. He found Claire making a banana cake and elbowed her aside good-humouredly; a little later, he produced a delectable banana cake from our oven.

Pawl, in his early 40s, was an entertaining and gregarious person. More so than many Pitcairners, he was also well read, and had an impressive collection of books and music. He loved the island, which he described as 'a magnet in the middle of nowhere ... Once you've experienced life here, you just want to keep coming back.'

Sitting on our front deck, Pawl voiced clear-cut views about the criminal case. 'They're trying to say it was a way of life — well, no way, not with children,' he said. 'It's different if two young kids are fooling around. But when a 12-year-old girl is with a man in his 20s or 30s, there's something wrong there. How can she consent?'

Although the atmosphere on Pitcairn had been tense and unpleasant, with Pawl himself labelled 'a Governor's spy', he saw the trials as a painful necessity. 'How long can you let it keep going on before things have to change?' he demanded. Pawl dismissed the idea that the boats could not be operated if men went to jail: the rest of them would simply be more selective about which ships they visited, he said. 'If there's big surf and it's too dangerous, you'd just say, "Sorry, forget it, look forward to seeing you next time."'

Pawl was trying to keep his distance from the trials. He explained, 'At the end of the day it's better for me not to know who's charged, so that I can still look them in the eye and face them as mates.'

Randy Christian, Steve's middle-born son, was the last Pitcairn-based defendant to go on trial.

It was Randy's actions, and those of his brother, Shawn, allegedly, that had led to the exposure of child abuse dating back generations. After putting up with their assaults for years, their victim had seized an opportunity to speak out — and within a few months the web of silence and collusion spun around the Pitcairn men had disintegrated.

That victim was Belinda, the awkward, anguished 15-year-old who had lit the touch paper in 1999, then watched her life — and the island — blow up in her face. On Wednesday, 13 October 2004, Belinda finally got to tell her story in public.

That she was still around, and willing to tell it, was remarkable. It was five years since Belinda had unburdened herself to Gail Cox; evacuated from the island, she had been looked after by grandparents in New Zealand but cut off by the rest of her family. Belinda had not seen her parents or siblings since 2000. She had not even been told about the death of another grandparent; instead, she had learnt about it third-hand.

Belinda's mother supported her, after a fashion. However, her own husband had been questioned after Belinda quit the island. She still had to live on Pitcairn with the rest of her family, in a community where her daughter was reviled.

While Belinda's mother had divided loyalties, her father just sided with his mates. He had even reminded Steve about Belinda nearly drowning in a well when she was a toddler. She had not been right in the head since then, he said; maybe Randy's lawyers could use it against her.

Belinda's father had also done his best to bully her into abandoning the case. After making threats as he said goodbye to her at The Landing in 2000, he had kept up the pressure in emails. Police warned him about intimidating a witness. A few days before the trials started, he emailed his daughter again. 'Don't you understand that we're fighting for our lives here?' he told her. 'This is your last chance to back out. If you give evidence, you'll never be welcome in this community and you'll never see your family again.'

Ten days before Belinda was due to testify, an aunt tried to telephone her for the first time in four years. Suspecting a last-minute attempt to dissuade Belinda from giving evidence, her grandparents declined to put her on the phone.

Randy, 30 years old, was charged with five rapes and seven indecent assaults. Simon Moore claimed that he had targeted

Belinda 'in a fashion that can only be described as calculated, cold and utterly indifferent to the pain and terror he inflicted'.

Like his father, Randy was 14 when he allegedly embarked on a career of sexual offending. Like his father, he allegedly abused for 11 years. Like him, he picked on girls who were much younger and unlikely to make a fuss. Belinda was ten years Randy's junior. But while Steve had waited until they were 12 or 13, Randy, allegedly, had no such scruples. He began molesting Belinda when she was five or seven years old, Moore claimed.

Randy was installed at the front of the public gallery, wearing dark blue shorts and a dirty T-shirt. He was taller than his father, and built like a rugby prop. His enormous arms and legs were speckled with white paint.

Belinda materialised on the satellite link. She had dark hair, pulled back from her face, and an English rose complexion. She wore a fluffy jumper, and spoke with a distinctive Pitcairn accent.

Simon Moore asked her to tell the court about an incident that allegedly occurred soon after her tenth birthday. Belinda visibly squirmed. In a low, clear voice, she related how, as a child, she liked to go for solitary walks around the island. One warm and sunny day, she climbed up to Aute Valley, the site of vegetable gardens and also a tennis court. Suddenly she heard a motorbike approaching. It was Randy. After a brief conversation, Randy stuck his hand down her skirt. Belinda pushed it away. He persisted. Then he 'picked me up by my waist and took me' into a banana grove, she said. He pinned her to the ground, one large hand on her stomach. 'I kept telling him to let me go. I was scared of him and I just wanted to leave . . . He told me to be quiet or he would hit me.'

Belinda fought as Randy prised her legs apart. But he was 'too strong for me', she recalled. He raped her, and the pain was so agonising that she blacked out; when she regained consciousness,

Randy was putting his clothes on. He ordered her not to tell anyone. And with that he departed.

She did not tell anyone. 'I was too scared to. I thought I would be the one to get into trouble.'

Belinda had not had any sex education, and she did not even know what had happened to her. What she did know was that she was frightened of Randy now. She could not avoid him, though, for their families socialised regularly. A few months after the incident at Aute Valley, Belinda's family was invited to Big Fence for dinner. Afterwards she fell asleep in the video room. When she woke up, she said, she was in Randy's bedroom and he was raping her again. On this occasion she managed to break free, and she fled into the kitchen, where the adults were congregated. But still she did not say anything.

Belinda then recounted an episode that took place shortly before she turned 11. She spoke very slowly, punctuating her phrases with audible sighs. Randy leant forward, massive arms on massive thighs, listening intently.

It was the time of year when the sugar cane was harvested and boiled down into molasses. Most of the islanders were gathered in a processing shed near the cemetery; nearby, but out of sight in a thickly wooded area, the children were playing hide and seek with Shawn and Randy.

Belinda found herself alone with the brothers. 'They cornered me against a bunch of banana trees ... At first I thought they were just playing,' she said. Then Shawn pulled off his T-shirt and stuffed it into her mouth, and the two men, nine and ten years older than her, thrust her to the ground. As Randy held Belinda down, forcing her arms above her head, Shawn raped her. Then, 'joking among themselves ... laughing', they swapped places: Shawn held Belinda down and Randy raped her.

Thirty-one years earlier, their father had raped Jennifer, allegedly, as two friends restrained her.

When Randy had finished, he and Shawn left the ten-year-old lying on the red volcanic earth. Traumatised and weeping, she got dressed and walked to the sugar cane shed. Her father was there, and so was Dobrey Christian, Randy and Shawn's grandmother. Again Belinda said nothing. Again none of the adults appeared to notice anything was wrong.

Randy raped her several more times, Belinda alleged, and indecently assaulted her until he moved to Norfolk Island in 1999. 'I asked him why he was doing this to me,' she said. 'He told me it was because he liked me.'

Somewhat perplexingly, she liked him too. When she was 13 or 14, Belinda admitted, she became infatuated with Randy. He was popular and he was funny. She sent him love letters. But she did not like what he was doing to her. Belinda attempted to explain. 'He made me feel special,' she told the judge, Russell Johnson. 'I was confused. It was like he had two sides to him ... a great friendly guy and a person that did these awful things to me.'

By this point Randy was involved with Leon Salt's daughter, Rachel. Allan Roberts, Randy's lawyer, suggested to Belinda that Rachel was 'an obstacle to your affections'. Did she make her statement to Gail Cox as 'a method to have him refocus on you and not forget you ... to draw back attention to yourself'?

'No, I did not,' Belinda replied.

Although Belinda became distressed during cross-examination, she did not cede any ground to Roberts. Parts of her story were corroborated by Karen, her childhood friend, who alleged that she, too, had been indecently assaulted by Randy. Karen also testified that when the two girls were teenagers, Belinda had warned her 'that I shouldn't let my [younger] brother and sister play with Randy any more 'cause he's not safe'.

During Randy's police interview, which was shown to the court, he denied any sexual contact with Belinda. He denied it 21 times. 'Actually I haven't even touched her,' he said.

Throughout Belinda's testimony, I could see Brenda Christian, who was sitting next to Randy, furiously scribbling notes. She spoke to Randy in loud whispers, offering a commentary on the evidence and shaking her head, mock-pityingly, at what she was hearing. Brenda had behaved in a similar way during previous trials, including her brother's and Len Brown's. Len ate dinner at her house every night. It was she and Mike — rather than Len's son, Dave, or his daughter, Olive — who mainly took care of the old man.

Brenda was the island police officer. She was also Randy's aunt. It seemed blindingly obvious that the two roles were irreconcilable. Brenda's job was to uphold the law in an impartial manner. She was only in court in her professional capacity: the public was excluded during the women's evidence. Brenda was supposed to be supervising the defendants, not conferring with them and giving advice.

I knew Brenda was a good person. I knew she had robust views on child abuse. Yet it was impossible for her, as it would have been for anyone in that situation, to remain detached when her friends and relatives were in danger of going to prison.

The awkwardness of her position was evident throughout the trials, as Brenda strove to do her job without alienating her neighbours. And she had not even investigated this case or brought it to court. How had her predecessors coped?

Brenda told us that, during her three years in the post, no one had reported a crime to her, or even a problem. 'It's because I'm a Pitcairner,' she said.

★ ★ ★

On Friday night, with the evidence in Randy's trial largely completed, Pawl Warren held a party. Pawl held a party most Friday nights. They were laid-back affairs: a few drinks, some music, and a game of darts with Pawl and his darts-mad mother, Daphne. Pawl told the media that we were always welcome at his house. 'Somebody's got to look after you guys,' he said.

As Simon Moore and his colleagues, who had also been invited, were walking along the road to Pawl's house, they were overtaken by a convoy of quad bikes. The defendants were conveying their lawyers to Big Fence for *their* Friday night party. The men were in fancy dress: white prison uniforms emblazoned with black arrows.

The verdicts were nine days off.

CHAPTER 10

Judgement day

All the evidence had been heard, but the verdicts were still a week off. In the meantime, I was distracted by a more immediate concern: food. I was not exactly starving: the Lodge, when the six of us moved in, had a larder stacked with tinned food and a freezer full of meat. But fresh fruit and vegetables were another matter. For those, we were dependent on the islanders. And most of the islanders didn't like us very much.

Grant Pritchard, the Governor's Representative, would buy produce from the locals, and he appeared at our door periodically with a box of bananas or cabbages. However, we never had enough fresh food, and I envied Simon Moore, who was constantly receiving gifts — strawberries, papayas, pineapples, sweet potatoes. Despite the fact that he was prosecuting Pitcairn's leading men, some of the locals seemed quite fond of Moore.

Notwithstanding our location, we rarely had fish; Pritchard once gave us some steaks off a big tuna caught by Len Brown. Meat was all imported. There are no sheep or cattle on Pitcairn, only wild goats, which are occasionally hunted for food. A few families keep chickens, mainly for eggs.

I would look forward to the shop opening infrequently for an hour, although it always contained the same meagre range of goods, just in progressively smaller quantities. Stocks of cheese declined until none was left; there would be no more cheese on Pitcairn until the next ship, which was weeks off.

Now and again, courtesy of Betty Christian, we varied our diet with home-made pizza and coleslaw. We would call up Betty on the radio and place our order, which she delivered on the back of her quad bike. We nicknamed her the Pizza Express.

I fantasised about fresh salad, particularly tomatoes. I hadn't seen a tomato for weeks.

During the week-long lull, we took the opportunity to get to know a few more of the islanders. Claire Harvey, Neil Tweedie and I visited an elderly couple, Reynold and Nola Warren, who lived on a hillside just up from our house.

Nola and Reynold were a window onto island life in decades past. They are the only people on Pitcairn without a computer. They have no running water, nor a back-up electricity supply; when the public generator shuts down, they light gas lamps. Reynold, in his 70s but fit and lean, walks everywhere and still uses one of Pitcairn's old wooden wheelbarrows, otherwise considered museum pieces. The wheelbarrows, specially adapted for the steep terrain, were the main form of transport until motorbikes arrived in the 1960s. Nola cooks on a 'bolt' — an enormous open range with a wood fire beneath it — and bakes in an ancient stone oven, heated by burning wood and raking out the hot coals. She showed us how to grate coconut with an oversized tool of Polynesian origin and gave us ripe banana to dip in the shavings. I asked Nola whether she enjoyed living on Pitcairn. 'Well, I have to, don't I?' she replied in her booming voice. 'It's my home.'

As we left, I caught sight of the couple's vegetable patch, with its rows of lettuces and ripe tomatoes. For a second I gazed at it, shimmering before me like a mirage. Then, with a sigh, I continued on my way.

Sometime later, Mike Lupton-Christian called round to the Lodge for a chat, along with Vaine Peu. Vaine, a Cook Islander, had got together with his partner, Charlene Warren, while on a contract to build the island's new medical centre. They now had four young children. Charlene, like her elder sister, Darralyn, had given a statement to police but then withdrawn from the case.

While Charlene was now 'anti-prosecution' and supported the men who were on trial, Vaine, to our surprise, was bluntly critical of them. Settling into our sofa, a cup of tea in his hand, he rubbished their claim that it was Polynesian culture to have sex with much younger girls. 'Sex with a 12-year-old, that's not normal,' Vaine declared.

Vaine was worried about his own children, particularly his two-year-old daughter, Torika. 'What I read in the papers, what they've done, I don't like the men still being around us,' he said, frowning. 'It's like a badge of honour with them, to be the first to have gone with a girl.'

Mike, who has three daughters from a previous marriage, all living in Britain, told us, choosing his words carefully, 'If this had happened in our street in the UK, I'd be a vigilante. I find it quite horrific. And if it happened to one of *my* girls, there'd only be one trial: mine. I'd be up for murder.'

Like Pawl Warren, Vaine and Mike believed the community would be able to function without Steve Christian and his followers. Simon and Shirley Young, who were away at that time, held a similar view, according to Mike. It was clear that this little group of 'newcomers' was hoping to benefit from a shift in power dynamics if the Big Fence gang went to jail.

The following day, I opened our back door to find a bag of juicy-looking tomatoes. I gasped. Some kind soul had left them there, but who? I later discovered, by chance, that it was Reynold Warren, whose garden I had admired.

Closeted in the Mission House, not far from the Lodge, were the three judges, pondering the fate of the defendants.

The judges had been cooped up for nearly a month in the pastor's quarters, a ramshackle beach hut with a back garden overlooking the ocean. Aside from Graham Ford, the court registrar, and Maureen Dawson, the stenographer, the only people they mixed with were Bill Haigh, the communications adviser, and his wife, Catherine. Ford once got on the radio and asked Bill if he would mind coming over to fix a technical problem; he should bring Catherine too, Ford suggested. When the couple arrived, the judges were waiting for them with gin and tonics.

The Haighs were also invited to dinner on Trafalgar Day, the anniversary of the great British naval victory, which fell three days before the verdicts were due. Jane Lovell-Smith, an amiable and vivacious woman, entered into the mood of the occasion, roasting some 'aged beef' — an out-of-date joint she had found at the bottom of their freezer. Speeches were given, and toasts were drunk to the Queen, England and Lord Nelson.

Day to day, the judges were in the same boat as other outsiders, and they divided up the domestic chores with shipboard efficiency. Chief Justice Blackie was in charge of lighting the copper and burying vegetable scraps. Russell Johnson vacuumed the floors and washed dishes, while Jane Lovell-Smith did the cooking and laundry.

On one occasion Lovell-Smith delegated the job of making bread to her male colleagues, who carefully read the instructions inside the bread-making machine. Johnson, who now heads the entire New Zealand district court system, weighed out the ingredients and added them in the sequence prescribed. But when the men removed the 'loaf', it was a sticky mess. 'It was a total disaster,' says Graham Ford, 'and we couldn't figure out why until we cut it open and found a metal part in the middle.' They had not realised they were supposed to pour the mixture into a teflon insert, not directly into the machine, with its delicate working parts that were now coated in sticky dough.

Every morning at 6 a.m., the judges set off on a two-hour walk, choosing routes that circumvented people's houses. Charles Blackie, a reserved and courteous man, told me later, 'We couldn't really enter into conversations with anyone, except for transitory greetings. We had to keep very much to ourselves. The challenge on Pitcairn was to play our roles 24/7. So it was rather like living the life of a monk.'

Ford, who slept at the prison but joined the judges for meals, chaperoned them on their outings. Sometimes the military police would scoot up and down the road first, to check that the coast was clear. Despite being so isolated, Ford says, 'We were never bored. We would sit on the verandah with a glass of wine or two after a day in court, watching the frigate birds gliding up and down the cliffs.'

The judges also read our news reports on their laptops. They knew they were making history, and history was rarely far from their consciousness. Once, in court, Charles Blackie addressed Fletcher Pilditch, one of the prosecutors, as 'Mr Fletcher'. Hastily correcting himself, he called him 'Mr Christian' — and then, finally, 'Mr Pilditch'.

We journalists were less cut off than the judges. Even so, by this stage — our fourth week on the island — I felt like an insect trapped in a glass jar.

I had spent my life in big cities and while I had visited plenty of small, out of the way communities, nothing had prepared me for the claustrophobic intimacy of Pitcairn — a place where it is impossible to be alone, where there is always a quad bike or two rattling past, even after a calf-searing hike up to some spectacularly secluded spot.

On Pitcairn, privacy is as scarce a commodity as solitude. The islanders — and outsiders, too, taking their cue from the locals — wander into each other's houses without knocking. Wherever you go, whatever you do, you are unlikely ever to be unobserved. 'I saw you up at Aute Valley this morning; you were wearing a red T-shirt,' someone will remark.

A hand-drawn map of Adamstown, produced for tourists, shows the network of dirt tracks and the location of people's homes. The houses are marked simply 'Royal and Mike', or 'Reynold and Nola', making Pitcairn seem a cosy, homely place — like Coronation Street. But this soap opera had dark undercurrents, and to me the map underscored the sense of enforced propinquity.

Even the islanders feel hemmed in at times. Betty Christian confessed that she loved to stroll along Queen Street, the main shopping street in Auckland, when she was in New Zealand. 'It's marvellous being an anonymous face in the crowd. No one watches you to see what you're doing or saying. Here you never know what you can say to whom. Everything is so personal on Pitcairn.'

While Betty was still friendly to us, in her slightly guarded way, the animosity of most of the other locals was getting me down. It was not as if the islanders knew any of us personally — they disliked us solely because of our jobs. The majority believed, or claimed to believe, that the media were writing and broadcasting fiction. My perception of reality seemed so different from theirs that I sometimes felt like I was going mad.

Ewart Barnsley appeared in the living room one day, looking anxious; he had lost some notebooks and feared they might have been stolen. Although he found them soon afterwards, the seed of paranoia had been planted. We had already been fretting about whether our emails, which were transmitted via the local server, could be read; now we discussed the possibility of an intruder destroying our laptops or satellite phones. It was a crazy thought, but not that crazy, and if it happened, we would be completely lost. We talked about locking the house, but there was only one key. I took to hiding my notebooks and computer among the clothes in my bedroom closet.

Three days before the verdicts, the *Clipper Odyssey* was scheduled to return to Pitcairn with a new load of passengers — and the word on the island's mud-caked streets was that Steve Christian was determined to keep us off the ship this time. We were equally set on enjoying another escapist foray, and besides, it would be Simon Moore's birthday. Matthew Forbes took the precaution of contacting the *Clipper Odyssey*'s captain beforehand to check whether outsiders could visit. He told Forbes that he would be glad to see us, and pooh-poohed the idea that any of us had misbehaved last time.

A band of lawyers, diplomats and journalists met at The Landing in the early afternoon. Once again there were souvenir stalls set up, and the jetty was thronged with passengers. We stood around, waiting for a longboat to take us out to the ship. Then word filtered through that we had been banned from the *Clipper Odyssey* by the tour operators.

Who says? Neil, Claire, Ewart, Zane and I collared the company's representative, Mike Messick. 'I'm just the messenger,' he protested, discomfited, as we converged on him with notebooks and television camera. The decision was based on 'logistical considerations', Messick insisted, trying to walk off with us in pursuit.

So the islanders could visit the ship, but outsiders couldn't: was that it?

'Yes, that's right,' he replied, feebly.

I noticed Dave Brown grinning nearby. It was Dave's birthday, too; in fact, it was his 50th. He was probably looking forward to a few drinks without us.

And that would have been that, except that those who had hatched this little plot had left Pitcairn's senior diplomat, Matthew Forbes, out of the equation. Forbes is a typically understated character. But the *Clipper Odyssey* was in British territorial waters, for heaven's sake. He could hardly allow himself meekly to be barred from a ship that was only anchored off the island with his permission. Forbes took Messick aside for a quiet word; Messick denied that Steve was behind the blackballing. In any event, the 'logistical problems' were resolved, and a few minutes later we were approaching the *Clipper Odyssey* in a longboat.

Ascending the stairway to the poolside bar on the rear deck, the first person I set eyes on was Dave, swigging a beer. Dave, who had departed before Forbes' intervention, almost dropped his bottle when he saw me. Soon our little group was sitting in the sun, slurping exotically hued cocktails.

Matthew Forbes, I noticed, was walking a little taller. He had just nipped in the bud probably the closest thing to a civil insurrection that the British colony had ever experienced — albeit one planned and carried out entirely in the shadows, which was the only way it would ever be on Pitcairn.

Since the island had been swamped by outsiders, the mayor and Deputy Governor had been locked in a silent power struggle, and Forbes had just won a decisive battle. The locals regarded the cruise liners as a private playground where they hobnobbed with wealthy passengers, often to their advantage; not long previously, Steve had come away from a ship with a crate of Bacardi.

That evening, back in Adamstown, Max Davidson, the Kent detective, sang 'Happy Birthday' to Simon Moore over the radio. Perhaps unwisely, he sang it on Channel 16, the frequency reserved for communicating with ships and making public announcements. Immediately a series of other voices rang out. First Steve's daughter, Tania, bawling, 'Get the hell off our radio!' Then Steve himself, calling up Brenda and, in a tone of cold rage, ordering his sister to take immediate action. 'This is not funny,' he shouted, as the whole island listened, rapt. 'We want to find out who did it, and put some sort of legal charge on them.'

Brenda set off to see Matthew Forbes, who was already on his way over to see her. Steve summoned Paul Dacre, who succeeded in pacifying him, thus averting the intriguing scenario of Brenda arresting Davidson, her superior in the policing hierarchy, although on what charge — singing 'Happy Birthday' without consent on Channel 16? — was hard to imagine.

The strain of recent weeks had clearly taken a toll on Steve. 'They can't control you, that's the problem,' commented Mike Lupton-Christian the following day. And it was true. There were journalists swarming around Pitcairn, interviewing anyone who was willing to talk and broadcasting the islanders' most unsavoury secrets. Outsiders were trespassing on their cruise ships; we were even misusing their radio network. And all that Steve could do was watch, impotent for the first time in his life.

Finally it was judgement day: Sunday, 24 October.

Only one of the seven defendants, Jay Warren, had given evidence, and only Steve Christian had called any witnesses. The others had left it to their lawyers to assert that the alleged incidents did not take place, or that the girls had consented. The defence case, which usually occupies a substantial chunk of a criminal hearing, had been brief, or — where some trials were concerned — almost non-existent.

None of the defence counsel had suggested, on behalf of their clients, that their behaviour was part of Pitcairn culture, or 'island ways'. As for the prosecution case, there was no physical evidence, nor were there any witnesses to the events. The verdicts would hinge largely on whether the judges believed the complainants. It was the women's word against the men's.

Meralda Warren had written a special poem to mark the day, which she distributed to friends and supporters via email. The poem was entitled 'Is Seven a Lucky Number?'

It went:

> *The Seven are tried before the world*
> *The day draws nigh for the Judges' word*
> *What fate will pass our tiny Isle*
> *What legal battles the Lawyers toil*
> *Most are seventh generation*
> *Why just these Seven here for Fell's condemnation*
> *There's never an age consent set in our Laws*
> *Oh 16 is in the British clause*
> *What book they choose*

> *What next law will they ruse*
> *Why must these Seven men be used?*
> *To clean up Britain's political Poo's*
> *Oh to be the gecko on the wall*
> *To hear the three judges hopefully say*
> *A pardon to you all*
> *Roll on Lucky Seven Roll on.*

The 'Lucky Seven' assembled at 2 p.m. Graham Ford, the registrar, had reminded the community over the radio that everyone was free to attend. Just five locals turned up, including one close relative: Jay Warren's wife, Carol. Jay's sister, Meralda, who longed to be 'a gecko on the wall', was absent.

It felt like a big day. The military police, and Brenda Christian, were wearing their Pitcairn Island police uniforms, rather than shorts and T-shirts. It was swelteringly hot, and the court was like a sauna; my glasses misted up immediately. Curtains and blinds were drawn against the glare, adding to the sensation of an airless box. The ceiling fans appeared to be moving in slow motion.

Steve Christian and Jay Warren were in the front row of the public gallery; they were to be dealt with first, by Chief Justice Blackie. Dave Brown and Terry Young were installed behind them. Steve looked nervous, sitting rod-straight, hands clasped in his lap.

Blackie entered, and Jay, wearing black jeans and a white shirt, stepped into the dock, which had been brought into service for the first time. Jay was accused of indecently assaulting Suzie at Bounty Bay. The judge briefly detailed the background, then he pronounced Jay not guilty. Jay's shoulders lifted. In the public gallery, Cookie Warren punched the air and hugged a pink-faced Carol.

Steve was next. Earlier, he had strolled across the square, tossing a jocular remark at Claire and me: 'Hope you get a good picture, girls!' Now he stood in the dock, shifting from foot to foot, rivulets of sweat running down his face.

Charles Blackie began by ruling on two counts of indecent assault. He dismissed each of them, calling the evidence 'equivocal'. Tension in the courtroom mounted, with everyone glancing at each other, not quite believing what they were hearing. Was Steve going to get off?

Then the judge turned to the six rape charges. First, the attack on Jennifer under the banyans, with two boys assisting. Blackie declared, 'Despite the endeavours of the defence to shake this witness, I find her evidence to be compelling ... The actions attributed to the accused were so gross as to be indelibly printed on her mind.'

The judge proclaimed the rape 'proved beyond reasonable doubt'.

Damp patches formed on Steve's blue short-sleeved shirt.

Blackie was equally convinced by Jennifer's description of being raped for a second time, in a garden shed. 'The way she gave her evidence made a deep impression,' he said. Altogether, he found Steve guilty of raping Jennifer on four occasions.

The Chief Justice also believed Steve's second victim, Charlotte. 'She was young, naïve and vulnerable,' he told the court. 'She was secreted into the bushes ... I am quite satisfied that the accused had his way with her, not caring whether she consented or not.' Only about the rape that Charlotte had alleged occurred at The Landing, in the boathouse, was he not sufficiently persuaded.

Steve was guilty of five rapes. He looked dazed.

Blackie rose to his feet. Steve marched outside with his face set, Paul Dacre following a little way behind. We ran after him, yelling out questions, which Steve ignored. He crossed the square and was halfway down the ramp leading to the main road when he realised he had left his bike at the top. He strode back up and retrieved it, feeling, no doubt, rather foolish, on top of everything else.

Jane Lovell-Smith took Blackie's seat at the front of the court. Dave Brown, in jeans and flip-flops, walked over to the dock. He was white-faced. Earlier, he had been heard to remark, glaring in my direction, that if I went anywhere near him, he would 'smash her fucking camera down the back of her throat'.

Dave had pleaded guilty to three charges; 12 remained. Lovell-Smith started by acquitting him of four indecent assaults. She said she was not certain that the girl had been under 13. Christine Gordon, who had prosecuted the case, looked dismayed. She stood up and informed the judge politely that age was not a relevant factor for those charges. The judge, with a face like thunder, turned to Charles Cato, Dave's defence counsel, who assured her that age *was* relevant.

Cato was wrong, as it turned out, but by then Dave was in the clear.

The next six counts, which were based on admissions that Dave had made during his police interview, Jane Lovell-Smith found 'proven'. However, the most serious charges — sticking his penis in five-year-old Isobel's mouth, and assaulting seven-year-old Marion in the church — she rejected. The judge had reservations about Isobel's ability to remember events from 30 years earlier: it was she who had recounted both episodes.

Dave left court in tears, his tough-man image discarded. They were tears of relief, for he knew that while guilty of nine indecent assaults, he was no longer in danger of going to jail. He mopped his eyes with a trailing length of toilet paper, and clung to Brenda Christian as she supported him down the steps of the public hall.

Next, it was Terry Young's turn. Terry, dressed in blue trousers and a bright yellow T-shirt, shuffled into the dock. He gave the impression of being somewhat slow, although he had surprised detectives, when they interviewed him, with his precise recall of dates. Terry owned a ham radio licence, and was sharp enough to have been left in charge of radio communications during an island emergency.

Lovell-Smith ruled Terry guilty of molesting 12-year-old Janet outside the school toilets, and Catherine on his quad bike when she was 13 or 14. She acquitted him of touching ten-year-old Sarah during a children's game of tag. Moving on to his main victim, Marion, the judge found Terry guilty on all counts: four indecent assaults and one representative charge of rape. She said, 'I find that the complainant was repeatedly raped by the accused almost every week on the island from the age of 12 years to 15 years, whenever they went to collect firewood.' Lovell-Smith added, 'He knew that she was the most vulnerable member of her household, subjected to physical and verbal abuse.'

Terry shuffled out, displaying no emotion.

Lastly, Russell Johnson handed down his decisions, first on Len Brown, then on Randy Christian. Len gripped the wooden handrail of the dock and craned forward, straining to hear the judge's words.

Johnson said Jennifer had described the two rapes in or near the watermelon patch 'in an emphatic, very emotional, but persuasive way'. He told the court, 'This was no seduction. It was a rough act of sexual domination by a tall, strong and fit man over a frightened teenaged girl.'

The judge proclaimed Len guilty of both rapes.

Len departed, his face as hard as the basalt cliffs that he had scaled in his youth. His son might cry, but he never would, not in public, and probably not even by himself. However, Brenda Christian, Len's friend and carer, appeared upset, and in the public gallery the jubilation caused by Jay Warren's acquittal had long since fizzled out.

Last to be judged was Randy, the biggest of those powerfully built men who had done as they pleased for most of their lives, using their brawn to tyrannise little girls. Now, like the defendants who had stood before him in the dock, Randy resembled a frightened boy. Like his father, he sweated profusely as, just like him, he saw prison loom.

Mosquitoes buzzed around the room as Russell Johnson pronounced Randy guilty of four rapes and five indecent assaults. He had found Belinda convincing, her credibility unimpaired by her 'so-called infatuation' with Randy, the judge said. He added, 'He [Randy] was for the main part an adult and she was a child . . . She was naïve and lacked knowledge of the world, and education.'

Randy left court looking outraged, eyes flashing.

Three generations of Pitcairners, from Len Brown, 78 years old and half deaf, to Randy, 30 and brimming with vigour, were guilty of a total of 35 offences.

The men were all descendants of the *Bounty* mutineers, and so were the women whose lives they had blighted.

At this point, anywhere else in the world, the guilty men would have been taken off into custody to await their sentences. But this was Pitcairn, where no one had yet spent a night behind bars, and that was not about to change. Jay Warren was discharged; the other defendants were remanded on bail. They were to be sentenced, along with Dennis Christian, five days later. The child sex offenders returned to their families. I saw Terry Young sitting outside his house in the early evening, listening to the radio.

Meanwhile, those who had watched the trials closely, even if they had not been present in court, gave their reactions.

Carol Warren was moist-eyed with relief, but angry that Jay's name 'has been dragged through the mud ... The whole world now sees him as a child molester.'

Tom Christian told me, 'I don't feel any differently about the men. I've known them all my life, and it happened a long time ago. People change. Anyway,' he added, 'we need all the men to operate the longboats in rough seas.'

Tom's wife, Betty, said, 'I'm pleased it's all over. But I don't see any sign of remorse.'

Robert Vinson, the detective in charge of the case since Dennis McGookin's retirement, said the verdicts had 'sent a strong message that the abuse of children is not acceptable in any culture, anywhere, and Pitcairn Island is no exception'.

In Auckland, Karen Vaughan told New Zealand television that the victims were 'extremely relieved ... overwhelmed ... On the whole, they feel justice has been done, and were extremely happy about it.'

Cookie Warren posted a message on Friends of Pitcairn, an internet chat site. 'We believe this whole thing was a set-up from the beginning and no matter how well the Defense argued the case they were fighting a losing battle,' he wrote. Cookie said there was 'a much bigger picture which is yet to emerge ... Contrary to what you might read in the news this thing is FAR from over yet.'

What did Herb Ford, snug in his book-lined office in California, make of it all? Ford had been uncharacteristically quiet during the trials: the Seventh-day Adventist Church had issued a press release emphasising that he was neither a spokesman nor a Church leader. I had dropped him an email, asking him whether, in the light of the evidence, he had revised his opinions about the case. Ford said that he was 'withholding judgement' until the verdicts, but added, 'My feeling about the basic good of the Pitcairn people is unchanged.'

After the verdicts, I emailed him again, posing the same question. Ford replied, 'Since the purpose of the Pitcairn Islands Study Center is to provide information about the Bounty Saga, which includes Bligh/Bounty/Pitcairn/Norfolk, it would be outside our purpose to provide any judgemental comment on this.'

The following day, the Pitcairn men took one of the longboats out to trade with the crew of a Dutch container ship. Steve and Randy Christian oversaw the operation. Steve's quad bike, with its distinctive canopy, was parked at the wharf, in the prime spot that it always occupied. Out at sea, Steve, Randy and Jay Warren staged a protest, refusing to hand up the locals' baskets of fish and bananas. Mike Lupton-Christian explained later, 'They were trying to prove a point, because we've been saying that we can manage without them [on the boats].'

The islanders came back to shore in a filthy mood. They appeared subdued but defiant. The atmosphere at The Landing was strained. People were barely speaking to one another.

The men glowered at Claire and me as we photographed them unloading cargo. Suddenly Randy got on his quad bike and reversed towards us at speed. I stepped aside, and Dave Brown sniggered; Randy changed direction just short of where Claire and I stood. Then Steve abruptly walked over to us, with his arm raised as if to strike us. At the last minute he turned away. It happened so quickly that I wondered if I'd imagined it. But I hadn't.

CHAPTER 11

'You can't blame men for being men'

Two days after the verdicts were handed down, the prosecution and defence lawyers were scheduled to present sentencing submissions. Claire and I headed to court, and since the shop was open, we made a detour to pick up some groceries. As we waited to pay, Tania Christian called out in a voice heavy with sarcasm, 'Shall I get you an arrows suit, Kathy? Is that what you'd like?'

I knew what Tania was referring to: a story of mine that had mentioned the men dressing up in mock prison uniforms. 'No thanks,' I replied, turning away. Tania, though, started to harangue Claire and me, and Meralda Warren, who was in one of the aisles, joined in. When we eventually left the shop, a little dazed, Pawl Warren — who had witnessed the altercation — appeared. 'It was outrageous, the way they talked to you guys,' said Pawl, who insisted on carrying our shopping home for us on his bike. But he hadn't spoken up to defend us: that wasn't the way that Pitcairn functioned.

At court, all three judges were assembled. Simon Moore spoke first, and rebutted the idea that jail sentences would 'close down the island'. Paul Dacre observed that none of the guilty men had re-offended, adding, 'The very nature of the prosecution ... has brought home to them in no uncertain terms that young women must be respected.' Dacre reminded the judges that all the men had held responsible positions, helping the community to 'survive in the face of very significant odds ... [It was] hard to imagine any community in the world where ... [people] rely on each other so fully.' He urged them to treat Pitcairn as a unique case. 'We're talking about 50 people on a rock, not 50 million people in England or four million in New Zealand.'

Dacre read out testimonials from, among others, Meralda Warren, who described how she had been rescued by Randy, Steve, Dennis and Dave after being washed away by a giant wave while fishing off some rocks in 2003. 'They're brave men', Meralda asserted. 'I regard them as friends, and will always continue to support them.'

The lawyers then turned to individual cases. Moore pointed to the 'aggravating features' of Steve's offending, including his use of violence, and said that the effects on Jennifer had been 'profound and enduring'. She had suffered 'depression, flashbacks, nightmares, panic attacks ... feelings of self-worthlessness', and had also attempted suicide. Paul Dacre responded by listing Steve's numerous talents: fishing, diving, rock quarrying, road cutting, demolition, welding, surveying, house building, explosives and longboat design. It was hard to envisage another case where one individual was so important to his community, Dacre said, or where a man had done more to compensate for his crimes.

Next, submissions were offered on Dave Brown, with Christine Gordon noting that Dave had lived for 11 years in New Zealand, 'so any comments about social mores need to be seen in that context'. Charles Cato, the defence lawyer, countered that Dave was 'an inherently modest man' who loved Pitcairn and 'doesn't want it to be seen in the light of the unfortunate picture that has been painted of it as a place that's unsafe for women'. Cato appealed to Jane Lovell-Smith's sense of history, saying, 'Many years ago, the events that made Pitcairn a part of folklore, of romantic and historic writing, were, at least allegedly, caused by one man's inhumanity and inability to understand other men. I ask for mercy for Dave Brown here, many years later.'

Christine Gordon moved on to Terry Young, whose principal victim, Marion, wished to see Terry rehabilitated rather than imprisoned, she said — thereby displaying 'a humanity that is in marked contrast with and significantly lacking in the offender's treatment of her'. In a statement to the court, Marion revealed, 'I carried a lot of shame about the sexual abuse. Now I feel more free than I have ever felt, because this shame has lifted from my shoulders by speaking out.' Allan Roberts, for the defence, said that Terry had sole responsibility for his 77-year-old mother, Vula, who was infirm, rarely left the house, and required twice-daily insulin injections. Contradicting Dacre's picture of a mutually caring community, Roberts claimed there were no alternative support systems.

The lawyers then addressed the delicate matter of Len Brown, once described by Paul Dacre as 'a man who will die if his feet are not in the salt water'. No one, not even the prosecution, wanted Len to go to prison. However, his crimes had been violent, callous and premeditated, Fletcher Pilditch told the court, and his victim had been 27 years younger than him. Roberts, his defence lawyer, suggested that jailing Len would be 'akin to caging a songbird'. The trial judge, Russell Johnson, a kindly, almost avuncular person, inquired, 'Are you able to say now there's remorse?' Roberts shook his head. 'That would be fraudulent.' Johnson's eyebrows shot up.

I felt quite tearful. Couldn't this old man, nearing the end of his life, admit that he had done wrong decades earlier and say sorry? Len, I later found out, was intractable. He was convinced that Jennifer had consented to sex, and swore that if he ended up in prison, it would be 'on the lies of that girl'.

Dennis Christian was dealt with swiftly, for his offences were less grave than some, and he had pleased the court by pleading guilty. He had also emailed his main victim, in what Fletcher Pilditch called 'probably the singular instance in these trials of an apology being given, deep remorse being expressed and that being accepted'. Russell Johnson said he had no intention of jailing Dennis.

Finally, Simon Moore drew the judge's attention to the many aggravating features of Randy's offending. Allan Roberts outlined Randy's record of community service, remarking that the tragedy, for him and for Pitcairn, was that Randy was 'regarded as the leader of a new generation'.

As Roberts spoke, I heard children playing in the square outside. There were only half a dozen of them on the island now, and only three of school age. The sound of their laughter sent a little chill through me.

The proceedings were adjourned. Sentencing would take place three days later.

Cookie Warren and his sister, Melva, who lives in Alaska but was back visiting, were in the public gallery, behind Claire and me. Earlier, they had been making caustic comments. I turned round and asked them if they would sit down with us and have a civilised discussion. They were always accusing the media of reporting one side of the story. Why didn't they tell us the other side?

Cookie seemed startled. Quickly recovering his composure, he retorted, 'You'll only twist our words.' Melva agreed. 'It would be like diving into a pool of sharks,' she told us.

★ ★ ★

We had been on Pitcairn for a month; it was almost summer. It was hot and dry, and the dust had returned. The mud had baked hard in the sun and then cracked; the dirt tracks looked like shattered windscreens. The warmer weather had also brought an invasion of insects. Convoys of centipedes proceeded across our kitchen floor. Claire and I found a gigantic spider in our bedroom. A crab clawed its way into the house through a flimsy screen door and attached itself to Zane's big toe. We were able to establish that the voracious reputation of the island's mosquitoes is well deserved. Andy Nicholson, one of the MDPs, had white Scottish legs that resembled a pair of pink polka-dot stockings.

Anyway, never mind creepy-crawlies: I was running out of alcohol and cigarettes.

Almost in the same breath as he had informed me that I was to be a member of the media pool, Matthew Forbes had enquired how much alcohol I planned to consume. I had to place my order right away, he explained, as a supply ship was about to leave Auckland. I had agonised. Under-ordering had obvious perils; on the other hand, I was reluctant to give the impression that I was some kind of dipsomaniac. I requested a crate of red wine and a bottle of whisky, which seemed an embarrassingly large amount.

Once on the island, the wine and whisky soon evaporated. Fortunately, Neil Tweedie came to my aid. Like a true hack, he had overestimated his needs, and had in his bedroom what looked like a small wine cellar. After my duty-free Marlboro Lights had gone, I tried in vain to stop smoking. Then I begged or bartered cigarettes, mainly from Vinny Reid, Nicholson's fellow officer, who was staying at the prison. ('I'm off to jail to get some fags,' I would announce cheerfully.)

Reid invited the media to a barbecue at the prison one evening. The six cells, we discovered, were spacious double rooms, with cooking facilities and ensuite bathrooms with flushing toilets. The walls and floors were pine, rather like those of a Swiss chalet. The jail was expected to be used as visitor accommodation once it had served its primary purpose. The wooden deck running along the front of the cells was a congenial place to relax and count the stars. In the distance was the foamy expanse of the Pacific Ocean.

Darralyn and Turi Griffiths planned to build their house on a block of land behind the Lodge. The site had been quiet throughout our stay. On 28 October, the eve of sentencing, it erupted in a flurry of activity. The whole island appeared and set about helping the young couple, the antagonisms of recent weeks apparently put aside. Steve Christian was in the pink bulldozer, turning over the earth. Others were mixing and pouring concrete for the foundations. It was an impressive display of communal togetherness at a critical time — and it was all photographed and filmed by us, as the Pitcairners had no doubt intended.

Sentencing was scheduled for 2 p.m. the following day. The islanders were back at the building site first thing. At lunchtime the six defendants vanished, and an hour later they were lined up in court, sitting in two rows like sullen schoolboys.

Again, only a handful of locals were present. Steve was first to enter the dock. His cheeks were covered in grey stubble. I noticed how large his hands were. As Charles Blackie began to speak, a thunderbolt — perfectly timed for dramatic effect — cracked overhead. Blackie declared that rape was 'a particularly serious offence'. However, he added, it was the court's task 'to impose sentences which are appropriate for this island'. Lengthy jail terms might have 'adverse effects' on the community.

The Chief Justice addressed Steve. 'You are the mayor of the island, you are the spokesperson of the island, and you have represented the island at a number of international forums,' he told him. 'The court cannot but be impressed with your contribution to island life over the past 30 years.'

Blackie jailed Steve for three years for the five rapes. He could apply for home detention after nine months, and parole after a year. Steve did not seem grateful for the judge's magnanimity. He left court with a face as stormy as the weather outside.

Russell Johnson took Blackie's place, and Len Brown replaced Steve in the dock. Rather unusually, Len had been at a barbecue hosted by Simon Moore the previous night. He got on well with the prosecutors and felt that they treated him with respect — more so, perhaps, than his own son, Dave, who was furious with him for fraternising with them.

Johnson informed Len that he had, in the main, led 'a worthy life of hard work in circumstances most would see as adverse'. However, he went on, 'Three decades ago you disgraced yourself and degraded a young woman ... a vulnerable member of the community picked on by a range of sexual predators, a matter I may imply came to your notice.' The judge told him, 'You are an austere, gentlemanly person around the community, hard of hearing, and, some of your testimonials indicate, hard in your attitudes.' He sentenced Len to two years, with the possibility of serving his term at home.

Next, Dennis Christian stood before the judge, who commended him for 'breaking ranks with the generally confrontational approach adopted by others'. Johnson said, 'It was courageous, and not an easy thing for you to do, in the circumstances that I perceive to exist here at the moment.' He ordered Dennis to undertake 300 hours of community service. Dennis looked shame-faced and relieved.

Johnson had sterner words for Randy Christian. 'As a young man, you seemed to believe you had some kind of right to sexually violate young girls when you felt like it,' he told him. The judge noted that Belinda had 'bravely' given evidence, while Randy himself had chosen not to testify. He also directed some pointed remarks at the community: 'Some people on this island who did not see or hear the evidence have publicly suggested that it is a fiction,' he said. 'The fact that the major complainant gave her evidence in the face of total rejection by her family is eloquent proof to the contrary.' Nonetheless, Johnson accepted that Randy had become 'a valued and respected member' of the community. He jailed him for six years. With good behaviour, he could be out in two.

Finally, Jane Lovell-Smith pronounced sentence. The weather had grown increasingly wild. Torrential rain now clattered on the tin roof. Through a window I saw a flash of lightning.

Dave Brown received credit for his guilty pleas, although they had been limited and late. Lovell-Smith observed, 'He has had the courage and decency to stand up in this courtroom and acknowledge his guilt.' She sentenced him to 400 hours of community service. Once again, Dave appeared tearful.

As for Terry Young, the judge told him that he had abused the position of trust that all adults occupied in a small community. Yet he had also overcome learning difficulties, she said, and was 'known to have a particular fondness for caring for elderly individuals'. She gave him five years.

As soon as sentencing was over, the storm passed.

Chief Justice Blackie had acknowledged, while sentencing Steve, that the penalties 'may be seen as far less than what might be expected in the world at large'. That seemed to me to be an understatement. In Britain, and similar jurisdictions such as

Australia and New Zealand, the worst offenders — Steve, Randy, Terry and Len — would probably have received prison terms of ten to 15 years. Dave and Dennis would almost certainly have been jailed, too. The sentences, Blackie claimed, were 'tailored to Pitcairn', taking into account 'factors unique to this island, such as its isolation, its permanent population of less than 50 people, its dependence on the manpower of its able-bodied citizens, the need for members of the community to be responsible for most of the facets of modern living'.

I wondered what that meant. The judges had made it clear they did not believe the community would collapse if men went to jail. So was Charles Blackie saying that the crimes were somehow less serious because they were committed on a remote island with a small population? Was he saying that the Pitcairners deserved such extraordinary leniency because ... well, because they were Pitcairners?

Blackie and the other two judges had cited the fact that the defendants had endured 'massive adverse publicity'. Yet it was the islanders who had courted the media for two years, depicting the complainants as money-grabbing liars.

The judges also said they were sure the men had reformed, and so the penalties did not need to act as a deterrent. However, Randy's offending was relatively recent, and only Dennis had expressed real contrition. If no child had been abused on the island for a few years, as appeared to be the case, might that not have something to do with the presence of police and social workers, rather than paedophiles turning over new leaves?

What signal did the sentences send to a community that had denied or excused the abuse, and particularly to the teenage boys growing up there? Did they not convey the message that the Pitcairners were special, and could — to a large extent —

get away with behaviour that would be severely punished elsewhere?

Simon Moore commented, 'No one will be able to say that they're beyond the reach of the law, because we've proved that they're not.' But one outsider described the sentences as 'a slap on the wrist', while Max Davidson, who had worked with victims of child sexual abuse, said, 'These punishments in no way reflect what the men did. Whatever their status on the island, no matter what public work they did, and what lives they saved, that doesn't help the victims.'

He was right. Many of the women who had waited for so long to get to court were deeply dissatisfied with the outcome.

After receiving his jail sentence, Steve Christian returned to the building site; that evening he had dinner with his lawyers at Big Fence.

Steve, Len, Randy and Terry were still free, for the defence's legal arguments — questioning, among other things, Britain's sovereignty over Pitcairn — had yet to be aired. The three judges would ponder the issues in Auckland in early 2005, and the Privy Council in London, the highest appeal body for British territories, had also agreed to hear them. If the defendants' arguments were upheld, the verdicts handed down on Pitcairn would be overturned and the sentences quashed. But it would be six months, at least, before the various courts delivered their rulings, and the judges had decreed that the guilty men should remain on bail until then. Until then, they would not be formally convicted.

The community faced another period of limbo.

Nola Warren, the wife of Reynold, our tomato donor, had been in court. A little group of people, among them Nola and I, fell into step as we walked home in the same direction. As we approached our respective houses, Nola said to me quietly, 'No one will ever want to come here again after what you've written.'

The judges and prosecution lawyers were departing the next day, with what seemed almost indecent haste. The rest of us would have to wait for the *Braveheart* to come back for a second run. The boat could only carry a dozen passengers. A long week lay ahead.

Although I longed to go home, I was uncomfortably aware that I appeared to have lost interest in the wider world. George Bush had been re-elected in the United States, and so had John Howard in Australia; neither event had really engaged my attention.

My world had shrunk to a 2-mile-square chunk of rock.

I was starting to comprehend why the Pitcairners were so insular, caring only about themselves and the weather and the next ship. I was starting to see how, in that environment, a different set of rules might evolve and come to be accepted, even by outsiders.

In our house, we were no longer a happy band of journalists. The atmosphere had been tense for a while. Neil, whose sense of humour had helped us survive thus far, had sunk into a deep gloom. Ewart had withdrawn into himself. Zane was downright sick of the place.

Each of us had hit the wall at different times. The spark was always trivial. In Claire's case, it was someone squashing her freshly made loaf of bread. In mine, it was the sight of a dirty pan left in the sink by a colleague. Unable to contain my irritation, I asked him to wash it up. 'In a minute,' he replied. I began shouting at him. He shouted back. Suddenly I could not bear the sound of his voice. I picked up a glass and threw it across the room. Then I stormed out, half in shock at what I had done.

Just outside the front door I stopped, feeling foolish. There was nowhere to go.

The whole community was at The Landing to wave off the *Braveheart*. One half stood on the jetty, saying their goodbyes; the other half stayed by the boatshed, just watching. It was a perfect reflection of the divided island that the legal teams were leaving behind.

The judges, attired in shorts and sunhats, were carrying walking sticks carved by Brenda and Mike. The prosecutors had given their custom to Len Brown, who had produced some of his intricately worked longboats and *Bounty* replicas.

As I said my farewells, I came across Russell Johnson, the judge with the benign smile and twinkly eyes. Rusty, as we journalists had taken to calling him among ourselves, apologised for having been so reclusive.

The minute the *Braveheart* was over the horizon, Claire and I dashed back up the Hill of Difficulty and raided the lawyers' pantry. Then we did the same at the Mission House, where we found a frisbee in the garden. Was that how Rusty and his fellow judges had whiled away their spare time?

Later on, we bumped into Dennis Christian, wearing a bee-keeper's suit. As he puffed little bursts of smoke over his hives to sedate the bees, we chatted to him briefly about honey production. We had heard that Dennis — but not Dave Brown, for some reason — was 'on the outer'; the other men considered him a 'woos' (coward) for pleading guilty. And while he would probably redeem himself over time, said one islander, Dennis would 'never be one of the boys again'.

British officials now had to tackle the tricky issue of Steve and Randy Christian — who, having been found guilty of serious offences, could not continue to hold public office, as mayor and internal committee chairman respectively.

Ever since the verdicts, Matthew Forbes had been dropping heavy hints to Steve and Randy that they ought to resign — noting that if they did not, Governor Richard Fell might have to intervene. When the pair showed no sign of budging even after receiving prison sentences, Forbes brought the matter to a head, requesting a meeting with them at the jail with their lawyers. For the last time, he asked father and son to step down. Both men refused. Steve declared himself the victim of a 'stitch-up by the British government', and said he knew 'what an innocent person feels like when wrongly accused'.

In Wellington, Fell issued a special ordinance sacking the pair. Forbes pinned it up on the public noticeboard. Steve's daughter, Tania, promptly stuck a Bible verse over the top. Forbes moved the verse aside, so that the ordinance was visible.

Tania's choice of Bible reading was Micah, Chapter 7, Verse 8:

> *Do not gloat over me, my enemy!*
> *Though I have fallen, I will rise.*
> *Though I sit in darkness,*
> *The Lord will be my light.*
> *Because I have sinned against him,*
> *I will bear the Lord's wrath,*
> *Until he pleads my case*
> *And establishes my right.*
> *He will bring me out into the light;*
> *I will see his righteousness.*
> *Then my enemy will see it*
> *And will be covered with shame,*
> *She who said to me,*
> *"Where is the LORD your God?"*
> *My eyes will see her downfall;*

> *Even now she will be trampled underfoot*
> *Like mire in the streets.*

Steve handed Matthew Forbes a letter stating, 'I do not intend to resign ... I have not been convicted of any crime.' In an email to his supporters that crackled with anger, he vowed that once the legal arguments were made public, 'the bigger picture will reveal the abuse and suffering that all Pitcairners have been subjected to since 2000 ... There will be some very shameful people in high places in the British government.' He never spoke to Forbes again.

Cookie Warren claimed in an email that 'the majority of the islanders still support Steve for mayor and Randy for chairman'. Meralda Warren accused Britain of trying to trample 'the true Pitcairners in the mud'. She proclaimed, 'We are a STRONG community. We are like the rock we stand on.'

Despite resistance from Steve, an interim mayor had to be appointed to fill the post until December, when an election was due. The island council held a secret ballot and narrowly elected Brenda Christian. Steve's allies, outraged, claimed that Fell had engineered the result. They labelled Brenda 'the Governor's puppet' and his 'special little pet'. Cookie's sister, Melva, wrote, 'The world needs to know that the elitist, power-mad overlords of the Colonial era are not a thing of the past. That attitude is alive and thriving on a tiny dot of land in the vast expanse of the Pacific Ocean.'

Over the VHF radio, Brenda announced that a cruise ship would be arriving in February 2005. Coordinating those all-important visits had been Steve's job. Now his sister had usurped him. The growing family rift exacted a price. Nadine Christian barred her son from seeing Brenda, although the little boy was fond of her.

* * *

The story, at least for the time being, was over. I would not miss the 2 a.m. satellite phone conversations with London to discuss how many words I should file, nor the nightly attempts to transmit pictures via Pitcairn's erratic internet connection. From the start, though, the *Independent* — and *New Zealand Herald*, too — had wanted not just daily news stories, but 'colour' (atmosphere) and analysis. Now, during that final week, I redoubled my efforts to find out how the community ticked; apart from my ongoing fascination with the place, I was gathering material for an Australian magazine feature.

Gratifyingly, I was able to shop in peace on one occasion — the reason being that I was escorted by Ewart. The islanders, I had noticed, were generally polite to him and Zane, possibly because Ewart was a familiar presence on New Zealand television. Then again, Neil was unknown to the people of Pitcairn, and he did not encounter the sniping that Claire and I did.

At the till, Carol Warren rang up my purchases. Curious to know her thoughts on the case, now that the trials were over, I mentioned the subject cautiously. A smile flickered across Carol's face. She seemed a little smug that Jay had been the only person acquitted. She had, I'd heard, sent a spiteful email to Jay's accuser, Suzie.

Carol leant over the counter conspiratorially. 'I saw these girls every day, and I know what they were like,' she told me. 'They threw themselves at the men. You can't blame men for being men, particularly when girls are acting so provocative.'

Why would women have gone to the trouble of testifying, I asked her.

'Money,' Carol replied, taking mine.

One morning, I found myself on a fishing trip with Len Brown at Tedside, on the other side of the island, Brenda Christian having invited Claire and me to join her, Mike and Len. It was a rare Pitcairn day with low wind and moderately flat seas: ideal fishing conditions. I watched Len skip barefoot across the jagged rocks, spear in one hand, fishing tackle in the other. He was dressed in the same grey trousers and threadbare cream shirt that he had worn for his court appearances.

Within a few hours, the three of them had accumulated a sizeable haul of nanwe, rock cod, trevally, whitefish and opapa (a little speckled fish). Brenda and Len cleaned the catch, sitting cross-legged on the ground. Mike demonstrated how to open a coconut by flinging a rock at it.

Later on, Mike and Brenda drove us back to their house for coffee. We admired their glass-walled duncan, with its fabulous ocean views, and Brenda's collection of dolphin knick-knacks, which filled two big glass display cabinets. Brenda often wore a necklace of gold dolphins, and in her home there were dolphins everywhere you looked — in photographs, posters and calendars, even carved into the concrete floor. In the bathroom, the soap dish and toilet-roll holder were dolphin-shaped.

Inevitably, we talked about the trials. Mike deplored the fact that the guilty men were still free. 'It's going to be very hard for the community to move on,' he said, 'and that's a real problem.'

The peculiarity of Pitcairn's situation had struck me at Tedside, where we had seen a small boat motor past as we stood on the rocks. Belinda's father was out fishing with Randy Christian, who had just been given a prison sentence for raping Belinda.

Belinda's father was not angry with Randy. Actually, most Pitcairners thought Randy was the one with reason to be cross. Randy's father, Steve, held a grudge against Belinda's father, because he had failed to control his recalcitrant daughter.

189

Randy had not only raped Belinda; he had also molested Karen. However, Karen's father felt sorry for Randy, he told friends. Randy had a young family himself now, so perhaps he could understand things from a father's perspective. Karen's father continued socialising with Randy, and with Dave Brown, even though Dave had assaulted his sister, Linda.

Dave had also attacked Janet, and so had Terry Young, yet Janet's father apparently bore them no hard feelings. Before the trials, he had voiced surprise that Steve, in particular, was being prosecuted. 'What's the problem?' he had asked. 'Steve was young and single then.'

Karen's father and Janet's father were both decent men. But it was difficult not to be shocked by their moral equivocation. I was beginning to wonder if everyone on the island — even the likes of Mike, who had no connection with the case — was not compromised to some degree. If Mike wished to enjoy the fruits of Pitcairn, he had to live and work with men whose actions he despised. On Pitcairn, there was no other way.

Another morning was spent in the company of Betty Christian, who showed Claire and me around the weather station at Taro Ground. Until 1992, the building had also housed the radio station; Morse code was in constant use for communicating with ships in the vicinity, sending telegrams to the British administration, and even placing grocery orders. Betty told us that she and Tom, both former radio operators, still practised Morse code, rapping 'Pass the salt, please' on the table at mealtimes.

Changing the subject, Claire asked Betty how important her ancestry was to her. 'I'm proud of the fact that Fletcher Christian stood up and fought for what he thought was right,' Betty replied. There were drawbacks, though: the Pitcairners were under constant scrutiny, 'like a goldfish in a bowl, or a monkey in a zoo', she said.

When she and Tom travelled overseas, people would come up 'and want to hug or touch you, just because you're from Pitcairn'. Betty sighed. 'I tell them that we're ordinary, we make mistakes like everyone else. But we're supposed to be unique and different. We're supposed to be the perfect community.'

Mindful of one significant loose end in our reporting, Claire and I decided to drop by Steve Christian's house and ask him for an interview. We figured that he might at least be willing to share his feelings about being sacked as mayor.

As we approached Big Fence, I glanced in through a window. Steve and his mates were assembled in the living room. It did not seem an ideal time to visit, but it probably never would be. We walked up the driveway towards the front door, which was open. Steve was sprawled on a sofa, holding court. When he saw us, he almost foamed at the mouth.

'We just want to request an interview,' I called out.

'GET THE FUCK OFF MY LAND!' shouted Steve, gesticulating with violent sweeps of his arm.

Dave Brown came to the door, highly agitated, and shooed us off like a couple of stray cats. 'Go away, you're not wanted here,' he scolded us, incredulous at our effrontery.

Retreating, we turned up a side road in the direction of Pawl Warren's house, where we had promised to drop something off. Almost immediately Brenda Christian drove past in the opposite direction, accompanied by one of the MDPs. They shook their heads at us reprovingly. When we reached Pawl's two minutes later, his mother, Daphne, asked us, by way of greeting, 'What have you two been up to now?' An apoplectic Steve had just been on the radio, summoning lawyers and police officers to deal with this brazen case of harassment and trespass. Before we had even sat down, the radio started up again, with Vinny Reid, the senior

MDP, trying to contact Claire and me. He needed to talk to us urgently, he said. We arranged to meet him at the Lodge. As we walked home, we were overtaken by Dave, haring to the prison to collect Paul Dacre.

Reid arrived with Brenda and another MDP. He wore a stern expression, and was carrying an official-looking file. He told us that Steve had made a complaint: we had been on his property and had refused to leave. 'That's not true, we left straight away,' I protested. Claire and I explained the sequence of events. Reid said, 'OK, we'll leave it at that, then. I just had to get your side of things.'

The three of them got up to go. 'Try to stay out of trouble, girls,' Reid said.

The *Braveheart* was on its way back, I was relieved to learn, and would arrive in a couple of days. I felt like I was suffocating — not merely trapped for six weeks in this tiny, out of the way place, but crushed by the weight of the women's testimony.

Reminders were all around us. Every time I stepped out, I saw the sugar cane processing shed. In a nearby banana grove, at the hands of Randy and, allegedly, Shawn, Belinda had suffered atrocities no ten-year-old should even know about. The shed happened to be near the Lodge, but there was barely a location on the island that was not associated with some harrowing tale of sexual violence. The crime sites all had postcard-pretty names: Doodwi Ground, Garnets Ridge, The Hollow, Jack Williams Valley, Highest Point.

I wandered the length of Garnets Ridge, nearly 1,000 feet above sea level, a spot as ravishing as it was lonely. I could see Adamstown way below, a few dozen houses sprinkled across a bright green hillside. As I looked down at this unremarkable rural settlement, framed by the savage beauty of the Pacific, I shivered.

* * *

Thick mist heralded the day of our departure. Every bit of the island above Adamstown had disappeared. Even Christian's Cave was invisible. It was as if Pitcairn was pulling a blanket over itself as the last visitors prepared to leave.

I walked past rows of crumbling gravestones in the little cemetery, located on a grassy slope with wide sea views. Beneath the ground lay generations of men whose crimes had gone unpunished, and generations of women whose stories remained untold. Some of their sons and grandsons had been brought to account now. But would the cycle of abuse on Pitcairn ever end?

At The Landing, the same two groups had formed. The islanders desperately needed closure, and none was in prospect. Some of those who had openly condemned Steve Christian and his followers were afraid for their safety once the outsiders had gone. Social workers, meanwhile, were not persuaded that the men no longer posed a risk to children. After all, paedophiles were notoriously recidivist. They had advised the judges to withdraw the men's bail; however, their advice had not been heeded.

Guilty but free, Steve must have felt invulnerable to a degree. As for Dave Brown, who had originally faced far more serious allegations, he probably thought he was the luckiest person alive. Allan Roberts told me later that immediately the threat of prison was lifted, Dave 'stopped being this persecuted, weepy figure and became a bantam rooster again, strutting around, trumpeting advice to everyone else'.

Roberts, his clients clustered around him, drove the boat that ferried our group out to the *Braveheart*. Steve stood at the engine, smiling for the first time in six weeks and guiding Roberts on a macho course that skirted dangerous rocks. The islanders could not contain their delight at getting rid of us. The atmosphere on the longboat was festive. After showing off their skill as sailors, the men slammed the boat sideways into a wave, to soak us.

We boarded the *Braveheart*: journalists, diplomats, police officers and the defence team. Dave produced a camera and began ostentatiously taking pictures of me. I blew him a sarcastic kiss. We glared at each other across the water. Vaine Peu reached over and grasped my hand. I was touched by this public gesture of friendship. Then Steve started up the longboat's engine.

As the Pitcairners set off, leaving a milky trail in their wake, Meralda Warren turned back to face us.

'We'll never rest until our men are free!' she yelled, a final message of defiance carried on the wind.

Part 2

Viewing Pitcairn from a distance

CHAPTER 12

How the myth was forged

'It was cultural, though, wasn't it?' asked a friend as we propped up a wall in the courtyard of a Sydney pub. It was December 2004. I was not long back from Pitcairn and had stepped out to a pre-Christmas drinks party. 'I mean,' said my friend, a fellow journalist in his 40s, 'it was part of their culture and everyone accepted it, even the women.'

'I don't know if everyone accepted it,' I said. 'The children who were raped didn't like it.'

'But,' said my friend, a father of two, 'they weren't actually children, were they? They were 12 or 13. That's the age when girls get married off in some countries.'

Another journalist joined us. 'Ah, Pitcairn,' he said. 'I was in two minds about that whole case. What they did was wrong, of course, but did they know any different? It seems like under-age sex was their custom. To go in there and have a big trial, I don't know if that was the right thing to do.'

Head whirling, I wandered off. I had not yet readjusted to a world with restaurants and traffic and pavements and shops. The conversation at the pub I had found quite baffling. However, as I was to discover, my friends' comments were by no means untypical.

I ought to have been prepared for it. While still on the island, I had read numerous opinion pieces defending the Pitcairn men. In the London *Times*, for instance, Ross Clark had attacked Britain for treating 'a genuine example of cultural diversity ... as perversion'. On the other side of the world, the *New Zealand Herald*'s Gordon McLaughlan had blamed political correctness for Pitcairn's woes, observing, 'High flights of imagination are not needed to grasp how someone raised in the island's extraordinarily introverted culture could settle in New Zealand, absorb our culture of victimhood and be persuaded she had been seriously wronged.'

McLaughlan's fellow *Herald* columnist, Garth George, had ridiculed 'all the tut-tutting and oh dearing and isn't it awfulling' that characterised 'the reports of the wide-eyed ingenue from whom we received our coverage'. (That was me.) George picked out a headline about the men's lack of remorse. 'Why on Earth would there be any remorse over what had obviously been part of Pitcairn culture since the place was settled?' he asked.

Then Colleen McCullough, the bestselling author, had weighed in. McCullough is Australian and lives on Norfolk Island, where she is married to a Pitcairn descendant, Ric Robinson. In an interview with the *Sydney Morning Herald*, she declared of the Pitcairners, 'They are as much Polynesian as anything else. It's Polynesian to break your girls in at 12.' She went on, 'The Poms have cracked the whip and it's an absolute disgrace. These are indigenous customs and they should not be touched. These were the first people to inhabit Pitcairn Island. They are racially unique.'

It was, it seemed to me, as if McCullough and the various columnists had not read any of the news reports from the trials. It was as if the evidence — ten-year-old Belinda gang-raped in a banana grove, 12-year-old Marion raped weekly while collecting firewood — had completely passed them by. Or maybe they didn't believe it? Maybe they believed, instead, that every one of these sexual encounters had been consensual, and that if some of the girls had been a bit young, well, that was simply the Polynesian way.

What about the guilty verdicts, though, I wondered. Didn't they count for anything? Of course, the police and courts didn't always get it right. But the island men were hardly the Birmingham Six. The judges on Pitcairn had found the evidence overwhelming, and the men had barely put up a defence.

Their crimes — raping and molesting children — would normally have had the public baying for their blood. Instead, the islanders were seen as victims of a miscarriage of justice, perpetrated by their over-zealous British rulers.

There were several factors at play, I came to realise. One, the knee-jerk instinct to side with the tiny island pitted against the big colonial power. Two, the reluctance by right-thinking people to condemn what they thought might be a cultural tradition different from theirs.

And three, the myth.

Every year, on 23 January, Maurice Allward torches a 7-foot replica of the *Bounty* on the back patio of his neat brick cottage in Hatfield, a dormitory town north of London. A select group of guests watches the ship go up in flames, while Allward's wife, Joy, stands by with a hosepipe, just in case. 'Maurice nearly burnt the house down one year,' says one regular at the midwinter gatherings. Another guest, backing away from the fiery spectacle, once fell into an ornamental pond.

The ritual incineration is the highlight of a party com-memorating the burning of the *Bounty* in 1790. On Pitcairn, the locals recreate the event by setting fire to a model of the triple-masted cutter in Bounty Bay. Maurice Allward builds his versions to a 1/15 scale. 'I went overboard on the first one,' he recalls. 'I even gave it rigging.' Since then he has refined the procedure. 'I get two big cardboard boxes, tie them together with three toilet roll holders for the mast, and then pack it with fireworks and cardboard. I make the bow, clip it on the front, then clip the stern on the back.'

For the Allwards, 23 January 2005 was no different from previous years. Their dog, Muffin, milled around as Maurice, a vigorous 82-year-old, played a tape of the Pitcairners' traditional welcome song. Joy served up breadfruit fritters; in the past, guests have sometimes eaten their Bounty Day meal off antique wooden plates. Allward on one occasion weighed out the food portions on coconut-shell scales, emulating Bligh's division of rations on the voyage to Timor. On this evening in 2005, everyone adjourned to the garden to see the *Bounty* burn.

It was two months later that I interviewed Allward; he had read reports of the recent trials, and even showed me some newspaper cuttings — plucked from a capacious file labelled 'Bountiana'. While he admitted that the case had changed his view of Pitcairn, it was clear that he loved the myth too much to let go of it.

Maurice Allward is not related to anyone on the island, nor has he visited: with two artificial knees, he cheerfully acknowledges, leaping into the longboat could be tricky. Nevertheless, since he retired as a civil aircraft engineer, Pitcairn and the *Bounty* have been his main preoccupations. Every shelf, coffee table and mantelpiece in his house is lined with ornaments and knick-knacks, among them a *Bounty* cushion cover, a William Bligh mug and a tin lamp modelled on the ship. Allward's collection of memorabilia — one of the largest in private hands — includes half a dozen greasy coils of hair: the sailors' pigtails, supposedly. Joy shudders when he produces them.

His fascination with the story, Allward told me, dates from 1936, when his father took him to see *Mutiny on the Bounty*, starring Clark Gable and Charles Laughton. He was 12. 'It was such a rip-roaring yarn, full of chaps being whipped and keelhauled,' he says. 'I'll never forget that scene when they carried on flogging someone after he was dead.' A poster from the film hangs in his office; on the door is the Pitcairn coat of arms. The room is stuffed with prints, photographs, rare books and relics, such as a fragment of the *Bounty*'s rudder and a shard of rock from Christian's Cave. A plaque outside the house commemorates a visit by Brenda Christian, one of many island friends with whom Allward corresponds.

The single-mindedness with which he pursues his hobby is almost fanatical, yet there are people all around the world who share Allward's fascination. For him, it began with an interest in oceans and shipping; for others, it was naval history or philately or the South Pacific or Seventh-day Adventism. Fans congregate in internet chat rooms, where they swap news about their favourite island and bicker about obscure details of the mutiny. They collect Pitcairn's stamps and subscribe to the local newspaper, the *Miscellany*, with its breadfruit recipes and fishing reports. And, like Allward, they haunt the big auction houses, hoping to pick up yet another memento.

To these devotees, Pitcairn is not just a lump of rock with a rich history and an exotic location. To them, it is a little piece of paradise in the South Seas, and nothing that ever happens there will alter their opinion.

I had first met Maurice Allward in London at the biannual meeting of the Pitcairn Islands Study Group. Set up 20 years ago by philatelists, the group nowadays welcomes anyone with a passion for Pitcairn and the *Bounty*; its members, mostly retired, include ship's captains, amateur historians and a vicar. The meeting was at the Union Jack Club, an imposing establishment for British service and ex-service personnel, near Waterloo Station. Squeezing past antiques and leather sofas, I found myself in the basement Gascoigne Room, where about 40 people, mainly middle-aged or elderly men, were assembled. I noticed a preponderance of beards and tweed jackets.

The day-long programme of events featured a talk on first-day covers based on the island's radio station. There was also to be a presentation on Pitcairn nautical charts by the group's honorary secretary, Captain Jeff Thomas. However, the star speaker was Maurice Bligh, the great-great-great-grandson of William Bligh of the *Bounty*.

Bligh was a dapper, intense man in a dark blue blazer, and it quickly became clear that he was on a mission. Although his lecture was billed 'The Bounty/Pitcairn Saga — Where Do We Go From Here?', he launched straight into a fiery speech denouncing Fletcher Christian and his men. The mutiny, he claimed, was a 'piratical seizure' by sailors who wanted to return to the fleshpots of Tahiti, while Christian was most likely suffering from laudanum withdrawal, having been prescribed the drug by the *Bounty*'s alcoholic surgeon to treat his venereal disease. Before settling on Pitcairn, Maurice Bligh said, Christian and his followers had embarked on 'a leisurely nine-month island-hopping cruise, like drunken millionaires, kidnapping, raping and flogging, and slaughtering more than 60 natives'.

I had the impression this was not the first time that Maurice Bligh had outlined these arguments in this company. Nonetheless, his audience listened politely, interjecting the odd 'Hear, hear!' or 'Disgraceful!'

Seated in the third row were two descendants of the person whom Bligh was criticising so robustly: Sheri and Darlene Christian, great-great-great-great-granddaughters of Fletcher Christian, and daughters of Tom and Betty Christian. On learning who they were, an elderly man in their row pulled out a camera and leant over to photograph them close up. The sisters smiled politely. Maurice Bligh, who said he had no interest in sustaining the two-centuries-old grudge between their families, shared a lunch table with the Christian women, and at one point could be heard telling them excitedly, 'This could be the start of something new.'

And how did those gathered in the Gascoigne Room, hemmed in by oil paintings of warships and battle scenes, feel about recent events? The trials had ended a few months earlier, but the subject had barely been mentioned. Over a cup of coffee, Jennifer Toombs, the group's president and the designer of many of Pitcairn's early stamps, told me, 'Those *beastly* trials. It was such a horrible shock. I know some of those men very well, and my prayers have been with them around this whole business.' Toombs had visited the island in the 1960s, she said, encountering 'nothing but absolute warmth and hospitality'.

Judging by the attention lavished on the Christians, the case had in no way lessened the island's appeal. I was a minor celebrity myself. 'Did I hear right?' inquired a man sitting beside me. 'You've actually been to Pitcairn? You are *so* lucky.' Applause greeted Jeff Thomas's announcement of a 'happy event': the birth of a baby boy to Randy Christian. Did those clapping, I asked myself, know that Randy had recently been found guilty of serial child rape?

'It's probably because of Hollywood that we're here,' someone at the Union Jack Club remarked. But the public was enthralled by the mutiny long before celluloid was invented. In fact, Britain was agog from the moment William Bligh arrived home following his odyssey in the *Bounty*'s launch.

It was the late 18th century; European exploration of the South

Seas had only just begun, and the descriptions of early visitors had conjured up visions of a tropical Garden of Eden. Now a group of English sailors had not only commandeered a Royal Navy ship; they had apparently sailed off to live with a posse of beautiful maidens on a palm-fringed island. The English press seized on the story, and Bligh's first brief published account, called *A Narrative of the Mutiny on board His Majesty's Ship 'Bounty'*, was an instant bestseller. The story inspired, among others, Lord Byron, who wrote an epic ballad, 'The Island', while the Royalty Theatre in London staged a musical, *The Pirates; Or, The Calamities of Captain Bligh*.

The outside world's interest was only heightened by the eventual discovery of the seemingly idyllic community on Pitcairn — particularly when it emerged that this was a Utopia with *Christian* values. Among those who filed extravagant reports was Walter Brodie, shipwrecked off Pitcairn in 1850, who wrote that the island was 'the realisation of Arcadia, or what we had been accustomed to suppose had existence only in poetic imagination — the golden age: all living as one family, a commonwealth of brothers and sisters'. However, it was not only starry-eyed visitors who helped to create the myth: from the outset, it was cultivated by interested parties exploiting the mutiny story for their own purposes.

On his return to England in 1790, William Bligh had been fêted as a national hero. He was presented to King George, promoted to captain, and absolved of any fault over the loss of the *Bounty*. Before long, though, he had fallen from grace, thanks to a propaganda offensive waged by the well-connected families of Fletcher Christian and Peter Heywood, the *Bounty* midshipman.

Heywood had been among the mutineers captured on Tahiti; back home he was court-martialled and sentenced to hang. After lobbying by his family, he was not only pardoned but later promoted, going on to enjoy a long and fruitful naval career.

According to Caroline Alexander, author of *The Bounty*, a definitive account of the mutiny and its aftermath, the Heywoods blackened William Bligh's name in naval circles. Christian's relatives, for their part, were determined to persuade the wider public that Bligh was to blame for the uprising. Edward Christian, Fletcher's older brother and a Cambridge law professor, conducted his own unorthodox inquiry, interviewing surviving *Bounty* crew members in a seedy riverside London pub. Plied with ale, the sailors praised Fletcher's virtue and courage, and damned Bligh as a foul-mouthed despot. Edward concluded, 'Captain Bligh is a detestable villain against whom ... every door must be shut.'

Public opinion had already started to turn following the trials of Heywood and the other mutineers, whom the newspaper reports had painted as underdogs. As a counterblast to Bligh's *Narrative*, in 1794 Edward published a partial transcript of the court proceedings, together with an appendix containing the sailors' alehouse statements. Bligh responded with a detailed rebuttal of Edward's claims, including depositions from the same crew members. Edward issued a counter-rebuttal. Bligh put out a longer version of his *Narrative*, and also published his private log.

While the attacks ended then, the damage was done. Despite a second, this time successful expedition to transport breadfruit seedlings from Tahiti to the Caribbean, Bligh was not promoted further. He had to wait nearly two years for his next commission. Lord Chatham, First Lord of the Admiralty, refused to see him.

Bligh had also lost the propaganda war, although he did not realise it yet, believing he had silenced his critics through a rational demolition of their arguments. Caroline Alexander writes, 'He failed to comprehend that he was doing battle with a force more formidable and unassailable than any enemy he would meet at sea — the power of a good story ... this fantastic tale of escape to paradise at the far end of the world.' The story would come to be known as 'The Mutiny on the *Bounty*', and the mutineers' version — constructed by the Heywood and Christian families, and cemented by Hollywood — would outlive Bligh's.

Edward and his friends had pulled off quite a feat: with the assistance of a receptive public, they had managed to rescue Fletcher Christian's good name. Two centuries later Fletcher's descendants, aided by *their* allies, would convince public opinion that they, too, were victims of tyrannical overlords.

The Pitcairn legend persisted well into the 20th century. For adherents of Christianity, the island remained a symbol of faith. It also had a strong appeal for secular souls. City dwellers mourning the fragmentation of their communities saw it as a place untainted by the West's materialism and modern vices, where people still lived and worked together in a spirit of genuine co-operation. The island was regarded as pure and wholesome: Maori children from Auckland's rough suburbs were sent there for a break from drugs and street crime.

Pitcairn attracted a stream of other visitors: anthropologists, archaeologists, film-makers, zoologists, sailors, adventurers, historians and the simply curious. Nearly everyone was charmed, and when the scandal broke, they were loath to believe that the men they were flattered to call friends were capable of such behaviour. Among critics of the prosecution have been the captains of supply ships: one English captain decried 'the back-to-front thinking changing this island from a Crown to a penal colony'.

Landlubbers were — and are — equally besotted. Herb Ford, the self-styled Pitcairn expert in California, receives up to 300 emails a day requesting information. Some 1400 people worldwide subscribe to the island's *Miscellany* newspaper, and another 1000 pay up to $US100 a year for a domain name and email address with the .pn suffix. And then there are the tourists. Daphne Warren told me about an occasion when some elderly cruise ship passengers nearly staged a mutiny because the captain had told them it was too rough to disembark. To placate them, the crew went ashore and filled up a dozen buckets with earth, then came back and poured it over the deck. According to Daphne, 'The passengers were tripping over each other to be first to step in the dirt ... They'd been looking forward so much to telling people back home that they'd set foot on Pitcairn.'

Just as in the 19th century, gifts constantly arrive on the island: pencils and sweets for the children, boxes of shoes for the adults — an American church group that saw a film of them walking around barefoot thought they couldn't afford to be shod. A family in the United States used to mail magazines to Steve Christian. Not a great reader, he used them as kindling. After a while the family announced, 'We're not sending you any more money, because you haven't come out to America to visit.' They had been cutting pictures out of the magazines and sticking in dollar bills. Steve will never know how much money he burnt.

The islanders assiduously nurture their myth. They even have a term for it: 'hypocriting the stranger'.

On the ships, the locals befriend crew members in charge of stores. One outsider who accompanied them aboard a cargo vessel watched open-mouthed as they reappeared with their haul: tables, chairs, five mattresses, and a new pair of shoes, still in their box. Day-trippers depart Pitcairn laden with souvenirs, some moved to tears by the islanders' kindness and hospitality. One observer says, 'They pretend to be simple, unsophisticated folk. But they're actually very shrewd and manipulative. They're professional charmers.'

On Pitcairn, 'hypocrite' is an adjective, too. John Harré, a New Zealand anthropologist who stayed on the island in the 1960s, remembers the church being given a 'hypocrite coat of paint' — to spruce it up for an official visit. The islanders also spoke of the 'hypocrite seas': apparently calm, but concealing danger.

The dissembling tradition began with John Adams, who claimed that he had not been 'in the smallest degree concerned in the mutiny, he being at the time it happened, sick in bed'. Adams hid flaws in his supposedly perfect society, and then, as now, out-siders colluded. According to Caroline Alexander, unfavourable reports — 'such as the account [by one early visitor] that the pious youths had been caught red-handed brewing spirits very much like whisky' — were ignored by Pitcairn's admirers. In later eras, the islanders camouflaged aspects of their lifestyle that they knew would be frowned on. A ship's captain in the 19th century discovered that the community had doctored birth records to mask the existence of illegitimate children.

The islanders were aware that their virtuous image was their main asset. They were especially keen not to alienate the Seventh-day Adventist Church, which had been unfailingly generous. Again, sympathetic visitors assisted. A New Zealand sociologist in the 1970s abandoned a thesis on Pitcairn, concerned that if he pub-lished it, the Church would cut its links.

After two centuries of feeding their own legend, the Pitcairners — with their *Bounty* T-shirts and their family trees at their fingertips — appear to have bought into it themselves. They believe in the glamour and the heroism. They talk about Fletcher Christian as if he were alive only the other day. Some proudly display *Bounty* tattoos.

Daniel Carnihan, husband of Sheils, the former teacher, says,

'They really believe they're living in paradise, and Pitcairn is the best place in the world. They keep on repeating it, and no one ever challenges them. It reminded me of the Emperor's new clothes.'

Unwilling to be disrobed, particularly in public, the islanders are ultra-sensitive about how they are portrayed by writers and journalists. One reporter in the 1990s was told, 'You'd better not bloody write anything we don't like, or we'll string you up. You'd better keep your bloody mouth shut.'

If the world learnt what Pitcairn was really like, the locals feared, the cruise ships would stop calling, and the parcels of new clothes would stop arriving, and wealthy ham radio contacts would no longer treat them to all-expenses-paid trips to the US and Japan. The myth would be exposed for what it was, just a myth, and the mutineers' descendants would be left to their own devices.

When the child abuse story broke, the islanders had to 'hypocrite' the outside world more than ever before. Their efforts paid off, as I discovered from some of the feedback to my own reporting.

In early 2005 I received an email from Lyle Burgoyne, the Adventist lay pastor and friend of Leon Salt. It was Lyle who had helped Steve Christian pin up a statement outside the Adamstown courthouse rubbishing the prosecution, minutes after charges had been laid inside.

Lyle and his wife, Jenny, who live in Australia, wrote that, after reading my reports and Claire Harvey's, they had realised that 'your ilk of journalist writes whatever they want so long as it is sensational & sells'. The couple told me, 'We now open any newspaper & read with great scepticism, knowing that most, if not all, could be fabricated. Even our 15-year-old daughter ... could not get over the absolute garbage and lies that were printed about the people she knows.' The Burgoynes took exception to a reference I had made to 'opponents of the criminal prosecution'. 'What is continuing to happen to Pitcairn people is criminal PERSECUTION,' they thundered, '& the methods used to persecute are considered illegal in all civilised countries — & that is what we are against.'

Not long afterwards, Jenny's mother, Margaret Head, sent me an email. Margaret informed me that she worked with victims of child sexual assault — by which, she said, she meant 'real sexual assault not the pseudo-sexual assault you have in this case [Pitcairn]'. Jenny had told her years ago, Margaret said, that Britain wanted to shut down the island. 'I laughed at that suggestion. How could they do that? NOW I KNOW HOW!!!!! Mention the words sexual assault and say it often enough and it becomes the truth.'

Margaret concluded, 'I don't know what your experience is with sexual assault. Maybe you know very little or maybe you have had some experience and are going to make every male pay.'

Around that time, I noticed an unflattering reference to myself on the internet forum Friends of Pitcairn. 'Don't believe all the BRITISH PROPAGANDA that you are reading in the media at present,' warned a woman named Anne from New Zealand. 'Kathy Marks for one, should be shot.' Feeling somewhat shocked, I read on. Anne revealed that one of the pieces I had written from Pitcairn had made her feel 'physically sick'. Not, it transpired, because it had contained a vivid account of a child being sexually assaulted — but because, to her, it had demonstrated that 'the British are BUYING into a power struggle that they don't really understand the dynamics of'.

Friends of Pitcairn had been set up in May 2000 by a Florida woman, Barbara Kuchau, and attracted members from more than 20 countries, including India, Germany, Sweden, Nigeria, Romania, Malaysia, Costa Rica and Norway. A handful had family links or had visited the island; most were drawn, simply, by a consuming interest in the *Bounty* story, and in the minutiae of contemporary life on Pitcairn. Quite a number were paradise myth junkies, like the Californian who sighed, 'I'm here because ... it seems as if we all have the same dream.'

'Friends' exchanged news about Pitcairn, debated its history and argued the relative merits of the Hollywood films. They purchased the islanders' products, and weighed such questions as 'Whatever happened to Fletcher Christian?' and 'Do Pitcairners have washing machines?' They cooed over photographs of children on Pitcairn, dispatched birthday greetings to elderly islanders, and when Nadine Christian, Randy's wife, went into labour, followed her progress step by step. No matter that they had never met Nadine or any of the other islanders; they felt as if they had, and they talked about them as if they were old friends or family members.

The message board received up to 1600 postings a month, with Herb Ford, the Californian Adventist, a leading contributor. It was he who first brought news of Operation Unique, warning that 'the demonic winds are blowing again about our favorite island'. A police investigation into child rape and incest was not, presumably, what Pitcairn's admirers had in mind when they became 'Friends'. Most of them coped with this turn of events by ignoring it: when Barbara Kuchau invited comments on a story in the *New Zealand Herald*, no one responded. Instead, a member called Brian reported, 'Today I received a shipment of 7 jars of Pitcairn Honey ... it's absolutely spectacular. I would recommend that all FRIENDS order some.'

Ford and Kuchau set the tone for what discussion took place, with the latter stating firmly that 'child abuse is a VERY serious charge but can be misunderstood and used for many reasons'. Members recalled cases in Britain and the US where allegations had turned out to be fabricated, and reminded each other about the importance of respecting other people's cultures. The few who dared to dissent were shouted down, with one Friend opining, 'We should hold back from condemning men whose only sin is potentially that of following island practice.' Melva Evans, the Alaska-based Pitcairner, squashed one man who tried to inject a note of reality. 'There is NO child abuse on Pitcairn,' she told him, tartly. 'There is nothing to discuss with respect to that subject.'

Melva was one of half a dozen islanders who joined the forum, giving star-struck Pitcairn fans a thrill. 'Anyone with Bounty lineage is a celebrity in my eyes,' gushed one woman. The islanders played up to the attention. Meralda Warren signed herself Maimiti, one of the names by which Fletcher Christian's wife was known. Melva told members, 'You can only push a Pitcairner so far. We inherited that gene from one who had the guts to take a stand against a bully.'

In 2005 Maurice Bligh popped up in the chat room, and soon he and Melva were crossing swords as they defended the honour of their respective ancestors. Within a few months Bligh had departed, claiming his presence had sparked whisperings about 'the enemy within'.

Many Friends of Pitcairn members championed the 'South Pacific culture/under-age sex' argument. And since that argument has been given such wide credence, it might be worth examining in some detail.

Central to the argument is the island of Tahiti, the archetypal South Pacific paradise, and its sexually liberal image, forged by the likes of Philibert Commerçon, a naturalist who accompanied the 18th-century French explorer Louis-Antoine de Bougainville. Commerçon wrote, 'The Tahitians know no other god but love.

Every day is consecrated to it, the whole island is its temple, all the women are its idols, all the men its worshippers.'

Other Europeans, including Captain James Cook and Paul Gauguin, the late 19th-century French painter, were similarly affected. Gauguin's paintings, together with novels and films produced about the South Pacific over the years, enshrined the notion of Polynesia as a haven of carefree promiscuity. In 1928 the American anthropologist Margaret Mead scandalised her contemporaries with a no-holds-barred report — since largely discredited — on the sexual mores of young Samoan women.

That background may help to explain why claims that the Pitcairners were only practising their island culture have fallen on such fertile ground. According to those claims, adolescents in Polynesia were encouraged to experiment with each other; the custom was then carried to Pitcairn by the Tahitian women and perpetuated by their mixed-race heirs. And while the Westernised world gradually took a dim view of youthful sexual activity, isolated Pitcairn remained in a late 18th-century timewarp.

The argument collapses once it is subjected to scrutiny, for it is not teenagers dabbling in sensual pleasures who were prosecuted, but adult men who had raped and assaulted girls allegedly as young as three. That has never been part of South Pacific culture — and even if it had been, few people would endorse it, presumably, any more than they would endorse female circumcision. As for isolation, the islanders have been travelling to and from New Zealand for nearly a century.

Sheils Carnihan, the New Zealand teacher who laid some of the groundwork for Belinda to make the first disclosures, says, 'If it was cultural and acceptable, why did they hide it? In India they have child brides. We might not agree with that, but at least it's out in the open. If this was really Pitcairn culture, then why keep it secret?'

'If it was cultural,' says Karen Vaughan, the Wellington detective, 'why didn't they all plead guilty and say, "Yeah, we did it, and that's what we do here, what's the problem?" It was no more cultural than what goes on behind closed doors in New Zealand and in communities all over the world.'

There is another reason why the cultural argument is a fallacy: Pitcairn is not a Polynesian community. In fact, the Polynesians' role in the Pitcairn story has only been recognised belatedly, and to a small degree. At the top of the Hill of Difficulty is a brass plaque inscribed with the names of the nine mutineers, together with the *Bounty*'s specifications; a new plaque listing the Tahitian men and women who co-founded the colony was not put up until 2005.

Although the women, in particular, kept the settlement alive through their understanding of the plants and the seasons, and their knowledge of how to grow food and catch fish, the sailors' influence predominated as John Adams fashioned Pitcairn into an English-speaking, Christian society. The mutineers' offspring saw themselves as transplanted Europeans. Britain was the mother country, and increasing contacts with New Zealand reinforced their English heritage.

Some Tahitian traditions have survived, including fishing and methods of food preparation. Dishes such as pilhi (mashed green banana or sweet potato, baked in a banana skin) are pure Polynesian, and so are surfing, kite flying and walking on stilts: all popular children's activities. To a visitor, though, Pitcairn appears almost entirely Westernised. There is no Tahitian dance or music, costume, language or architecture. Tahitian stories and legends have not been handed down. 'The Polynesian side was never encouraged,' says Betty Christian. 'It's an island in the Pacific, but it's not a Pacific island,' says Ewart Barnsley, TVNZ's former veteran Pacific correspondent.

A few islanders, notably Meralda Warren and her mother, Mavis, consider themselves Polynesian, and take a keen interest in the language and crafts and music. Others seem ambivalent. People with dark complexions are given derogatory nicknames, and a Pitcairner who moved to New Zealand was offended to be mistaken for a Maori.

One Polynesian aspect of life is the way children are cared for communally. All the adults watch out for them, and they can walk into anyone's house and be given a meal and a bed. On the other hand, it is clear that children were not looked after properly. And the communal set-up facilitated the sexual abuse. Adults had easy access.

In spite of recent events, and in spite of — to my mind — obvious flaws in the apologists' arguments, the Pitcairn myth remains intact. 'People need that dream of perfection, and I don't think it can ever be destroyed,' says Mary Maple, a New Zealander who taught on the island from 2004 to 2005.

Dea Birkett, the author, says, 'People find it hard to disentangle the myth from the reality, even after they've been there. It doesn't matter what anyone writes about Pitcairn, or what the Pitcairners do. The legend is bigger than the reality, and it always will be.'

CHAPTER 13

Politics, poison and power plays

'Get down!' yelled Pawl Warren as the longboat hurtled towards the jagged rocks at the mouth of Bounty Bay. Leslie Jaques, the Commissioner, threw himself to the bottom of the boat, and so did others, including Vinny Reid, the military policeman. As they crouched there, petrified, a large wave caught the boat at the last minute and pitched them to safety.

The trials had recently ended, and the longboat had just transferred the last batch of visitors, me included, to the *Braveheart*. Steve Christian was at the tiller; delirious, perhaps, at getting rid of us, he drove back to the island at high speed and almost caused a serious accident.

Many of the islanders were incensed with Steve: they knew how closely they had avoided catastrophe. Some were even convinced that his actions had been deliberate — aimed at demonstrating to Leslie Jaques how dangerous the surf could be, and how badly the community needed people of Steve's calibre. At a meeting of the council's internal committee, Vinny Reid complained about his conduct. Steve was outraged. 'Are you saying that I drove my longboat dangerously?' he demanded.

For Steve, the row was a petty distraction from his main preoccupation: the indignity of being ousted as mayor. Although guilty of serial child rape, sentenced to a prison term and fired by special edict of the British Governor, the man who had run Pitcairn as his own little kingdom for so long was not about to give that up lightly.

Two days after we left the island, Steve stalked up to the Lodge, where Reid was now living with his fellow MDP, Lee Smith. Accompanying him was Stephen Bews, the new pastor, whom Steve had asked to be an independent witness. Also present at the Lodge were Jaques, who had recently arrived on Pitcairn, and Brenda Christian, in her capacity as police officer. Steve was sweating and seemed 'almost deranged'. He brandished an email from Paul Dacre which, he claimed, proved that his dismissal had been illegal. He raged at the injustice of his situation and demanded to be reinstated. Jaques calmly explained that was out of the question.

The following day, a public meeting was held to invite nominations for a new mayor. One after another, Steve's supporters took to the floor to express fury at his sacking. They even made semi-farcical efforts to nominate him, although he was, of course, ineligible. As Brenda, the interim mayor, struggled to keep order, they shouted that she had no right to be in the chair. Reid and Smith fingered the handcuffs and batons that they had taken to carrying.

Two days later, another meeting was attempted, this time with Leslie Jaques presiding. The Commissioner began by reading out a message from Richard Fell, emphasising that Steve and Randy had been legally removed and appealing to the islanders to 'act in the best interests of the entire community'. Steve then stood up and proclaimed that he had been 'working my butt off for this community for the past 30 years'. Then Randy got to his feet, with his little daughter, Emily Rose, in his arms, and said that he, too, had been slaving away for Pitcairn. No one else — not even those who were pleased that the family's grip on power was being loosened at last — said much.

Usually a mild-mannered, easygoing person, Jaques lost his temper. 'A few people have been running this place for years and the silent majority still aren't saying anything,' he exclaimed. But the meeting at least achieved its purpose. Three candidates were nominated: Brenda, Jay Warren and Cookie Warren.

Jay had been itching to regain power. In fact, the day after Steve's showdown at the Lodge, Jay had proposed that *he* be appointed mayor, since, he said, only he was capable of taking charge at this tempestuous time. Cookie, a wily character intent on self-promotion, had positioned himself as an ally of Steve's, although he was kept at arm's length by the Big Fence crowd. One thing Cookie did, reportedly, was to record, from the vantage-point of the site of the Griffiths' house, where work was continuing, the names of 'pro-British elements' visiting Leslie Jaques at the nearby Government Hostel. Consequently, islanders who wanted to speak to Jaques privately, but without being spotted, took to calling on him before breakfast.

In this immediate post-trials period, tensions on Pitcairn reached an unprecedented high. Some outsiders were deeply concerned about Steve's mental stability, and they believed that certain of his followers were capable of violence. The MDPs loaded up the pistols that they kept inside a locked cabinet at the Lodge. According to some sources, Richard Fell contemplated bringing in the New Zealand police, or even *gendarmes* off a French warship. There was also talk of deporting Steve, it is said. British officials deny any of those measures were considered.

Mike Lupton-Christian, meanwhile, had begun carrying a hammer for self-defence. Mike had told journalists that if it had been one of *his* daughters who had been abused, he would have killed the man in question — and his neighbours were so angry with him as a result that Mike feared for his own welfare.

The atmosphere was poisonous. The three families deemed to have 'associated' with the media and prosecutors — in other words, to have treated us with basic civility and kindness — were nicknamed 'Dogs Incorporated'. The families — Mike's, Pawl Warren's and Tom Christian's — were subjected to 'general nastiness ... some of it veiled, some of it obvious', says one recipient. Tom and Betty were given a particularly hard time because they had signed affidavits confirming that, as far as they were concerned, Pitcairn was a British possession. The statements would be used by the prosecution to rebut the guilty men's legal arguments, and in the eyes of many islanders, Tom and Betty were traitors. Pitcairners at home and abroad told them as much in colourfully phrased emails.

The strain showed on Leslie Jaques, who not long after the mayoral nomination meetings drove his quad bike over a cliff. He managed to jump clear and was unhurt, although shaken. The bike was written off.

In December 2004, a month after the trials ended, elections for a new Pitcairn mayor and council took place. The outcome was an emphatic victory for Steve's camp — or the 'old guard', as one journalist called them. Jay, widely seen as Steve's puppet, won the mayoral contest; Cookie was elected chairman of the internal committee, the second most influential political position; and the council was stacked with like-minded locals, including Steve's wife, Olive, Jay's wife, Carol, and Dave Brown's wife, Lea.

Brenda's short spell as interim mayor had been difficult. But despite incessant attacks and vindictive gossip, she had performed her duties with skill and good grace. Daphne Warren says, 'Pitcairn has never been so well governed as when Brenda was mayor. She was totally fair. She has broad shoulders and a heart of gold.' But Brenda's qualities were immaterial, for the guilty men and their allies — representing the majority of adults on the island — were profoundly hostile. She was female, and most Pitcairners did not believe a woman could lead. She stood for change, and most islanders opposed that. And she had 'sucked up' to the prosecution. Brenda could not even count on her mother's vote: Dobrey Christian was Steve's mother, too.

The British were dismayed. To them, Brenda embodied the community's best hope for the future. She recognised the need to acknowledge past wrongs and go forward. Her 21–11 defeat, a landslide in Pitcairn terms, indicated that most of her fellow islanders did not.

The winning candidates vented their exasperation at the way the election result was interpreted. After all, the process had been open and democratic. Why were outsiders still obsessed with the sexual abuse thing? Why couldn't they just accept that 'the voice of the people spoke and was heard loud and clearly around the world', as Cookie put it. For the 'old guard', the court case had altered nothing: the guilty verdicts were just regarded as further proof of a British plot to emasculate the community. In emails, the islanders accused British diplomats and Crown prosecutors of persecuting them and tarnishing Pitcairn's name. They compared their plight with that of the Chagos Islanders, the inhabitants of a British territory in the Indian Ocean who were evicted from their home to make way for an American military base.

Dissenters remained in the background. One man, who asked not to be named, said the court had left 'a smouldering cauldron' in its wake. He told me, 'We are now no better off than before the whole investigation started ... The chasm that divides the island is now wider than the Grand Canyon.'

As 2004 drew to a close, Steve announced that he was cancelling Christmas. Trees were planted in the square and hung with presents, but Steve's family boycotted the festivities; others, such as Cookie and Dave, only went along fleetingly. Contrary to the custom of everyone giving everyone else gifts, some people received next to nothing.

By early 2005 official sources were describing the island as 'ungovernable'. It was even hinted that Britain might impose direct rule. 'At the end of the day,' said one source, 'it's up to us how much autonomy we give them ... and if things get too extreme, we may cut them out altogether.' In February, Grant Pritchard, the Governor's Representative, was succeeded by Richard Dewell, whose previous posting had been to the United Nations. Some observers remarked that Pitcairn would test the skills of the highest-level UN negotiator.

However, it was not only diplomatic but also economic talents that were required at this time. In November 2004, just as the *Braveheart* departed and Steve Christian narrowly missed impaling his longboat on the rocks, Pitcairn had gone broke. Income had declined to almost zero, while the island's running costs remained substantial. From now on, it would be dependent on 'budgetary aid': a lifeline of £500,000 a year from the British government.

Britain had no intention of subsidising the community indefinitely, and Leslie Jaques set about investigating ways to reinvigorate the economy. The most promising option seemed to be eco-tourism, which would offer visitors the chance to immerse themselves in Pitcairn's history and natural environment. Tourism would generate new jobs, Jaques hoped, while improved transport links would encourage young people to stay and more newcomers to settle.

First the place needed to be smartened up. The infrastructure — especially the Hill of Difficulty, which was dangerous after heavy rains — was in an atrocious state. For years Britain had done the bare minimum for Pitcairn in terms of upkeep, and the locals had asked in vain for funding for various projects. Now the road was to be concreted, and the jetty and slipway rebuilt, at a cost of NZ$5 million (£1.85 million); what was more, the feasibility of constructing a breakwater, enabling smaller boats to land, was to be explored. Some of the finance would come from Britain, and some from the European Union's development fund. Britain denied that the large sums being pumped into the island amounted to 'guilt money'. Privately, though, one or two officials admitted that it was the criminal case that had made it all happen.

The infrastructure programme, which began in early 2005 and was overseen by a New Zealand contractor, alleviated frictions temporarily. For seven months the men were occupied from morning until night, while everyone else was diverted by the spectacle of the new road, growing longer by the day — and by the company of some New Zealand builders. The locals were also given a taste of a different work culture. There were good wages to be earned, and for once the jobs were not divided up by Steve and his mates, but allocated on the basis of skills and experience. Rather than Steve being the boss, there was a project manager, Tony Price. Price reprimanded Steve when he was late for his job interview. The islanders had to turn up on time to work, and were not permitted to take their customary extended lunch break.

Other changes were introduced. Vaine and Mike finally got to drive the tractor. New faces were seen at the helm of the longboats. A job in horticulture and biosecurity was created for Simon Young.

Matthew Forbes visited in February 2005 with Leslie Jaques, whose previous sojourn had been brief. Some of the guilty men, including Steve, refused to speak to them, despite the fact that Jaques was spearheading the effort to transform Pitcairn's fortunes. Steve called him 'Jaq-ass' behind his back. During their stay, two cruise ships arrived on the same day, discharging a record 750 tourists. The weather was unusually calm, and for the first time in Pitcairn's history the ships lowered their tenders and transported passengers to shore. The event was heavy with symbolism. The local men no longer controlled exclusive access to the island.

In August Richard Fell visited for the last time. His posting to New Zealand would be finishing in early 2006. While the islanders put on a public dinner for him, many people treated him coolly. A cartoon of the Governor that had been published during the trials was blown up and pasted on the front wall of Big Fence. Of all the British officials involved with the child abuse case over the years, Fell was the one most bitterly disliked. He had not ordered the investigation, nor taken the decision to prosecute; he had merely been the senior diplomat in post during a critical period. He told me, 'I am seen as one of the people who have destroyed the myth.'

In September the New Zealand contractors went home, leaving behind NZ$1.4 million (£518,000) of equipment, including a bulldozer and rock crusher. The Pitcairners were informed that it was a gift from the British — at which Cookie Warren, the acting mayor, inquired who would be expected to maintain it, and whether they would be paid.

★ ★ ★

The trials had been supposed to signal to the islanders that the British government was determined to uphold law and order. Little over six months later, in June 2005, Britain's resolve was tested.

The builders threw a farewell party for one of their number who was about to go back to New Zealand. It was held at the jail, where the contractors were staying, and quite a few of the locals attended; so did the crew of the *Southern Salvor*, the *Braveheart*'s sister boat. During the party, Nigel Jolly needled Meralda Warren about the Pitcairn men who were facing jail. Meralda was extremely drunk. She is a well-built woman. She punched Jolly three times: left, right, left. 'The guys have not been convicted, they are innocent!' she bellowed repeatedly.

Jolly walked away. As the evening progressed, however, Meralda punched Pawl Warren, then Brenda Christian. She called Brenda — who had been about to take Meralda home, at her own request — a 'whore' and a 'fucking bitch'. When Tony Price, the works supervisor, urged her not to drive her quad bike, Meralda replied, 'There's no fucking law here and I don't care.' Vinny Reid, who had just returned to Pitcairn for a second stint as MDP sergeant, was summoned to the prison; Jolly and Pawl declined to make formal complaints, but Brenda was set on pursuing hers. That put Britain in a quandary. The incident was a minor drunken assault; then again, the victim was a police officer, and it was the first reported crime since the trials.

A New Zealand magistrate, Hugh Fulton, was scheduled to visit the island in September to train the newly appointed Pitcairn magistrate, Simon Young. Fulton agreed to hear the case against Meralda, but he insisted that lawyers would also be required. Notwithstanding the enormous expense, British officials reluctantly authorised Allan Roberts to travel to Pitcairn to represent Meralda. Simon Mount, one of the Crown prosecutors, would accompany him.

The trial lasted five days. Meralda was found guilty and fined NZ$60 (£23). The case cost the British more than NZ$40,000 (£15,600). Matthew Forbes told the *New Zealand Herald*, between gritted teeth, that 'at the end of the day, the principle is more important'.

The affair provoked lively debate in the Friends of Pitcairn chat room, where many members argued that Meralda was the real victim. Cyberspace had grown even noisier since the trials. Following an attempt to ban that topic on Friends of Pitcairn, several breakaway forums had sprung up, largely attracting people who were disgusted that FoP members were still defending the abusers. The migration of serious debate away from the main message board was welcomed by, among others, Dave Brown. 'I reckon it is much better after the other board started and took all the nonsense with it,' declared Dave. The serial child molester added, 'There is still great things to talk about here and get on as Ladies and Gents should.'

Photographs of Steve and Randy celebrating Christmas with their wives and children were posted on the FoP site. (No mention was made of their boycott of Pitcairn's communal Christmas festivities.) And the island continued to win new converts. Peter from Sweden joined FoP, saying, 'I thought it would be both interesting and fun to get to know and learn about how the daily life is today on this special and so mythical island.'

In June 2005, after months of planning, members of the chat room gathered for a three-day conference in St Petersburg, Florida. More than 120 people, from as far away as Russia, Jamaica and Germany, participated. Maurice and Joy Allward flew out from

England, and five Pitcairners were present: Tom and Betty Christian, and Nola and Reynold Warren, then on holiday in the US, and Melva Evans, who flew over from Alaska.

Herb Ford from California delivered the keynote speech, and others presented talks on genealogy, stamps and the Panama Canal. There were Pitcairn goods to buy and admire, and real Pitcairners to fawn over. No one mentioned the elephant in the room — until Betty got up to speak.

Betty had chosen the role of Pitcairn women as her subject. She recalled the contribution of her Polynesian foremothers. She described the historic divide between 'women's work' and 'men's work'. Then, unexpectedly, she turned to the trials. She told the conference, 'The present case of sexual exploitation of women and young girls is a sad chapter in our history. This is not something that is unique to Pitcairn, as it happens in every country and small community in the world, but that does not make it right or acceptable. It is evident that this sort of activity has been carried on all throughout the history of Pitcairn, because of the amount of adolescent pregnancies that have occurred. It is an issue that should have been dealt with years ago, but I supposed it was considered too hard an issue to deal with.'

Betty added, 'I know what I am saying, because it happened to me and it is something that you don't forget. I believe that if our people are not prepared to accept and acknowledge that this sort of behaviour has happened, and that it is not acceptable, we have no future.'

Most members of the audience were diehard Pitcairn fans who believed the anti-British conspiracy theories. But afterwards many of them praised Betty's speech, calling it the best of the conference. I asked her later why she had decided to reveal that she had been a victim. 'I had gotten sick of people from overseas giving their opinions on the trials and what was going on here, when most of them had never been here and didn't have a clue what life was like,' she said.

Compared with the people she was talking about, I had a slightly better insight, having visited Pitcairn and met some of the personalities. But I felt sure that I had only scraped the veneer. I wanted to know more about this extraordinary place and the disturbing events that had gone on there. The story had got under my skin, and I picked away at it, trying to understand the darkness that lay at its core. As well as reading every book on Pitcairn that I could find, and carrying out dozens of interviews in Britain, New Zealand and Australia, I spent weeks poring over the colonial archives in London and Auckland. I also travelled to Norfolk Island for the 150th anniversary of the arrival of the 193 Pitcairners who migrated there in 1856.

During the week-long celebrations I came across Steve Christian's eldest son, Trent, who lives on Norfolk with his wife and three sons, and has a part-time job entertaining tourists at Pitcairn-themed dinners and 'fish fries'. Trent shook my hand and smiled broadly, displaying perfect white teeth, when I introduced myself at the Sunday markets, where he was serenading shoppers on an electric guitar. Later, Trent — who sells CDs of himself singing 'songs from Pitcairn Island, Norfolk Island and other favourites' — spoke frankly about the impact on the Pitcairn community of the long-running criminal case. 'It's been really, really hard on them, actually,' he told me. 'It's really ruined, basically, the island in a lot of ways, all the publicity — I mean, all the wrong publicity. They've just ruined Pitcairn, and they don't care what measures they take.'

It must have been difficult for his own family, I suggested. 'Gosh yes. We're all trying, taking each day as it comes, just waiting for the end of all this rubbish. So we can try and start getting our lives back on track. It's gone on for so long and hurt a lot of people.' Shawn and Randy's elder brother expressed optimism about the outcome of the defence's legal arguments, which could see the men reprieved. 'It's something that we all do hope for,' he said. 'To see it come to a good end, that will be a real treat. And for people to be compensated.'

Back on Pitcairn in 2005, Jay Warren was mayor and Cookie Warren was chairman, and both were walking around with a swagger. However, no one had any doubt as to who was really in charge. 'Boss, we are ready to start, will you be long?' Cookie inquired anxiously over the VHF radio, as the rest of the community, assembled at the school for a concert, waited for Steve Christian's family to arrive.

Despite Britain's new focus on the island, and its commitment of vast sums of money to haul Pitcairn into the 21st century, little had changed. Key decisions continued to be made at Big Fence, while at council meetings, said one islander, 'Jay would bring things up that were clearly prompted by Steve ... It was almost like Steve had his hand up Jay's arse.' Another commented, 'Jay is like a jellyfish. He's got no backbone.'

Some Pitcairners yearned for change, but no one was willing to take on Steve — not least because it was unclear when, if ever, he would be going to jail. 'Steve still controls a large chunk of people, and a lot of it's to do with fear,' said one outsider. 'He has an aura of invincibility, and it's only been reinforced by the trials.'

To some, Steve was a martyr. On Friends of Pitcairn, Meralda Warren likened him to the late Diana, Princess of Wales. 'Next she will have him walking on water,' one local observed.

While Steve still had many admirers, some outsiders were horrified that he and the other men remained at liberty, with access to children — in some cases, living with children.

A psychologist who works with convicted paedophiles told me, 'I can't think of any other Western jurisdiction where this would be allowed to happen. If child safety was the priority, the men would be put in jail or removed from the community while the appeals were sorted out.' He added, 'You have to ask who's in charge here, and it's fairly clear that they are. They're running the agenda, and it's a nightmare scenario. You've got sex offenders roaming free, you've got a community that doesn't accept that sexual abuse occurred, and you've got a bunch of professionals on the island who would be almost powerless to challenge it.'

CHAPTER 14

Britain's 'ineffective long-range benevolence'

In November 1970 the Pitcairn Island council held a special meeting. All parents on the island were required to attend, as were all children aged ten and over.

The purpose of the meeting was to remind everyone present that it was illegal to have sex with a child under 16. The magistrate, Pervis Young, explained that a complaint had been lodged about the 'raping or illicit carnal knowledge of a girl aged 11 years'. The case could not be pursued because there was no 'definite proof'. So he had decided to issue a general warning.

As was routine, a copy of the minutes was sent to the Governor's office in New Zealand. However, no response is recorded: it seems that news of the possible rape of an 11-year-old was received with equanimity in Wellington. British officials did not request any further information, nor did they take steps to ascertain whether the complaint had been properly investigated.

After the trials on Pitcairn, I spoke to many people who had followed the case, and they were perplexed by certain aspects of it.

In particular, they wanted to know why the sexual abuse, about which the women had testified so movingly, had remained hidden for such a long time. Why had no one felt able to speak out until 1999? Who had let the girls of Pitcairn down?

Pitcairn was extremely isolated, but it was not as if no one in authority had been keeping an eye on the place. Then there were the girls' parents — why had they not shielded their children from harm? What about the New Zealand teachers and pastors who had lived on the island for decades? And how much blame was to be laid at the door of the British government, given that Pitcairn had been a British colony since 1838? As I tried to piece together the story of neglect, I began with that last question first.

After the police inquiry was completed, the Foreign Office conducted its own post-mortem. It concluded that Britain's supervision of Pitcairn had been 'light and distant'. Governors had visited occasionally, and after the radio station was built in 1944 there had been regular two-way telegram contact with Fiji and then New Zealand. But the community had basically governed itself for a century and a half, running its own affairs, including law enforcement. It was a style of colonial administration that one former Governor, Sir Robin Byatt, called 'ineffective long-range benevolence'.

The old Colonial Office documents suggest an attitude of casual disregard. During the French nuclear tests in the 1960s and 1970s, for instance, when dozens of weapons were exploded in the South Pacific, a British Royal Air Force team was stationed on Pitcairn — just 520 nautical miles downwind — to monitor radioactive fallout. But the Ministry of Defence refused to provide a ship to stand by in case of 'an emergency resulting from a miscalculation by the French'. British officials just crossed their fingers; fortunately, no accidents occurred.

A few decades earlier, during World War II, the islanders had effectively been cut off when commercial shipping in the Pacific was halted. After reports emerged that they were starving, a US Navy ship steamed to their rescue and established that they were 'badly in need of certain food and medical supplies'. Forty people were treated, some for 'diseases in advanced stages'; the locals were said to be 'virtually in rags'.

To Britain, Pitcairn was a burden, and from 1945 onwards the government actively considered emptying it or offering it to New Zealand. The options were debated with increasing urgency as the population dropped, amid fears of insufficient able-bodied men to operate the boats. The removal of the islanders to New Zealand or elsewhere was regarded as inevitable, and the feasibility of evacuating them against their will was even discussed.

Oblivious to these clandestine machinations, the locals continued to give Britain their undivided loyalty. 'The Pitcairners have never wavered in their allegiance to the Crown and the Union Jack flies proudly on the island for every passing ship to see,' noted Ted Dymond, the Commissioner, in 1972. Over the years, certain colonial administrators did their best to reciprocate. Elderly islanders fondly recall the likes of Harry Maude, a senior Fiji-based official who spent seven months on Pitcairn in 1940–41, implementing a new legal code and overseeing the first stamp issue. He and others who took an almost fatherly interest in the island saw it as their opportunity to make a difference, it seems — to transform a little corner of the world. They got to know the locals well, and tried to train them in local government and court procedures. They submitted detailed recommendations to the Colonial Office on how the place could be better administered.

There was a limit to what visiting officials could achieve, though, and the attention that Britain gave the island — a minute outpost of an Empire that at its height covered one-quarter of the globe — remained sporadic and superficial. There were always more pressing colonial issues: Indian independence, the Communist insurgency in Malaya, post-war decolonisation. Why worry about an insignificant and exceedingly remote speck of rock that appeared to be running itself without major problems?

Governors who visited did not delve below the surface. Typical, perhaps, was Sir David Aubrey Scott, who in 1973 spent four days on Pitcairn, the territory that he ruled from 3,300 miles away in Wellington. Scott told the Foreign Office before setting off that his wife, Lady Vera, planned to 'examine the social conditions under which the young people, and especially the girls, tend to leave the island for an easier life in New Zealand or elsewhere'. During their stay, Scott explored his microscopic realm and presented the locals with a table and chairs of polished Fiji hardwood.

Scott's report on his visit contained much to divert desk-bound officials. There was his first sight of Pitcairn, 'with columns of spray rising 300 feet into the air from the headlands', and there were the 'tiresome strictures' of the Seventh-day Adventist Church, which — the Governor was gratified to discover — most islanders disregarded. Scott, who welcomed the Pitcairners' 'cheerful and disrespectful attitude to sexual as well as dietary restrictions', did not say whether his wife found out why so many girls left and never went back. But no one in London remarked on the omission.

His first and only trip to Pitcairn took place at a time when the sexual abuse of children was at a peak. Scott was not aware of that, of course, and it would hardly have come to his notice during his whirlwind tour of the island. Like most official visits, his was a short, stage-managed affair, and the locals — experts in the art of 'hypocriting' — behaved impeccably.

At least he bothered to go. Many governors did not, and long stretches — sometimes more than a decade — elapsed without the islanders seeing a single British official. A report in the 1950s by Donald McLoughlin, a senior British lawyer, was gratefully received by the Colonial Office for supplying 'very much needed background information on this isolated territory ... Our information on Pitcairn is very scanty.'

Notwithstanding that observation, there is evidence in the archives that Britain was warned repeatedly that all was not well on Pitcairn. Outsiders reported that the islanders' pious image was a sham, and urged the colonial power to supervise its far-flung territory more closely. 'If Her Majesty's Government intends to take any further interest in the island, it would be best to send someone from home to govern it,' advised Bouverie Clark, a Royal Navy commander, as far back as 1882. In 1919 the British consul in Tahiti, HA Richards, deplored 'the environment of incest, sloth and mental depravity, which makes Pitcairn Island one of the blotted pages in our colonial administration'.

In particular, colonial authorities were told time and again that the criminal justice system was a farce. 'Of law there is almost none, every man does practically as he sees fit,' declared the British Consul, HG Simons, in 1904. Harry Maude attended a trial where there was no prosecutor present and the defendant 'sauntered in' after the main witness had testified. He wrote, 'The general public gave their views freely ... I have been informed that when the public gets really excited the noise can be heard at a considerable distance while on at any rate one occasion the Chief Magistrate has been physically assaulted by the accused.' As for the custodial regime, Maude judged it necessary to stipulate that 'prisoners are to live in future in the prison and not in private homes'.

Most cases did not even reach court, for it was 'almost impossible to get any one person to give direct evidence against another', lamented a Pitcairn elder, James Russell McCoy, in 1905. McCoy told British officials in Fiji he suspected that 'really serious matters are being deliberately hidden in this way'. Little had changed, apparently, by 1942, when the Seventh-day Adventist pastor, Frederick Ward, observed that 'cases are hushed up and culprits are let off'. Anyone who reported a crime 'would find one of his trees cut or one of his goats gone the following day', according to another outsider.

If law enforcement was wanting, local government was at best ineffectual, at worst corrupt. Not many people were willing to stand for public office, and those who did were subjected to family pressures. The few who discharged their duties conscientiously found themselves extremely unpopular. One colonial official, Harry Dobbs, condemned the island council as 'composed of ignorant men with little or no conception of public service but a very keen eye on the main chance of personal gain'. Another, JB Claydon, concluded in 1954 that the word anarchy, 'shorn of emotional content ... does, I fear, adequately describe the administration situation on Pitcairn'.

Britain claimed to be starved of information about its distant colony, but it did not have to rely solely on officials who visited intermittently. From 1949 it had its own employee on the ground: a New Zealand teacher. Yet teachers were not heeded, it seems, unless they told colonial authorities what they wanted to hear — that Pitcairn was getting along fine.

Albert Moverley was the first incumbent at the new school; his wife, Jane, was also a teacher. They formed strong views about the island and communicated them to Fiji and London, even petitioning British MPs. 'You could scarcely be proud of the record of rape, incest, abortion, adultery ... credited to this community of less than 140 souls,' wrote Mrs Moverley, who found the islanders 'without religion, without standards, without principles' and practising 'ever increasing injustices'.

The couple alerted Fiji to the plight of one woman, Alta Warren, who was being beaten by her husband, Alwyn, with such regularity that she begged the policeman 'to lock her in the jail for a few hours'. Alwyn was chairman of the internal committee and a friend of the magistrate, who refused to assist Alta in securing a divorce; when she tried to escape to New Zealand, community leaders convinced the captains of passing ships not to allow her on board. Colonial Office correspondence records that Alta was being 'brutally mistreated' and 'without the faintest shadow of a doubt ... held on Pitcairn against her will'. However, it was several years before the authorities helped her flee to New Zealand, where a doctor who examined her said she would only have survived another six months.

Alwyn's behaviour towards Alta was shocking enough, as was the fact that British officials dragged their feet for so long. But the resident teacher also informed the administration that Alwyn had allegedly strangled his previous wife, Myrtle. Several mentions of this affair appear in the old island documents — yet Alwyn was never prosecuted, and Britain did nothing about it either. Other killings may have been concealed, too. For according to the Moverleys, when they appealed to the magistrate's wife to let Alta leave Pitcairn, if only to save her from being murdered, the woman 'tolerantly remarked ... "Well, there have been other murders here and no one worries."'

The couple also notified the Governor's office that a member of the magistrate's family had raped a ten-year-old girl so brutally 'as to cause the child physical injury'. Again the culprit had not been pursued, and again Britain took no action.

The Moverleys' letters — indeed, all official correspondence concerning the island — would have been seen in London, where several officials had specific responsibility for a small clutch of Pacific colonies. Of those, it might be reasonable to suppose that Pitcairn, the only one with a British population, was of particular interest. Yet the teacher and his wife, who continued to lobby Britain after leaving the island, were treated as a nuisance at the highest level. 'I hope this will be the last instance of my having to waste my time and yours with the Moverleys' importunity,' the Governor of Fiji told the Colonial Secretary, a British Cabinet minister, in 1953. The latter replied tersely, 'Every effort is being made to terminate correspondence with Mrs Moverley.'

Albert Moverley's successor, Roy Sanders, adopted a more detached attitude. After he returned to New Zealand, he wrote a doctoral thesis about the community, and among the incidents he recounted was the death in childbirth in 1952 of a 15-year-old schoolgirl, Vanda Young. According to Sanders, the baby was 'too big for her', and the island nurse was unable to deliver it. By the time a ship's doctor came ashore, Vanda had been in agony for five days and the baby was dead. Vanda was taken to New Zealand for surgery but died in hospital.

At a public meeting, Vanda's grandfather, Andrew Young, castigated his fellow islanders for 'immoral conduct'. Vanda was Steve Christian's older sister. Their mother, Dobrey, had got pregnant at an even younger age. (Vanda was given her mother's maiden name.) Another woman of Dobrey's generation had had four babies by the age of 15.

Schoolgirl pregnancies were common on the island: Pitcairn's birth records, which Britain would have seen, show that most women had their first baby at a young age. This was, and is, a universal occurrence, of course, but what was striking on Pitcairn was that the teenage pregnancies mostly involved adult men. And they were merely a symptom of a wider problem, for not all girls who were having sex got pregnant. George Allen, who succeeded Sanders as teacher, told British officials — and it is difficult to imagine a more explicitly phrased warning — that 'if such interference with children by grown men continues, then there is bound eventually to be a breakdown in the health and social structure of the community'.

Allen's successor, Alan Wotherspoon, told the British administration that there was a feeling in the community that young girls ought to be better protected. Nevertheless, he wrote, 'The circumstances are such in every case, that no move can be taken for fear of offence against a relation. And therefore the offending man goes absolutely free. This causes other young men, by the way, to regard the offender as a hero.'

Britain drew its own conclusion, which was that Pitcairn girls were promiscuous. A briefing paper circulated by the Governor's office in 1971 noted, 'Female children mature rapidly and tend to seek out male partners early in their teens ... Unattached girls are not backwards in offering their friendship to visitors.'

By most accounts, the girls *were* forward, and maybe it was — as some have suggested — to do with their Tahitian ancestry, or the tropical heat. However, in the light of what is known now about Pitcairn, it seems probable that more sinister factors were at play.

What about Pitcairn's laws? From 1904 they prohibited the 'seduction' of a girl aged under 14. The offence was later renamed

The three Supreme Court judges in court on Pitcairn: Jane Lovell-Smith, Chief Justice Charles Blackie (centre) and Russell Johnson.

Prosecutors Christine Gordon, Simon Moore and Fletcher Pilditch (obscured) set off to court from home, carrying their documents in front.

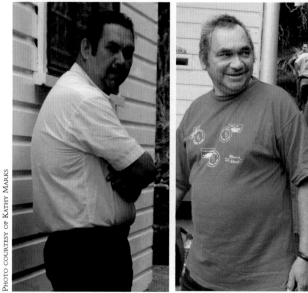

(Top, left) Jay Warren, the only Pitcairn defendant acquitted, outside court during his trial. Two months later, Jay was elected mayor.

(Top, right) Dennis Christian (left) and Steve Christian emerging from the courthouse in Adamstown, both wearing Pitcairn Island T-shirts.

Chief Justice Charles Blackie (left), escorted by court registrar Graham Ford, heading up the 'main road' of Adamstown towards the square.

Tom and Betty Christian dressed up for a Sabbath service at the Seventh-day Adventist church.

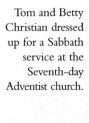

LAST RESTING PLACE OF
H.M.S. BOUNTY
50 M

A sign at The Landing points to the spot where the skeleton of the *Bounty* — scuttled and burnt by the mutineers — lies in shallow water.

Gail Cox, the English policewoman who received the first sexual abuse disclosures in 1999, outside court in Auckland in 2006.

Courtrooms

Track leading to Jack Williams Valley, near the banyan grove where 12-year-old Jennifer was raped by Steve Christian in about 1964.

Operation Unique investigators: Robert Vinson (left), Karen Vaughan and Peter George outside court in Auckland in 2005.

Pitcairn's British Deputy Governor, Matthew Forbes, in conversation with Christine Gordon, the Deputy Public Prosecutor, outside court during the 2004 trials.

Pitcairn's new jail, where the defence lawyers slept during the trials. It was built by locals, including men now serving sentences inside.

Shawn Christian and his Australian partner, Michele Purvis, during his trial in Auckland. Shawn was convicted of three rapes (one conviction was later overturned).

Photo courtesy of Simon Runting

Photo courtesy of Simon Runting

Shawn Christian's aunt and uncle, Clarice Oates and Kay Brown, outside court during Shawn's trial in Auckland. Indecent assault charges against Kay had been withdrawn.

Randy Christian heading to court to be sentenced for four rapes and five indecent assaults. He was jailed for six years.

Brian Young, later convicted of six rapes and three indecent assaults, walking towards court during his trial in Auckland in 2006.

The eight lawyers involved in the trials on Pitcairn: (left to right) Hugh Roberts and Charles Cato (defence), prosecutor Simon Mount, Deputy Public Defender Allan Roberts, Deputy Public Prosecutor Christine Gordon, Public Defender Paul Dacre, prosecutor Fletcher Pilditch, Public Prosecutor Simon Moore.

The author's four media colleagues who were on Pitcairn for the duration of the trials: (left to right) Zane Willis, Ewart Barnsley, Neil Tweedie and Claire Harvey.

'carnal knowledge', and from 1965 was treated as rape — and had to be handled by a British court — if the girl was under 12. If she was 12 to 15, the man could be dealt with by the local court, where he faced a maximum penalty of three months in prison.

The severity of the punishment indicates how that crime was viewed by the islanders — and by the officials who drafted Pitcairn's laws. In Britain, unlawful sexual intercourse with a girl aged 13 to 15 carried a maximum sentence of 14 years under the 1956 Sexual Offences Act.

Harry Maude reported in 1941 that 'carnal knowledge' of a girl aged under 14 was 'not regarded locally as a very serious offence'. He wrote, 'This crime, together with various other sexual offences, is far from uncommon among the islanders.' During the 1950s, nonetheless, half a dozen men were prosecuted and jailed, including Clive Christian, who had previously got Vanda Young pregnant. (She was the schoolgirl who died in childbirth.) Like other court proceedings, these had an element of the absurd. Clive was one of *three* men sent to trial over a pregnant 13-year-old.

They were unlucky. Most men got away with it, for the custom of 'breaking in' girls was widely tolerated. The rare prosecutions that took place had as their primary aim the assignment of financial responsibility for a baby. There was no real stigma about under-age pregnancy or an illegitimate child, and the offspring of very young mothers were often adopted by grandparents.

The spate of court cases in the 1950s was down to Floyd McCoy, the first local police officer to be appointed by the British administration, rather than the island council. Floyd's elevation to 'Inspector of Police' represented Britain's one attempt to address the climate of lawlessness on Pitcairn. He was considered 'one of the few men of integrity on the island', and already 'sufficiently unpopular ... not to be worried at the prospect of incurring further unpopularity through doing his duty'.

While Floyd was determined to uphold law and order, his was a lonely task. The islanders were hostile, and he received no backing from the council, which 'can't stand to principle for fear of relatives, or ridicule', he told Fiji. The magistrate, Warren Christian, and island secretary, Andrew Young, encouraged other men to threaten and goad Floyd. Almost friendless, he was excluded from social gatherings, and when he injured his foot and could not leave the house, only the pastor offered assistance. Frustrated, he told his superiors, 'We are not progressing, we may as well go back to the Bounty time, and have no Laws at all.'

Floyd was trying to lay bare the seamy side of Pitcairn life, and — just like when Kent Police started digging half a century later — the locals were not prepared to tolerate it. They undermined Floyd relentlessly, and Jane Moverley, the teacher's wife, warned that he was in danger of becoming 'one of those victims of "accidental death" which few on the island dare question too loudly'.

Britain gradually withdrew its support from Floyd. Like the Moverleys, he had become an irritation; like them, he was raising too many awkward issues.

Despite all the obstacles to the administration of justice, for much of the 20th century the island magistrate did sit regularly. During the 1960s the number of cases sharply declined. In 1972 a group of teenagers was formally rebuked for setting fire to some undergrowth — an incident mentioned during Steve Christian's trial. Then that was it. There were no more court hearings until the Ricky Quinn affair in 1999.

There was still a policeman on Pitcairn, but he never prosecuted anyone. There was still a magistrate, but he never presided over any trials. There was still a courthouse, but it was only ever used as a public hall. There was still a jail, but it was never occupied.

Not once during those years did colonial officials question why the machinery of justice had fallen into disuse. No one, it appears, stopped to marvel at how the islanders had managed to wipe out crime overnight. No one queried the monthly police reports that for nearly three decades logged nil complaints.

Instead, Britain praised Pitcairn's 'splendid record of freedom from crime'. Governor Sir Robin Byatt remarked in 1990 that 'so far as I know the prison has never held a convicted occupant', and that 'the present magistrate, who has been in office for five years, tells me that he has never had to sit on the bench'. That magistrate was Brian Young.

It seems that after Floyd McCoy died in 1963, no one else was interested in enforcing the law. And colonial authorities gave up grappling with the problem. Floyd's successor was Vernon Young, who, according to a Foreign Office paper in 1971, 'has little work to do ... His main duty consists in patrolling the village streets in the evening to preserve the integrity of family life.' The then magistrate, Pervis Young, was said to be 'a very big man ... who gives [law-breakers] a good talking-to and this is considered sufficient'.

The abandonment of the formalities of law and order coincided with the shrinking of the community from the early 1960s onwards. Leon Salt commented in 2002 that 'since the population fell below around 100, few if any complaints have been laid ... No one has a clear copy book and the possibility that someone may in retribution expose their past misdeeds, is discouragement enough for anyone to complain.'

Nearly all the offences of which Pitcairn men have been convicted were committed during the decades when there was ostensibly a zero crime rate.

★ ★ ★

Publicly, Britain still defends the way Pitcairn was governed. Richard Fell told me, 'The perception was that they were a happy, self-contained, religious island community that could be dealt with with a soft touch. They had their own mayor and elected council, they had community leaders, they had teachers, they had a Church that was supposed to provide moral guidance.'

Senior figures also insist that there was no concrete indication of children being sexually abused. 'Clearly there were cases of under-age sex that the administration was told about, but not the sort of thing we've heard about recently, girls being gang-raped and so on,' says one. 'I'm not sure that alarm bells rang at the time. There were reports, people feeling uneasy, saying they weren't sure everything was quite right. But it didn't really come together. Nobody really came forward with the evidence on which the authorities might have taken some action.'

Yet there *was* evidence. On top of the examples already given, here are two more. In 1927 a passenger off a visiting ship, the *Rotorua*, informed officials in Fiji about a rape that the magistrate, Richard Christian, had allegedly failed to investigate. The High Commissioner was content to take Christian's word that 'there is no such happening on the island'. In 1942 Pastor Frederick Ward reported that the main aim of Pitcairn's young men was 'to be the first to "break in" the young girls [sexually]', or 'to associate sexually with all the girls on the island'. In addition, Britain was told about teenagers cohabiting with adult men, attempted abortions by girls of 13 or younger, and women and girls prostituting themselves — or being forced to prostitute themselves — on passing ships.

No action was taken; meanwhile, colonial officials found time to exchange copious correspondence with the islanders on subjects ranging from a dispute about an overhanging coconut tree to the number of passengers who could legally be carried on a motorbike. As far as sexual abuse was concerned, they ignored the warning signs. Were the allegations of girls being raped simply too hard to confront? Or did Britain dismiss the Pitcairners as a bunch of natives with loose morals who could not be expected to behave any better?

The government was repeatedly advised that its 'soft touch' approach was ineffective, and the same remedies were advocated time and again. Improve communications and landing facilities. Encourage young people to stay and outsiders to settle. Establish stronger links with neighbours in French Polynesia. Arrange more frequent official visits. And provide Pitcairn with a full-time administrator. Britain's large colonies had a resident governor. Small ones, such as Tristan da Cunha in the South Atlantic, had an administrator. Pitcairn had no one — not until Operation Unique. The idea was rejected as 'wasteful' and nonsensical for a community that size.

Would the child abuse have come to light earlier if the island had had a resident official? The answer is: quite possibly. The abuse was hidden, but it was not invisible. It was picked up by a number of outsiders. Over the decades, the subject — once taboo — was more openly discussed in wider society. A British official living in the community would surely have realised what was going on and, perhaps, taken steps to address it.

Things might have turned out differently, too, if Pitcairn had had independent policing. It was ludicrous to expect the island to police itself. Yet Britain, with the exception of Floyd McCoy, did not even train the local officer — or, for that matter, the magistrate, who oversaw the justice system. The presence of an outside administrator or police officer might have acted as a deterrent;

at the least, children would have had someone independent to confide in.

Ultimately, British authorities were complacent. 'With a European schoolmaster resident,' wrote one official, 'and with radio communications and full postal facilities it is difficult to imagine any serious breach of the law taking place without the Governor hearing of it.'

CHAPTER 15

'I just did my job and minded my own business'

It was a Saturday morning in the mid-1930s, and 12-year-old Elizabeth had just been to church. As she made her way home, skipping along the back lanes of Adamstown, she met Elwyn Christian, a Pitcairn man well respected in the community (not Alwyn, the wife-beater). After chatting to Elizabeth for a while, Elwyn, who was in his mid-20s, grabbed her and pulled her into the undergrowth. He raped the little girl, ignoring her screams, and then left her lying on the ground, covered in mud and blood.

Sobbing, Elizabeth ran all the way to the house of the Seventh-day Adventist minister. He and his wife were the only outsiders on the island, and the only people who would believe her, she thought. As the couple cleaned her up, the pastor told the distraught girl, 'It was your own fault. You were wearing a pretty dress to church.' He added, 'You'd better not tell anyone, or Elwyn will get into big trouble. Just forget about it and don't ever mention it again.'

Elizabeth obeyed, for the pastor was a man of authority. She later moved to New Zealand and got married. However, she never had children, a fact that always saddened her profoundly.

In 2003, after reading about Operation Unique, she exclaimed to her younger brother, 'Nothing has changed.' As he listened in astonishment, she broke down and described the events of that bright Sabbath day on Pitcairn. Weeping, she explained that was why she had never been able to conceive. Elwyn had raped her so violently that he had caused internal injuries. A few months later Elizabeth died, aged 80.

This incident, related to me by Elizabeth's brother, is but one example — although possibly the worst — of the way in which the girls of Pitcairn were let down by outsiders living in their own community. For while British officials visited infrequently, and the islanders did not have a resident British administrator, they were not left entirely on their own. For much of the 20th century there was an Adventist minister on Pitcairn, sent out from Australia or New Zealand. From 1949 onwards, there was also a New Zealand teacher stationed there full-time. Both of these outsiders were in a position to offer guidance. Both had professional obligations, particularly towards the children.

The teacher and pastor were posted for two years, sometimes longer, and lived at the heart of the Pitcairn community. They worked alongside the islanders, manning the boats with them, worshipped with them on Saturdays and socialised with them. Several dozen individuals rotated through the two jobs during the half-century before the police investigation. Some, especially those who had daughters with them on Pitcairn, were later interviewed by British detectives. I talked to a number of them, and it is clear that certain individuals knew that girls on the island were being sexually abused; others harboured strong suspicions.

But apart from a few early teachers, such as Albert Moverley, none of them, apparently, voiced their concerns. They did not alert the British Governor, or the Commissioner, or the Foreign Office, or Adventist Church officials. Sheils Carnihan and Neville Tosen played a crucial role in the events that led to Belinda confiding in Gail Cox. The rest, for the most part, just did their jobs, went home to their families and forgot about Pitcairn.

It did not take long for outsiders to realise all was not well. The wife of an Australian pastor says she soon became aware that it was 'common practice' for adult men to have sex with young girls. The daughter of a teacher heard rumours of girls in her class being 'dragged into the bush'. Another teacher recalls a 12-year-old pupil arriving at school inexplicably upset; she was crying and sobbing all day, but would not tell anyone what was the matter. A pastor's wife was scandalised to catch a six-year-old girl lying on top of her son, who was a similar age, simulating sex.

Outsiders warned each other about the risk posed by the Pitcairn men. Before travelling to the island, one teacher was advised by a senior official 'to keep a careful watch on my girls'; another, after being briefed by his predecessor, gave his daughter 'a list of men I was never to be alone with'. During the voyage from Auckland, the family of one newly appointed teacher got to know a New Zealand woman whose husband was a Pitcairner. The woman warned the teacher's wife, who had two daughters, aged nine and ten, to beware of the local boys and men. The teacher's wife duly instructed her girls to be careful, but was concerned about them throughout her family's stay on Pitcairn; years later she told police that, as a result of what she had witnessed, she had 'no doubts' that girls on the island were being sexually abused.

Debbie Baronian, whose husband, Barrie, was the teacher from 1996 to 1997, sought advice from Leon Salt before the family left for the island. Debbie told me, 'We asked Leon, "What's the moral conduct like?" And he said, "Well, they live in isolation and they do have loose morals, you know. You've just got to be careful."' The

Baronians were on Pitcairn when 11-year-old Caroline accused Shawn Christian of rape. They sent their 14-year-old daughter home. 'We thought she was in danger,' Debbie says.

Debbie was 'not surprised at all' when multiple allegations of abuse surfaced a decade later. 'We knew that it's going on,' she says. 'We knew fairly early in the piece about [one girl] who'd been abused since she was a little wee girl. It was something that was talked about among the locals.' One islander confided to Debbie that she believed her own daughter had been 'interfered with'.

Tony Washington, who taught on Pitcairn from 1991 to 1992, was not surprised to learn about the investigation, either. 'No one ever told me about it [the abuse], but there are little things that you just put together,' he told me recently. Tony recalled one of his pupils, saying: 'She was a pretty girl, and you could think, "Now what's going to happen to her on this island?" . . . It just seemed that that was what was destined to happen.'

Once he and his wife, Christine, returned to New Zealand, though, they drew a line under their Pitcairn experience. 'I had the feeling that an interlude of my life was over,' Tony says. 'I look back on it and I've sort of closed it off, if you know what I mean, I've got no connection with it any more.' Christine told police in 2000, 'I never want to go back to that place.' She never did, and after her family left Pitcairn the sexual abuse continued — until the lid was lifted by Belinda, who was being molested by Randy Christian while she was in Tony's class.

Teachers not only failed to protect Pitcairn's children; with what seems like a horrible inevitability, one of them allegedly joined in the sexual predation. That person was Albert Reeves, from Dunedin, on New Zealand's South Island, who arrived on Pitcairn in 1967 with his wife, Margaret, and their son, Craig. Within a few months, allegedly, Reeves had homed in on one of his pupils, 13-year-old Jennifer. He would find pretexts to get her on her own and molest her, Jennifer says. The assaults were constant. When she was 14, he raped her at the back of the schoolhouse.

Reeves was a sadist, allegedly, humiliating Jennifer in ways so cruel and sordid that they stand out even in this story — and, 40 years on, it is still Reeves who features most prominently in Jennifer's nightmares. For he not only raped her; he betrayed her trust. He was her teacher, a figure of authority. He was also the Government Adviser, since from 1954 onwards the teacher was Britain's representative on Pitcairn — a shallow nod of acknowledgement by the colonial power that the island needed a resident official. Reeves, says Jennifer, used to gloat that if she told on him, no one would believe her because he was the Government Adviser.

In 1969 Reeves was replaced by Russell Henry. Reeves had left under a cloud, and Henry soon found out why. The pastor, Walter Ferris, told him that Reeves had been 'caught in a compromising position' with a pupil. Ferris did not say precisely what had occurred, but he made clear that it was something sexual.

That was all Henry knew, apparently. It was plenty, though: a teacher discovered *in flagrante* with a 14-year-old schoolgirl. Even in the late 1960s, that would have been treated very seriously by police and education officials, had they known about it. But Henry did not notify the authorities, and neither did Pastor Ferris, who was credited with bringing about a spiritual revival on Pitcairn. Neither, for that matter, did any of the locals. The incident would have been common knowledge in the tiny community.

Reeves returned to Dunedin and carried on teaching — and, possibly, abusing girls in his care. And until Jennifer spoke to police 30 years later, no one had any reason to doubt his integrity.

One of the six 'off-islanders' who were charged, Reeves denied all the allegations in 2000.

For the past 25 years, New Zealand teachers have been trained to recognise the signs of sexual abuse, and schools in that country are legally obliged to report suspected cases. Many of the teachers stationed on Pitcairn would have picked up signs; some, it seems, gained quite detailed insights into behaviour that, apart from being against the law, was unacceptable in New Zealand. None of them, apparently, felt impelled to share that knowledge with anyone official after they departed.

Instead, when the island was pitched into the headlines following the police investigation, many former teachers campaigned on behalf of the offenders. As noted in a previous chapter, Leon Salt and Allen Cox, who had both taught on Pitcairn, went to some effort to derail the prosecution. Eleven ex-teachers wrote to Richard Fell in 2003, attacking the 'oppressive ... [and] increasingly abhorrent ... manner in which the [legal] process is being applied'. The process was 'totally inappropriate' for Pitcairn, they said in a three-page letter, and would kill off the community — which was what Britain intended, they claimed. The signatories stated that 'during the periods that we were resident on Pitcairn we were not aware of *widespread* sexual abuse of children [my italics]'.

Tony Washington put his name to the letter. So did Barrie Baronian. So did elderly Ernest Schubert, who had been on the island during the spate of carnal knowledge prosecutions in the 1950s. So did Allen Cox, who four months earlier had remarked to his son, Andrew, that 'undoubtedly the sexual offences took place'.

The letter was organised by Pippa Foley, who had taught at the school in the mid-1990s and gone back there in 2002. Foley herself seemed not to doubt that there was substance to the allegations. In a letter to the British Governor, she proclaimed that 'as for the women of the island, most of them are victims'. She also acknowledged that 'these men have done wrong' and proposed that, rather than being put on trial, they should undergo compulsory counselling.

Yet by 2006 Foley was urging the women to deny publicly that they had ever been abused. 'How about Pitkern women declaring on email that "I am not the victim of Pitkern men, but I feel I am a victim of the British Police, who have harassed and hounded me",' she suggested. 'Then send your individual story to all the media outlets ... It is up to you all to fight for the truth, your island and its reputation.'

Foley had been the teacher in the period immediately before Belinda was raped by Randy and, allegedly, Shawn.

Leon Salt had taught on the island in the mid-1980s. One of his pupils, a 14-year-old, became entangled with a married man. His solution was to remove her from the island, packing her off early to school in New Zealand. The man, who had already raped three girls, remained on Pitcairn.

Dennis McGookin, the retired Kent Police superintendent, calls it 'Pitcairn fever'. Others dub it 'island fever' or 'going native'.

Many outsiders fall under Pitcairn's spell — intoxicated by the cachet of the place, perhaps, or by the giddy sense of being so far from anywhere. They suspend their critical judgement and lose touch with conventional values. And the infatuation with the island continues even after they leave.

Men seem particularly susceptible. Carried away, possibly, by the raw macho culture, they yearn to be accepted by Steve Christian and his mates. 'He was desperate to be one of them,' says one islander of a former pastor. Women succumb too. Once the locals work their legendary charm, it is hard for a visitor, insulated from competing influences, to resist. A former teacher warns, 'They hook you in, like a spider into its web. After a while you start to think like them. You start to side with them. You start to believe their version of events.'

McGookin's former colleague, Peter George, says, 'It's almost like Stockholm Syndrome.' It may be a survival mechanism too. As one observer points out, 'Those men are the most powerful people on the island, and if you're not in with them, God help you.'

The syndrome cannot be unique to Pitcairn, but very probably is magnified by its appealing history and extreme isolation. And it may help to explain why outsiders kept quiet about the abuse, and why many of those who already knew the community chose to support the men. Tom Scantlebury, a Canadian doctor, was rescued from a cave in 2004 after a boat in which he had been circling the island with Randy Christian capsized. Scantlebury, who is certain that Randy saved his life, is a staunch champion of the islanders.

Lyle Burgoyne, the nurse and Adventist lay pastor, went to Pitcairn with his family in 1996. His daughter, Sarah, has married Timmy Young, Brian and Kari's son; at the time of their wedding, Brian was awaiting trial in Auckland on child sex charges. The entire Burgoyne family — all of them practising Seventh-day Adventists — caught Pitcairn fever, it appears. Like Pippa Foley, Lyle has lived and worked on the island twice. Lyle and his wife, Jenny, insist that no one there was ever abused. Sarah defends the guilty men in online forums. Not long ago she asserted that, with one exception, 'the men weren't over 25 and the girls weren't under ten. The largest age gap was eight–nine years. That's hardly very old or very young ... I guess the Pitcairn men are paedophiles theory goes out the window.' (In fact, four of the complainants were under ten when they were assaulted, including two of Sarah's father-in-law's victims.)

Allen Cox has had three stints on Pitcairn — the first in 1978, when several girls were being badly abused. While on the island in 2003, Bill Haigh had a heated discussion with Cox over dinner. 'He said it was a unique culture, a special culture, and it needed to be preserved,' recalls Haigh. 'He said the British had always neglected the place and now they were interfering.'

The worldwide headquarters of the Seventh-day Adventist Church are located in Silver Spring, Maryland; its South Pacific division, which is responsible for Pitcairn, is based in Sydney.

The Church maintains that it knew nothing about the child abuse until Operation Unique. It would appear that it did not debrief its own pastors very thoroughly. For more than a century, moreover, the Church portrayed the Pitcairners as model Christians and the island as a credit to its missionary work. 'The policeman has the easiest job in the world, for these people are all sincere Christians,' enthused the narrator of one of its promotional films. After the Kent Police investigation, the division issued a statement noting that 'only a small percentage of the island population are practising Seventh-day Adventists'. It went on, 'The isolation of the island makes it difficult for the Church to know about these matters ... The Church ... is not trying to cover anything up.'

Neville Tosen was posted to Pitcairn shortly before the allegations emerged. I asked him what he was told about the community by senior Adventist figures. 'Nothing,' he replied. 'There was nothing from the Church. There was no word about loose morals, or people stealing equipment and money. We were only told that they were all good Christians. The Church just told us to be friends with them.' Tosen added, 'I think over the years there were little indications that things were not right. But Pitcairn was seen as such a citadel of Adventism in the Pacific, so those little worries were discounted. And perhaps that was not the best thing; perhaps they should have been investigated.'

While the Church claims to have been oblivious to what was going on, many of its pastors had at least an inkling. Like the teachers, ministers were trained, certainly in recent years, to detect the symptoms of sexual abuse. Their wives were usually registered nurses, and worked in that capacity in the community. Pastors got to know the children well and had daily contact with them. Some — such as Walter Ferris, who informed Russell Henry about the alleged misconduct of his predecessor, Albert Reeves — knew about specific incidents. Alfred Parker attended the council meeting in 1970 where the alleged rape of an 11-year-old was discussed. Walter Ferguson's wife, Phyllis, was told by an islander in 1978 that Brian Young had raped her young daughter.

One or two were conscientious. Owen Brown, who was on Pitcairn from 1995 to 1996, notified Leon Salt about the attempted rape of an adult, as well as liaisons involving young girls. Many looked the other way — or, like the minister in Elizabeth's time, actively covered up the abuse. And pastors, like the Church itself, persisted in romanticising Pitcairn. 'Are you tired of hearing about assaults, rape, robberies and hold-ups?' wrote Oliver Stimpson in the *Miscellany* newpaper in 1980. 'How would you like to live where no locks are needed? No crime! No jails! No police! No fears! Yes, there is such a place ... Pitcairn Island.'

When Neville Tosen returned to Australia, he contacted two ministers, Lester Hawkes and Rex Cobbin, who had served on Pitcairn in the 1950s. Both were well respected and had chalked up many years of mission service. Tosen regarded them 'as the kind of person who would stand up for what's right'. He says, 'I asked them point-blank, "Why didn't you see the problem and do something about it? Why was it left so late?" They said, "Look, we suspected something was going on. We saw things that worried us, but we had no proof." ' Cobbin, now retired, told me that he and his wife, Win, were 'very surprised and quite shocked' to learn about the sexual abuse. If they had known about it when they were there, he said, 'we could have done something about it'.

Like every Christian denomination, the Adventist Church has faced revelations of child abuse within its own ranks. And, like most big organisations, both religious and secular, it now has its own protocols. Drawn up in 1997, they state that the Church 'trains ministers and members to recognise the warning signs ... and to respond appropriately', while creating 'opportunities for children to report sexual abuse'. That did not happen on Pitcairn.

Rex Cobbin's son, Kendell, who lived on the island as a toddler in 1959, is a ministerial secretary in the Church's New Zealand–Pacific Union Conference, supporting roving ministers. Kendell said that the Church hierarchy had 'followed recent events with a great deal of consternation ... It's been an incredibly painful process for one and all.' I asked him whether, in his opinion, pastors should have reported their suspicions. 'No,' he said. 'When you've got this sort of dysfunction happening, you can maybe have an innate sense that there's something not right. But to put your finger on it would be very hard.'

Kendell added, 'I'm not saying that individuals ought to wimp out. That would certainly not be our position as a Church. But there's a powerlessness. What can you do about it? As a minister, you're not there as an investigator. You're there to care for the community.'

Rick Ferret, who was posted to Pitcairn in 1989 and stayed four years, became aware of adult men having sex with young girls. Although he did not convey his concerns to the Church, he still believes that he acted properly. 'There was never anyone who came to us and said, "This is happening to my child"', Ferret told me recently. 'There was never anything explicit. You may have a hunch, but what do you do with a hunch? When do you go in there with a magnifying glass?'

Ferret added, 'Hindsight's a great teacher, and I wonder whether all of us, the outsiders, were a symptom of the same thing. I wonder whether everyone was caught up in the Pitcairn myth.'

Did the Church let Pitcairn down? Sitting in the garden of their Queensland home, Neville Tosen and his wife, Rhonda, both retired, laugh sadly. After a pause that seems to last forever, Neville says, 'We've pondered this for a very long time, and my conclusion is no. The Church has stuck by the island through thick and thin. It wouldn't keep a minister in a town that size in Australia.'

It is a difficult conversation. Tosen feels torn. 'I just want to be loyal to the Church,' he says. 'And to the island, as far as I can be. But I can't be blinded against what I found: I have to face reality, and the reality is not very pretty.'

Did the Church let Pitcairn down? I asked the same question of another pastor who was on the island more recently. 'The Church is not an administrative organisation,' he replied. 'The Church is what happens between those walls. So yes, the Pitcairn Church did fail the people. It was not as effective as it would like to have been.'

The Church, as an institution, has now distanced itself from Pitcairn. Spokesmen emphasise that it is 'not an Adventist island' any more. An article on the Church's website, headlined 'Adventist Pastor, Wife Find Paradise on Tiny Island', states euphemistically that 'recent years have seen a well-documented departure from Church practices by some'.

★ ★ ★

For much of the past century, teachers and pastors were the only outsiders living on Pitcairn. Only they had any idea what was going on; only they could bring news of it to the outside world. The question still gnaws at me: why did none of those people do anything?

It is true that none of the girls went to an outsider for help. But that rarely happens, according to experts in the area of child abuse, which is why professionals are taught to pick up the signs and be proactive. The inescapable fact is that if even just one of them had alerted the authorities and convinced them to take the problem seriously, many of the island's children might have been spared the misery of sexual abuse. Instead, at least one dissuaded his own daughter from giving evidence.

Teachers and pastors 'were indoctrinated into the Pitcairn way of life, or they didn't want to be the one to destroy the myth ... No one was willing to stand up and be counted,' suggests Dennis McGookin. It is difficult, of course, to stand up and be counted. Whistleblowers are rarely thanked. More often they are shunned and denigrated, and some lose their jobs. In the case of Pitcairn, they would have risked being forever branded as the person who had destroyed the community. Gail Cox has been pilloried for years, simply because she was conscientious.

I asked Tony Washington, one of the former teachers, whether he felt he ought to have raised the alarm. 'I didn't think there was anything I needed to report,' he said. 'If a child comes to you in New Zealand and says, "This is happening to me," then you go and do something about it. But on Pitcairn, I mean, looking back on it, it seemed to be a fact of life. I didn't get involved in any of that. I just did my job and minded my own business.'

Washington added, 'If someone had picked up something big, like if something had happened to my daughters, I would have been hot on the case.'

Towards the end of our conversation, I mentioned the fact that two girls had been abused from age five and three. 'Did you say five and three?' Washington interrupted. '*That* shocks me. And if I had got any word of it, I would certainly have put my head on the block for that.'

Debbie Baronian, the wife of another former teacher, says, 'Barrie and I talked about it — what if you told? But if I ever thought about the logistics of bringing it to the fore, it was just like too big a thing for me to cope with, or envisage something actually being done, without destroying the island. And I think there's also in your mind that that's Pitcairn Island, that's their life, that's the way they want to be.

'In my mind, if I had done something, nothing would have changed. What could we have done, Barrie and I, to have changed the way things happened on Pitcairn Island? Nothing. Not a thing.'

In one of its policy pronouncements on child abuse, the Seventh-day Adventist Church states that 'to remain indifferent and unresponsive is to condone, perpetuate, and potentially extend such behaviour'.

Or, as Edmund Burke, the 18th-century philosopher, expressed it in one version of his famous quotation, 'All that is necessary for the triumph of evil is that good men do nothing.'

And so it was diffident, damaged Belinda who whispered the truth and bore the consequences.

CHAPTER 16

Interdependence + silence = collusion

It is, perhaps, the hardest question of all. Why did parents on Pitcairn not protect their young? Why did they allow the island to become a viper's nest of sex offenders, with their own children the defenceless prey? As I tried to fathom the Pitcairners' mentality, I remembered the men going out to sea to trade just after the verdicts. Back at The Landing, unpacking their spoils, which included crates of beer and big sacks of rice, their swift and fluid movements brought to mind an impeccably disciplined dance troupe. Yet those working shoulder to shoulder, heaving boxes from longboat to jetty, were the guilty men and the fathers of girls they had raped and assaulted. As soon as they had unloaded the goods, the islanders stalked off in different directions. They had barely spoken a word to each other — but despite the toxic atmosphere they had got the job done.

I realised that the necessity to co-operate, whatever the circumstances, is the most fundamental reality of Pitcairn life. Without such co-operation, the community would not survive. People and supplies could not be brought to shore. The locals would be unable to export their souvenirs or trade on the ships. The island itself, without regular upkeep, would revert to nature.

On the longboats, in particular, teamwork is essential, and so the men somehow manage to set their antipathies aside. Roy Sanders, who taught on the island in the 1950s, wrote evocatively that 'in a rough sea, the harbour mouth is negotiated with three crews of 14 men, rowing with clockwork precision, and in deathly silence'. Even with engine power, says one islander, 'you can't carry your differences past the next ship ... You have to be able to catch the eye of the man standing beside you, and know you can trust him.'

On Pitcairn, feuds are waged mostly beneath the surface. Dave Brown and Vaine Peu, for instance, 'hate each other's guts'. But when Vaine discovered that his papaya trees had been poisoned, he did not accuse Dave, whom he suspected, nor did he make an official complaint. He just brooded, and the bad feeling between the two men flourished like the prickly lantana weed strangling the native vegetation.

Not only are open confrontations avoided, but the pressure to conform to communal norms is intense. And those norms have to be accepted even if they become warped: anyone who challenges the 'Pitcairn way' risks being made an outcast. A former teacher says, 'The Pitcairners can be incredibly mean and vindictive. If the community turns against you, it is absolute hell.'

Like a family that is determined to stay together, the islanders have to take whatever communal life throws at them. They have to be able to accommodate any kind of behaviour — and that includes their children being abused.

The interdependence of the community is the key to under-standing why generations of parents failed to keep their children safe, and why older women, including those who were victims themselves, insist on defending the men.

But while co-operation is vital, and every person plays their part, not everybody on Pitcairn is equal. The island basically runs on male muscle power, so able-bodied males are at the top of the hierarchy, and women — however capable and assertive they may be — defer to the men. That is not to say that the women are not tough: Betty Christian, for instance, grew up in the 1950s, when wheelbarrows were the only form of transport. 'It took all day to collect firewood, once you'd pushed your barrow up the hill, chopped the wood by hand, and then wheeled it home,' she recalls.

While motorbikes have made life easier, women still perform physical work, labouring in the gardens, painting public buildings and joining the road-clearing teams. However, it is the men who dredge the harbour and drive the heavy machinery; it is they, in the main, who unload supplies, often in rough seas and sometimes at night. The longboats are an almost exclusively male domain — 'the phallus of power on Pitcairn', as one prosecution lawyer calls them.

'Yes, we're strong, but we need the men,' says Meralda Warren, herself an intelligent and physically imposing person. The mayor has to be a man, contends Meralda, because he communicates with ships and advises their captains where to anchor. And, she told Sue Ingram of Radio New Zealand, 'sometimes when you go alongside the ship, it's not calm. You have to make that leap from the boat to the ladder. I can't do it.'

In a place where 'it's always the main act, never the dress rehearsal', as one visitor puts it, the women are reliant on the men for survival. And so the men, until Operation Unique, at least, were able to do just about whatever they liked.

Eleven-year-old Isobel arrived home one afternoon in tears. It was 1978, and she had just been raped by a neighbour, Brian Young. Beside herself with anger and upset, Isobel's mother, a New

Zealander, gave her daughter 'a real belting'. When Isobel got undressed to have a wash, her mother noticed that her knickers were stained. She seized them and stormed down to the Mission House, where she showed them to the pastor's wife, Phyllis Ferguson.

Isobel's mother also interrupted a council meeting, producing the soiled underwear and brandishing it in front of everyone, including the magistrate, Ivan Christian. She told them this was Brian's work. The councillors, who included Brian himself, then chairman of the internal committee, turned their backs. Isobel's younger sister, Jeanie, told me, 'Brian denied it and no one took any notice of Mum. They weren't interested.' Isobel says, 'They're all islanders, so nothing happened. It's such a small community, and everyone is tied up with each other.'

Although Phyllis Ferguson was a registered nurse, she did not give Isobel a physical examination. The episode was not recorded in the council minutes, and on being asked about it many years later, surviving councillors claimed not to remember it.

A few days later Brian approached Isobel, who was sitting on the steps of the public hall. A games evening was in progress inside. Brian carefully positioned himself above Isobel and farted on her head. Everyone around them laughed.

Not long afterwards Brian married Kari Boye in a ceremony performed by Pastor Ferguson, who also helped the young couple to build a house. Isobel's mother was snubbed by other islanders, and her family slipped further down the pecking order. Isobel overheard a furious argument between her mother and Brian's, with the latter vowing that 'nobody's going to drive my son away from the island'.

Ivan Christian, who rebuffed Isobel's mother at the council meeting, served as the island's magistrate for eight years. Ivan —

Steve's father — was not the subject of any allegations. But his predecessor, Pervis Young, was one of those named by women who spoke to police, along with numerous other magistrates and prominent figures. In fact, the list of past office-holders on Pitcairn is practically a roll-call of child sex abusers, alleged or proven. Many offenders were in positions of authority, which is one reason, no doubt, why they and others were able to abuse with impunity. 'There was a power base of influential men, and no one would go against them,' says Robert Vinson, the Kent detective.

Locals say the island has always thrived under strong leaders. However, Pervis, for example, who was magistrate for nine years, did nothing to restrain the likes of Steve Christian, who was busy 'initiating' all the young girls then. According to one British official, Pervis, also an elder of the Church, was 'so far outside the moral fortress ... that he could not even cast a small stone'.

With magistrates abusing, and allegedly some police officers, too, it is hardly surprising that prosecutions and court cases ceased. Ron Christian, whom Meralda Warren replaced as police officer, and Kay Brown, who was in the post before Ron, were both charged following Operation Unique. During the Pitcairn trials, one complainant, Janet, was asked whether she had reported an assault to the magistrate. Janet burst out laughing. The magistrate was Brian Young, another of her assailants.

While anthropologists have never identified any negative effects of inbreeding within the Pitcairn population, the islanders are interrelated to a degree that is incomprehensible to most outsiders. The Pitcairn family tree is a chaotic jumble of interlocking lines, virtually impossible to unravel.

Imagine being a girl growing up on the island. Very likely you would be related to the men abusing you. If you made a fuss, the repercussions would touch your entire extended family, along with almost everyone else in the community. Everyone would get to hear about it. Pitcairn is such an intimate little place. And you would still encounter those men every day. In effect, you were imprisoned on that rock, for the nearest English-speaking country was a week away, and the next ship probably not due for months — not that you would be allowed to board it.

Parents must have been in a similar position. Not only were they dependent on other adults; they were also related to most of them. Speaking out in an environment so isolated and so close-knit would have been almost unthinkable. As a parent, if you had pointed the finger, the atmosphere in the tiny community would have been awkward, to say the least. Moreover, others might have felt inspired to follow your example. Someone else might have accused *your* husband or father or brother or son.

Pitcairn operated like one big family. 'And if you're a Pitcairner,' says one who knows the place well, 'you don't go against the family. You don't want to be the one to bring the island down. You don't betray the family's secrets.' When the police investigation began, dozens of women did just that. Carol Warren, a lifelong island resident, was incredulous. Their actions were 'definitely ... *not* the Pitcairn way', she spluttered.

The Pitcairn way was to deal with problems 'inside the family', as Gillian discovered when she was very small. Gillian told her parents that her uncle had been molesting her. Her father spoke to his brother about it, and the brother was 'apologetic'. Unfortunately for Gillian, he did not leave his young niece alone.

Gillian's case seems to have been unusual: few children confided in their parents. Nonetheless, most — if not all — members of the community surely knew what was going on. Not much remains under wraps on Pitcairn. As Royal Warren, one of the matriarchs, puts it, 'Everyone else's business is known, and you know everyone else's business.' The men were quite brazen. They whisked girls off on motorbikes, in full view of other islanders. They assaulted them in public: in the square, at the school. They pounced during birthday parties, picnics and fishing trips.

Some of the women now denying the existence of child abuse are either being disingenuous or have short memories. After Jay Warren was acquitted, Carol wrote to Suzie, his accuser, suggesting that she might have mistaken Jay's identity: Carol revealed to Suzie that she had seen another man assaulting her when she was very young. Charlotte told her friend, Meralda Warren, that she had been raped by Steve Christian, yet Meralda testified that she 'never saw or heard of this kind of thing' as a child.

The picture that emerges is of a society where abuse was, if not accepted, at least widely tolerated. Men climbed in through girls' bedroom windows, apparently unafraid of their fathers' wrath. Dave Brown, while working on a neighbour's house, wrote a 'love note' to the man's 11-year-old daughter and left it on her pillow. Randy and, allegedly, Shawn Christian raped Belinda a few yards from a shed crowded with adults. They must not have cared too much whether they were spotted. They must have known they had nothing to fear.

Then there was Morris Christian, or 'Mento', as he was rather cruelly known. Morris was a mentally disabled man who used to ambush schoolgirls. His conduct, and that of other men, was common knowledge, Jeanie says. She told me, 'All the adults knew about it, but they were probably scared of saying anything, and anyway, who would they tell?'

Those Pitcairners who were not themselves abusing closed their eyes to it. Some were unhappy, but 'everyone who disapproved was a silent voice', suggests Max Davidson, the Kent detective. 'They didn't want to rock the boat, because it was quite clear that certain families could make life unpleasant for others. It was easier to bite your lip and get on with it.'

So while the islanders would denounce a neighbour who stole fruit from someone else's tree, or mistreated a dog, no one was prepared to condemn a child molester. But then theft and cruelty to animals were aberrations; what men did to girls had an inevitability about it. 'There was no one to say, "That's not normal",' says Davidson's colleague, Robert Vinson, 'because there was no one for whom it wasn't normal.'

In 1996 a Pitcairn woman, Annie, was the victim of an attempted rape. Annie was reluctant to make a complaint, according to the pastor, Owen Brown, 'for fear of being made a laughing-stock or the butt of every joke on the island'.

To the locals, an episode like that was comical, and if you protested, you would most likely be ridiculed. Even the abuse of children was 'turned into a joke ... No one took it seriously,' remembers Jeanie, for whether you were a child or a grown woman, you were a Pitcairner, and Pitcairners were supposed to be tough. 'To show emotion is to be weak,' says a social worker familiar with the island. 'The whole culture is that when there's trouble, you harden up, suck it in and just get on with it. You don't show pain or distress. What's valued is bravery and resilience and strength.'

Pitcairners are trained from an early age to keep their feelings in check. Outsiders are sometimes shocked by the lack of affection displayed to children; they also remark on the way that certain parents routinely tease and belittle their offspring. Children are regarded first and foremost as workers, performing domestic chores that include chopping wood and lighting the copper. From the age of 12 or younger, they make carvings, crew on the longboats, and help with the gardening and trading on ships. Parents 'make [their children] into "useful" adults as soon as possible', says Karen Wolstenholme, the former Deputy Governor. Most have little interest in their children's education. According to outsiders, some encourage children as young as 12 to drink alcohol.

Adults seeking to shield their children from fellow islanders felt impotent. Some did what little they could. Janet's father offered Dave Brown a collection of his carvings to sell, if he would only promise to stay away from his daughter.

Other parents seemed not to object. When 15-year-old Josephine got pregnant in the 1960s, her father told the police officer, Floyd McCoy, that the man, who was 25, had the family's blessing. There were so few unattached males, he explained, and so many young women for them to choose from, so 'when this chance came for [Josephine], he and his wife were more than delighted'. The pastor and teacher told British officials that 'if his attitude [Josephine's father's] is the one accepted by the rest of the population, it would appear that once a girl reaches puberty, the parents encourage the single men to take her'.

What a girl then endured was immaterial, it appears. What mattered was for her to find a mate and produce children. The more breadwinners a family had, the more clout it carried. And the more babies born on the island, the more secure were its prospects. Staying single was not a viable alternative. One reason why Pitcairn girls needed a husband was to shelter them from predatory men.

The coda to this particular tale is that, nearly 40 years later, police — as part of their efforts to trace potential victims — approached Josephine's two daughters. Immediately they received a call from Josephine's solicitor warning them to back off. The girls had grown up in New Zealand, but one had confided in a friend that she had been gang-raped during a visit to Pitcairn at the age of 16 or 17. Thanks to her mother's intervention, she was never given the chance to recount her story to police or tell it in court.

The necessity to co-operate; the interrelatedness; offenders in positions of authority; the culture of not showing emotion — powerful as they may have been, these were not the only reasons why parents did not confront their daughters' abusers or report them to outside authorities. The spell cast by Pitcairn itself may also have played a part.

One of the things that struck me while on the island was how in tune people seemed to be with their environment. I watched Carol Warren, wearing a dirty blouse and baseball cap, fishing with a reel and line off the jetty one afternoon; Carol was hauling in dozens of nanwe, slashing their heads and flinging them into a bucket in one smooth movement. The bond that the Pitcairners feel with their surroundings is very apparent. They know the landscape intimately. And every rock, every tree, every gully is significant to them, either as a marker in their mental map, or by association with some event.

Even an outsider can perceive the island's attractions. As well as its history and spare, harsh beauty, there is the indisputable appeal of the lifestyle. A ready income, no tax, no one looking over your shoulder — and if the weather is glorious, you can drop everything and go fishing. Many Pitcairners leave, but many yearn to return, and some do, having found only menial jobs and a mediocre existence elsewhere. They realise that nowhere else will they enjoy the same freedom. What is more, on Pitcairn they can *be* someone; in Auckland they're just an anonymous face.

Almost every islander has a deep-seated affection for home, together with a sense of belonging that borders on the fanatical.

Although Meralda Warren has travelled widely, Pitcairn represents her roots, her identity, everything she stands for. As far as she is concerned, 'It's my rock, and nobody's going to shift me.' Betty Christian talks about the island as if it were another of her brood. 'I love it and I would never do anything to hurt it,' she says. 'It's such a gorgeous place.'

One of my lasting impressions is how besotted the locals are with their chunk of rock. And I wonder: has that most fundamental instinct, the instinct to protect one's young, been superseded by a pathological attachment to place — and a blind determination to remain there, whatever the cost?

If someone has an accident, 'the whole island is behind you,' says Betty. If an old or sick person requires round-the-clock care, everyone takes turns to watch over them. On Pitcairn, even your worst enemy will dive into the surf to rescue you from drowning.

This system of reciprocal support is often cited as one of Pitcairn's finest traditions. But, like everything else, it is all about survival. The islanders know that if they save someone's life, that person will repay the favour one day, if necessary. Pitcairn's much-vaunted community spirit is a chimera, some believe. Robert Wade, an economist who spent three months on the island in the 1960s, says, 'They did the minimum to get the boats in and out, and that was it. The idea of this community of people all pulling together is bullshit.'

The only thing that really unites the islanders is survival, and when it comes to survival, community takes precedence over family and individuals. Yet it is debatable what community means to the people of Pitcairn, or what they are so intent on preserving: the collective well-being, and their common history and culture, or simply their own self-interest?

In order to preserve communal harmony and maintain the status quo, certain parents effectively opted to sacrifice their daughters. But while some kept quiet out of a misguided sense of loyalty, others, it seems, were not prepared to give up their lifestyle and status. The sexual abuse is 'the price you pay for bringing up children on Pitcairn', suggests Robert Vinson.

One man who moved to New Zealand returned to the island with his wife and baby girl. He knew what the place was like; he must have known what awaited his daughter. Sure enough, she was raped by relatives. 'He served her up like a piece of meat,' the woman's partner told me recently. Her grandparents had attempted to keep her in New Zealand as a young child; her father had insisted that she go back to Pitcairn. The grandparents showed detectives a photograph of their daughter and son-in-law, the victim's parents. Karen Vaughan says, 'They wanted to tear him out of the picture.'

When I came home from Pitcairn, many people asked me why the women on the island were standing by the men.

The story of Catherine's mother may be instructive. When she was eight or nine years old, this middle-aged woman was molested, allegedly, by Fletcher Christian, Steve's elder brother. Fletcher, who is now dead, settled in New Zealand; Catherine's mother never told anyone about the incident. No doubt she felt sick and ashamed, and, as most victims do, she probably blamed herself and tried to forget about it. Then along came Operation Unique, and back came those excruciating memories.

And not just memories. Her own daughter was among the younger women speaking out about the abuse they had suffered — which, in Catherine's case, included a particularly nasty rape.

On learning that Catherine had given a statement, her mother's first reaction was to accuse detectives of putting words into Catherine's mouth. They quietly told her what was in the statement. Catherine's mother was horrified. Then, recovering her composure, she said she was certain her daughter had 'moved on' and was experiencing no ill effects.

Had anything happened to *her* in childhood, police asked. Her face changed. Catherine's mother described the episode involving Fletcher and shuddered, saying that she still had nightmares about it. When police observed that Catherine had been abused far more seriously and more recently, and was quite likely to be badly traumatised, her mother agreed. By the next day, though, she was once again claiming that her daughter was not in the least affected. And before long she was saying that all the women, including Catherine, had led the men on.

For her, and for many other women of her age, the reality of the situation must have been too much to bear. It would have meant facing up to their past, as well as acknowledging that the same thing had happened to their daughters — and that they had failed to prevent it. If they did that, comments one outsider, 'You'd have to accept that your life has been rotten, and that the place where you've always lived, and brought up your children, is rotten. It would be like denying your whole existence, like saying that your whole life up to this point has been completely worthless.'

It was easier to deny the fact of sexual abuse or dismiss it as a harmless rite of passage. (Moreover, the Pitcairners — like many people not so long ago — associated rape with a stranger in a dark alley, probably armed with a knife, not with someone they knew.)

Olive Christian's example offers another kind of insight. Olive has a choice between two versions of reality. According to the first, her husband Steve, son Randy, brother Dave and father Len are rapists and child abusers, while her other male relatives, including

271

her other two sons, are all suspected of similar behaviour, having been charged at one time. According to the second, her family is the principal target of a British plot to evacuate the island — a plot hatched in collusion with the New Zealand government, British and New Zealand police, the British and New Zealand judiciary, and at least nine Pitcairn women.

Olive has been one of the most outspoken supporters of the Pitcairn men.

If you were Olive, which version of reality would you choose?

Outsiders who are married to Pitcairners have defended the men with equal passion, despite not carrying the same psychological baggage. After arriving on Pitcairn and starting a relationship with Brian Young, Kari Boye had to return home to Norway for a while. According to Jeanie and Isobel, Kari warned their mother to 'watch the girls', as Brian had told Kari that if she did not come back, 'he would have to get his way somewhere else'. Jeanie and Isobel were seven and nine, yet to Kari, apparently, it seemed unremarkable that Brian should consider 'getting his way' with them.

Isobel's mother later flourished her daughter's soiled knickers at Kari, who refused to believe Brian was responsible — instead blaming Dennis Christian, 'because I knew Dennis liked them [the two girls]', she explained. Seemingly she saw nothing untoward, either, in Dennis's alleged interest in this pair of pre-pubescent mites.

When Brian and Kari had their own daughter, Anette, that was different. Kari told outsiders she was worried about the possibility of her being sexually abused. She made sure the family moved to Auckland not long after Anette's 12th birthday.

Of Albert Reeves, the former teacher, Kari later declared, 'We all knew about him and his preferences for young girls — there were several "victims" and several eye-witnesses.' She claimed, furthermore, that many visitors had behaved in the same fashion, including 'British [nuclear test] monitors, the Royal Engineers ... American satellite monitors ... certain doctors ... yachties and ships' crew'. Quite a list.

Kari initially approved of the investigation. She gave a statement and pronounced herself willing to testify. She also assured police that Brian would plead guilty 'at the earliest opportunity' — and when Brian angrily accused Karen Vaughan of 'fucking up my life, my marriage, my career, everything', Kari backed up Vaughan, who retorted that Brian's victims were suffering more than he was.

Anette's elder brother, Timmy, who had been a teenager on Pitcairn, told police what he knew about the sexual abuse of his contemporaries, which appeared to be a great deal. Brian gave a statement too. He had been at school with Jennifer, and said he had seen her and Albert Reeves together. Then Brian was charged, along with other men including his brother, Terry. Kari withdrew her statement. Timmy withdrew his. Brian withdrew his. And Kari embarked on her campaign to convince the world that the case was about nothing worse than under-age sex.

Another female outsider was Dave Brown's wife, Lea. After Dave was charged, Lea, a New Zealander, reportedly shrugged his alleged crimes off as 'island culture'. She already knew about her neighbours' worst skeletons, it seems, for when Leon Salt on one occasion warned Dave that he would 'go away for life if Darralyn laid a complaint', Lea snapped at him, 'If an investigation was started, it would uncover incest and all.'

There was also Lorraine Brown, the wife of Kay Brown, who warned at least one outsider of the danger that the local men represented. By the time of Operation Unique, the Browns had emigrated to New Zealand: they had a daughter and Lorraine wanted her off the island. Like Kari, she left the Pitcairn girls to their fate.

The conclusion is bleak. Parents knew what was happening, but, with one or two exceptions, they kept silent. That silence — enforced by powerful males and communal pressure — did not necessarily mean approbation. But the demands of raw geography fostered a different morality. The first law of Pitcairn life was survival. And the second was 'pulling together'.

By not speaking up, parents, it could be argued, made themselves complicit. But, as one of the trial judges said in relation to one victim, 'I consider that her reticence is not surprising in a closed community dependent for its survival . . . on the brawn of relatively few fit males.'

Who let the girls down, I asked a former diplomat. 'You pay your money and you take your pick,' he replied. 'Were they let down by their families? Were they let down by community leaders? By their teachers? By the Church? By the British government?'

He paused. 'Or were they let down by everyone?'

CHAPTER 17

Making legal history

In November 2003, seven months after charges had been laid, defence lawyers for the Pitcairn men claimed that the island was not a British colony. It was an independent state with its own laws, they said, and Britain had no business meddling in its affairs and prosecuting its inhabitants.

This intriguing proposition had been dreamt up by Adrian Cook, a QC and retired Australian judge in his 70s. Until not long before, Cook, who lives on Norfolk Island and is married to a Pitcairn descendant, had sported a ponytail and gold earring. In 2003 he had offered his services to the defence team.

The 'sovereignty' argument was first unfurled before the Pitcairn Supreme Court, consisting of the same three judges who were to hear the criminal case. First, Cook maintained, Pitcairn had never been formally claimed by the British. Although first sighted (and named) in 1767 by the captain of a British sloop, HMS *Swallow*, the ship's crew had not attempted to land. Secondly, the island had not been settled by British subjects, since the mutineers, in committing treason and piracy, had severed their links with the Crown. Thirdly, subsequent generations had not been British either, because the sailors had not married the Tahitian women, so the children had assumed their mothers' nationality.

Prosecution lawyers, led by Simon Moore, countered that British sovereignty was a political reality. They pointed to the islanders' frequent expressions of loyalty to the Crown and noted their acceptance of financial aid from Britain, as well as the fact that most Pitcairners — including the six guilty men — held British passports.

Unconvinced by Adrian Cook's reasoning, the Supreme Court formally rejected it in April 2004. The defence team immediately appealed to the Pitcairn Court of Appeal, composed of three senior New Zealand judges. These judges described the notion of Pitcairn not being British as 'somewhat startling', and observed that Britain had governed the island 'without protest from any quarter until the present challenge'. They dismissed the appeal in August, clearing the way for trials to commence in Adamstown in September.

Despite this setback, Paul Dacre, still spearheading defence efforts notwithstanding the arrival of Cook, did not lose heart. From the outset he had indicated that he would fight the case on every front, and he had already come up with seven or eight legal arguments, quite apart from the territorial question. Now Dacre attempted to delay the trials on the grounds that permission was being sought to appeal to the Privy Council, the highest court for British Overseas Territories. Unsuccessful, he produced yet more arguments while judges and lawyers were in transit in Tahiti, obliging them to convene in their hotel, with vacationers sipping cocktails a few yards away by the lagoon-style pool.

The new points Paul Dacre raised were Britain's alleged failure to 'promulgate' English law — in other words, to make sufficiently clear to the Pitcairners that English law applied to them — and the 'inherent bias' of a machinery of justice set up specifically to deal with the sexual abuse charges. These were deferred to be heard in Auckland in early 2005 and the trials went ahead, but only after one final bid by Dacre to have them adjourned. This time he cited 'apparent judicial bias' — the result, he said, of a meeting between Chief Justice Charles Blackie and Baroness Scotland in 2000. The judges retired to consider whether they were biased, and emerged to announce that they were not.

Now the Supreme Court had reassembled in surroundings markedly different from the palm trees and mosquitoes of Pitcairn: the district courthouse at Papakura, an ethnically diverse South Auckland suburb. It was 18 April 2005, and the lawyers were about to tackle the new arguments which, however arcane they might seem, were of vital importance to the six men who had in the meantime been found guilty. If the defence managed to persuade the court that the legal process was flawed, the men would be reprieved; if not, the sentences handed down on Pitcairn would take effect — possibly.

Outside the courtroom a sign proclaimed, 'No gang patches or insignia to be worn'. Inside, draped across the front wall, were the British and Pitcairn flags. A photograph of the Queen was perched on the judges' bench, like a family snapshot. Outside I could hear the muffled roar of traffic.

Bill Haigh was supervising a satellite link with Pitcairn which would allow the islanders to follow proceedings. And there they were, on a monitor screen at the side of the court, which showed the public hall in Adamstown — crowded, although hardly a soul had watched the trials. Steve Christian, in his best short-sleeved blue shirt, was seated in the front row, right in the centre. Close by were Randy Christian, Terry Young and Len Brown, like Steve all facing jail, along with Dave Brown and Dennis Christian, sentenced to community service. A second monitor displayed a wide-angle view of the courtroom at Papakura, which was what the islanders were able to see at their end. I noticed myself on the screen, in the public gallery. I could see them; they could see me.

Sitting around me in the gallery were Pitcairn supporters and expatriates, who included Leon Salt and Kari Boye Young. A few days earlier I had contacted Kari and another Auckland-based islander — Julie Christian, Dennis's sister — to request interviews for this book. I received a scornful reply from Kari, who had been quoted in a New Zealand magazine article describing my reporting on the Pitcairn trials as 'drippingly negative'. Kari copied her response to other islanders, which prompted Melva Evans in Alaska to drop me a line, saying, 'May I gently remind you, Ms Marks, that there are precedents to your plans to profit by the exploitation of the Pitcairn people, and all I can say is that your status has sunk to a new low because of this endeavour.'

Leon Salt had won his unfair dismissal case against the British government, which had not complied with New Zealand disciplinary procedures. But the tribunal had halved his NZ$32,700 (£12,000) award and refused to reinstate him, criticising his email exchanges with Allen Cox, the island schoolteacher, as an apparent 'attempt to thwart due legal process'. The men and their families regarded Salt, who had resumed his teaching career in New Zealand, as a martyr to the Pitcairn cause.

There was another interested party present: Richard Quinn, whose son, Ricky, had indirectly sparked Operation Unique in 1999. Ricky had been convicted of unlawful carnal knowledge of Karen after pleading guilty at the court case arranged by Gail Cox. Richard, who had travelled from his home in the Bay of Islands, was hoping to hear something of benefit to his son.

At the defence table, relations between Adrian Cook and the other three counsel — Paul Dacre, Allan Roberts and Charles Cato

— were chilly. Cook's speciality was the sovereignty issue; however, he had recently appropriated the role of defending Shawn Christian, one of six 'off-islanders' yet to go to trial. Although Dacre's original team had defended their clients robustly, discontent had been rumbling around them for some time, with the men suspicious of the fact that they had been appointed by the British Governor and were on his payroll. Some of the defendants had decided to seek 'independent' representation: Brian Young, another off-islander, had instructed Grant Illingworth, an Auckland QC. After the Pitcairn trials, Brian's brother, Terry, switched to Illingworth too, as did Ron Christian, one of the New Zealand-based accused.

Adrian Cook was acting *pro bono*, but quite reasonably wanted his expenses paid, while Grant Illingworth was charging a discounted fee. Still, significant sums had to be found. A newly formed Justice for Pitcairn Group had launched an appeal, setting up a website with links to international human rights declarations. A letter on the site, signed by 20 island women, warned that the community was 'in extreme peril', and donors were invited to buy a special CD featuring Meralda Warren singing Pitcairn songs. Donations would be placed in a trust fund; among the trustees were Ric Robinson, Colleen McCullough's husband, and Trent Christian.

Proceedings got under way at Papakura, where defence lawyers argued that the men had not been aware that English law applied on Pitcairn, nor that it could be used to prosecute and punish them for serious criminal offences. Consequently, the lawyers said, they did not know that it was illegal — or even wrong — to rape and sexually assault children.

In support of this, the defence cited some of the many hundreds of documents relating to Pitcairn affairs — some historical, some recent — that had been disclosed by the Foreign Office and other sources. The papers, they said, proved that the community had been neglected, especially when it came to law and order.

The prosecution argued that they demonstrated Pitcairn was a developed and civilised society that would have understood the gravity of rape and incest. If the defence arguments were upheld, the island would effectively be a 'zone of criminal immunity where serious crimes can be committed without consequences', declared Simon Mount, one of the Crown prosecutors. Mount gave examples of English law being applied on Pitcairn, beginning with the Harry Christian murder trial in 1898. (Christian was hanged the same year in Fiji.) Also dealt with by Britain, because they had been too weighty for the local court, were an abortion in 1940, a divorce in 1958 and an attempted burglary in 1971.

Then there was the bizarre case of Eldon and Julia Coffin, who in 1936 had allegedly tried to murder each other. Julia claimed to have spiked her husband's tea with liniment. She told a British judge sent from Fiji, 'I thought it might kill him and no one will find out as there is no doctor on the island.' Eldon, for his part, testified, 'I drink those drink and that is the best time I feel in my whole life.' He admitted firing a shotgun in the kitchen, narrowly missing his wife, but told the judge that he had been aiming at a stray chicken.

During the intervals, spectators in Papakura waved to their relatives on Pitcairn. I, too, glanced occasionally at the video-link monitor. Meralda Warren emailed me to say that several people on the island had 'noticed that whilst Simon Mount droned on you Kathy was busy scribbling your piece which came out rather quickly in the papers'. Then, when it was the defence's turn, 'you seemed bored and we noticed'.

The first witnesses were Tom and Betty Christian, who would

be giving evidence in person, having made the long trip from Pitcairn. The couple had been excoriated for their decision to testify 'against their own people', as one critic called it, but not everyone shared that view; quite a number of islanders were content to be British and wanted to stay that way. British-born Mike Lupton-Christian was indignant that the locals had not been consulted about a legal strategy that could strip them of their nationality. 'Just to get a few people off, they're willing to change everything, to give up Britain and all the security it offers,' he told us during the trials.

Tom and Betty's standpoint was that they did not wish to undermine the men's case but felt strongly that Pitcairn Island was British — and they could not envisage how the place would survive without Britain's support and protection. Betty, who entered the box first, looked gripped by nerves. Speaking in Pitkern, she greeted her fellow islanders, who were gazing out at her stony-faced from the television screen. No one responded. The public hall in Adamstown was full again, Steve Christian having reportedly let it be known that everyone was expected to attend throughout the hearing.

In her affidavit, Betty had stated that it had 'always been obvious that serious crime (including serious sexual offending) would be prosecuted under English law'. She told the court that Pitcairn had interacted 'almost constantly' with the outside world, and 'our beliefs and standards of behaviour have been no different to those of any other modern community'.

Next, Peter George took the stand. When George flew to the Antipodes for the first time in April 2000 to interview Shawn and Randy Christian, he expected it to be a one-off. He was about to retire from the Kent force; he did retire but agreed to see the Pitcairn case through, little imagining how long it would go on. As of early 2008, George had visited New Zealand at least 14 times (he has lost count) and Pitcairn on half a dozen occasions. The other detectives were similarly well travelled.

George was cross-examined by Charles Cato about Britain's failure to furnish the islanders with independent policing. With 'no police presence for about 200 years', Cato suggested, people would be less likely to realise that 'you're in trouble if you break British law'. Peter George replied, 'You don't need a police presence to tell you that it's against the law to rape a child.'

But it helped if you knew the penalties, didn't it, Cato insisted.

George said, 'As a child in the UK I wasn't educated about the law. No one told me what the Sexual Offences Act was ... [or] the Theft Act ... And I expect if you were to ask any member of the public ... they'd say the same thing. They would not know what legislation covered what offences. But they know what a crime is.'

It had become evident from the documents released to the prosecution and defence that even British officials had been confused about the age of consent on Pitcairn. The former Governor, Martin Williams, apparently realised during the Ricky Quinn affair that the age was not 16, but 15. Before Quinn's trial, he wrote to Leon Salt, warning him that, since Karen was 15, 'we cannot insist on the charge'. However, Williams added, if no one challenged Cox, and Quinn pleaded guilty, 'we would be presented with a *fait accompli*'.

This was what Richard Quinn, patiently sitting in the public gallery every day, had been waiting to hear. It was plain that Ricky's conviction could not stand. Three months later he received a royal pardon — the first in decades — and an undisclosed sum in damages.

In May 2005 the Supreme Court ruled against the defendants. The judges said they were satisfied that, on Pitcairn, 'rape and various sexual offending were known to be criminal ... [and] violations of universally accepted standards'. They also rejected a suggestion that the men's human rights had been infringed.

With the six convictions formally recorded, Kieran Raftery, for the prosecution, asked that sentences now be served. The judges, though, decreed that bail should continue pending the Privy Council appeal, for which a date had yet to be fixed. Some locals were dismayed. 'It's terrible, all this waiting,' one of them told me. 'When is it going to end? Steve and Randy are acting like they're never going to have to go to jail.'

In late 2005 the islanders recommenced the propaganda campaign, posting online many of the case papers that had been copied by Leon Salt and given to Christopher Harder, the Auckland barrister. The documents — which Harder had attempted to use to scupper the Pitcairn trials — contained 'the truth' that Britain was trying to hide, they claimed. However, the papers did not live up to their sensational billing, and most of them were already in the public domain.

Harder, who was struck off in early 2006 following his eighth appearance at a disciplinary tribunal, later gave an undertaking not to publish or distribute the documents. Salt refused to do so, and it was not until early 2008 that he and the British Government finally reached a settlement. In May that year his appeal against the halving of his unfair dismissal award was rejected.

In March 2006 the Court of Appeal threw out an appeal by the six Pitcairners against their convictions. The next stage was the Privy Council, which had finally scheduled its hearing to begin in London on 10 July. Paul Dacre had only two clients left: Steve Christian and Len Brown. The rest had defected to Adrian Cook and Grant Illingworth. Cook had resigned from Dacre's team.

The case had been painstakingly followed by lawyers, law students and academics: it seemed bound to make legal history, given Pitcairn's unique origins and the constitutional issues that it raised. Eminent counsel in both hemispheres, including Geoffrey Robertson, the Australian human rights QC, had expressed an interest in joining the defence team.

While Robertson decided against it, other lawyers jostled to get involved 'for their own glorification', says Allan Roberts, the Deputy Public Defender. Roberts told me in an interview in late 2006 that it had felt like 'vultures were circling behind us and waiting for us to fail'; Adrian Cook, he claimed, was 'trying to deal us out of the equation so that he could finish off in the Privy Council for his last hurrah and . . . be seen as the great redeemer for this poor oppressed nation'. After living at close quarters with the Pitcairn defendants, it had been 'gut-wrenching' when some of them instructed other lawyers, added Roberts, who became a district court judge in 2007. Randy Christian had not even bothered notifying Dacre's team.

In mid-2006, shortly before the Privy Council met, the islanders held a fund-raising event in the Adamstown square. They sold each other goods such as home-baked cakes, and there was no question of anyone not taking part. According to Justice for Pitcairn, the hearing would cost the Pitcairners and their supporters NZ$100,000 (£33,000) in legal fees and expenses.

Passing through the security cordon into Downing Street, where the Privy Council is located, I reflected how far the Pitcairn men had come. Rapists and child molesters rarely got the chance to appeal to the most senior judges in the Commonwealth — and that was what these men were, regardless of the outcome on points of law.

Outside, it was a scorching English summer's day. Upstairs, the oak-panelled chamber was gloomy, its high walls covered in lugubrious portraits. Kari Boye Young was already installed in the public gallery: she had flown to London to be the island's eyes and ears. She sat by herself in the middle of a room of mainly strangers, looking anxious and rather overawed. A dozen barristers in wigs and gowns were planted on heavy maroon leather chairs. In front of them was a bank of computer screens. This would be the first Privy Council case to make use of digital technology; the judges had to navigate their way around 4000 pages of documents.

The five judges — all members of Britain's House of Lords — entered, led by Lord Hoffman, President of the Privy Council's Judicial Committee. Paul Dacre stood up and asked if he might relay a message from Pitcairn's mayor, Jay Warren, who wished to 'acknowledge the historical significance of today's hearing'. Dacre added, 'Although it has been 216 years since the arrival of the mutineers, this is the first time the court has sat in Britain to consider constitutional issues about Pitcairn. It is also the first time there has been an appeal in Britain from a criminal trial on Pitcairn.'

Adrian Cook then got to his feet to argue that Britain had no jurisdiction over the island. Almost immediately Lord Hoffman interrupted him. 'If the Crown says a certain territory is a British territory, it's not for the courts to question that,' he remarked. 'It's a question of the separation of powers.' Cook responded that, in his opinion, Pitcairn had never been a British possession. One of Hoffman's eyebrows shot up, and he started to laugh. He said, 'I must confess that I have (ha ha), I mean (ha ha), seldom heard a more unrealistic argument (ha ha), in view of the message with which you began, and so on and so forth.'

Cook tried to explain that the mutineers, as a result of their seizure of the *Bounty*, had actually been pirates. Hoffman squashed him again. 'A lot of things have happened since 1789,' he declared.

Cook: 'Piracy is still rampant in the world ... It was certainly a very despicable act, a dastardly act in 1789.'

Hoffman, chewing on his spectacles: 'Well, there it is. Thank you very much.'

The five judges were briefly addressed by Simon Moore, after which they retired to weigh up the submissions. Barely five minutes later they returned to the chamber. Hoffman announced their ruling. Sovereignty argument dismissed.

Kari's face crumpled. She looked as if she had just been informed that a close relative had died. Adrian Cook seemed equally stunned. He rose. 'My Lords, I feel somewhat like the sea bird that's been clipped of all his feathers,' he said plaintively.

Hoffman rejoined, 'No feathers left. Oh, dear.'

The process of deliberation had not been quite as brutal or cursory as it appeared. The Privy Council had had months to peruse and discuss these issues; the verbal sparring was, to some extent, a formality, and while two weeks had been set aside for it, Lord Hoffman had a reputation for brisk efficiency. A casual spectator, though, might well have come away with the impression that this highly distinguished judge had reacted spontaneously, and in the same way as would any sensible layperson, to a proposition that seemed inherently absurd.

Surely it had been obvious all along that Pitcairn was British? Adrian Cook's argument must have had some merit, I reminded myself, otherwise it would not have got this far. On the other hand, judges were notorious for being fascinated by the novel. Had the Privy Council been unable to resist toying with the idea before throwing it out?

Other matters remained to be debated, such as 'promulgation' of the English law and 'abuse of process'. All the submissions had been completed by mid-afternoon the following day. The proceedings had lasted little over a day and a half.

The island's colonial status was the only question on which the Law Lords were willing to make up their minds on the spot. For the rest, the Pitcairn men — and everyone else, including the victims, who had still not received justice — had to wait another three months.

In October 2006 the Privy Council handed down its decision. It was Monday morning in London and the middle of the night on Pitcairn; many islanders stayed up to read the judgement online.

Lord Hoffman ruled on behalf of the committee, then two other judges, Lords Woolf and Hope, delivered separate judgements. All three dismissed the appeal. Lord Woolf called the evidence that Pitcairn was a British territory 'overwhelming', and said it was clear from the volume of documents, and from the decisions of the lower courts, that 'every issue which could be raised on behalf of the appellants has been fully canvassed and justice has been done'. He considered it 'reassuring that such care has been taken to achieve justice for a small community of limited means'.

Lord Hope observed that the case had highlighted 'some fundamental issues about the rule of law in remote communities'. He said, 'Let me not mince words. This case is about child sexual abuse on a grand scale. The extent to which it was practised on Pitcairn is deeply disturbing.' Moreover, it was 'impossible to believe' that the men were 'not aware that what they were doing was wrong', and 'scarcely credible that the population of the island as a whole was unaware of what was going on'.

Hope added, 'The fact that this scale of offending, of which the offences that have been proved in this case were almost certainly the tip of the iceberg, was tolerated for so long in such a small, isolated and closely knit community is an indication of the poor state of supervision exercised over its affairs by the colonial authorities.'

It was, as Matthew Forbes put it, 'the end of the road'. Two years had elapsed since the men had been found guilty. The investigation, trials and legal challenges had cost the British government nearly £7 million — a sizeable portion of that spent on efforts to prove the island was not British.

Five days later, at the request of the Pitcairn Supreme Court, Steve and Randy Christian presented themselves at the gate of the prison. They alighted from their quad bikes and said goodbye to their families. Then 'they walked in calmly and surrendered themselves in a dignified way', according to one witness.

Carol Warren, who was also watching, wrote, 'Let me tell you those families are not alone, we were all crying ... I rang Tom and Betty and told them that they must be feeling very proud of themselves for what they have done. I hope they can hear the kids crying at night especially, for their daddy and that it haunts them for a long while to come.' Just in case Tom and Betty had not got the message, Melva Warren wrote to the couple, denouncing them for their 'Judas role' and the part they had played in 'the living hell that [the Pitcairners] have been forced to endure'.

In the Pitcairn way, Steve and Randy were already acquainted with their jailors. Seven corrections officers from New Zealand had been on the island for the past month, in anticipation of the Privy Council ruling. Father and son, along with other locals, had helped the officers to put the final touches to the prison: concreting the yard, reinforcing the fence and building a workshop.

A month later, Terry Young joined Steve and Randy in jail, after his sister, Pauline, had arrived from New Zealand to look after their elderly mother, Vula. Len Brown was given leave to serve his sentence at home, under conditions that included no girl under 18 being allowed to visit his house unsupervised. Len, aged 80, was also granted special permission 'to fish for self or commercial reasons one day per week'.

Dave Brown and Dennis Christian began their community service. The long saga of the Pitcairn-based offenders was over, apart from their sentences. But the fate of the other six men, living in Australia and New Zealand, was yet to be determined.

CHAPTER 18

The final trials

The six 'off-islanders' kept a close eye on the legal skirmishes that began in Auckland and culminated at the Privy Council. A decision favourable to the Pitcairn-based men would mean an end to their worries, too.

Moves were afoot to bring those six accused to trial, but within little over a year of charges being laid, two of them had been reprieved. In June 2004 the last of four women who had made complaints against Trent Christian withdrew from the case. Fiona had accused Trent of raping her; Trent had denied all the allegations against him. Now the charges against Steve and Olive Christian's eldest son were dropped. Four months later Olive's brother, Kay, was in the clear too, thanks to a judgement in an unrelated case by a court on the other side of the world.

The ruling concerned a 12-month time limit for laying a charge of unlawful sex with a girl aged 13 to 15. It was common practice for prosecutors to circumvent the limit by charging men with indecent assault; in October 2004 the House of Lords, Britain's highest appeal body, closed that loophole. Only a fraction of the Pitcairn charges had involved consensual under-age sex, Simon Moore having decided to prosecute only when there was a substantial age difference. But all of those had been laid as indecent assaults; as a result, prosecutors were obliged to withdraw all the charges against Kay, along with some of Brian Young's and Ron Christian's. In addition, four of Dave Brown's convictions were wiped and his sentence was cut to 250 hours of community service.

That left four off-islanders still to go to court: Brian and Ron, against whom other charges remained in place, Shawn Christian, and Albert Reeves, the former teacher and sole non-Pitcairner. Reeves was seriously ill, and it was not clear whether he would be fit to stand trial. In January 2005, two months after the Pitcairn trials ended, authorities in two countries swung into action against Shawn. Trent and Randy's younger brother was arrested by police in Newcastle, north of Sydney, where he lived with his Australian partner, Michele Purvis. The couple had met on Norfolk Island, and Shawn had moved to Newcastle in 1999 to be with Michele.

With bail declined, Shawn, who had been employed as a manager in a large computer company, spent nearly two months in Sydney's Silverwater jail; the 29-year-old was the first person to be locked up since Operation Unique had started five years earlier. He agreed to be extradited, and Karen Vaughan and another New Zealand detective flew to Sydney to take him back across the Tasman; once in Auckland, he was granted bail by the Pitcairn court but was not permitted to return to Australia. Shawn's trial was set down for October 2005 at Papakura, then for December, then for March 2006. In March it had to be deferred again: Belinda, by this time living with a partner in New Zealand, went into labour the day she was due to give evidence.

In November 2006, a month after the Privy Council judgement, Shawn's trial was finally set to go ahead, with breaks arranged for Belinda to feed her baby. It would be followed by

Brian Young's trial. Ron Christian had pleaded guilty to his outstanding charges and would be appearing for sentence.

Steve and Randy Christian had gone to jail three weeks earlier, and feelings in the Pitcairn community, on and off the island, were running high. So venomous were the emails flying around that the new Governor, George Fergusson, issued a statement urging people to cease their attacks and instead 'work towards healing the community's wounds'. Fergusson received a flurry of indignant replies.

Shawn Christian, aged 31, was charged with three counts of rape, one of which related to aiding and abetting his brother, Randy. On the morning of his trial, the first week of which had been taken up by yet more legal argument, he stood outside the courtroom, chatting with his partner, Michele, and other well-wishers including Kari Boye Young and his sister, Tania Christian, now living in New Zealand.

Shawn seemed somewhat different from his father and brothers — more compact in build, and quieter, less brash. His court attire, a dark blue suit and yellow tie, was more conventional than theirs. He had a boyish, smiley manner, and as he sat down in the isolation of the dock he looked completely out of his depth. When Simon Moore stood up to deliver his opening address for the prosecution, Shawn flashed a grimace of mock horror at the public gallery.

The first witness was Belinda. She took a seat in the jury box, obscured from Shawn's view. Belinda was now 22. Her thick, dark hair was pulled back in a ponytail.

For the second time, she recited the horrific events that had allegedly occurred near the sugar cane shed. Then, in a soft, clear voice, she told the judge, Jane Lovell-Smith, about an evening when her family was invited to dinner at Big Fence. Belinda was 11, and after dinner she went into Shawn's bedroom to stroke the family cat, Animal. The next thing she knew, 'I remember seeing Shawn, and I remember the door being closed ... [and] Shawn was on top of me.'

Simon Moore questioned Belinda about her relationship with her family in recent years. 'How supportive has your father been in relation to this case?' he asked.

'Not very supportive. My understanding is he has not wanted anything to do with me,' Belinda said in her little girl's voice, of the father whom she once idolised.

'And your mum?'

'She's been a little supportive. She ... I know she's there.'

For the rest of that day and much of the next, Belinda was cross-examined by Adrian Cook. She sat stiff-backed, arms clenched by her sides, as if literally holding herself together. At one point Cook produced a handkerchief and, with a theatrical flourish, stuffed it into his mouth, to demonstrate, he said, that Shawn could not possibly have gagged Belinda with his T-shirt.

Almost seven years to the day after telling her story to Gail Cox, Belinda left the witness box for the last time. 'I can't believe it's over,' she told Karen Vaughan.

And now standing there in the witness box was Gail Cox herself, the catalyst for the whole affair, the police officer who had been in the right place at the right time, the sympathetic outsider in whom Belinda had felt able to confide. Cox had been a pivotal figure but she was also a mystery woman: although her name had featured in hundreds of news reports, she had, up until this day in New Zealand, refused to talk about Pitcairn publicly.

Cox felt anguished by the events she had triggered, and by their devastating impact on the Pitcairn community. Her actions had been picked over in the international media, on the internet, and

293

by her own colleagues in Kent. She loathed the high profile that the case had given her and avoided all contact with Operation Unique. In 2006, after an extended period of sick leave, she retired from the Kent force on health grounds, still in her mid-40s.

And that would have been that — except that the prosecution learnt that Adrian Cook was planning to query the circumstances surrounding Belinda's statement. Lawyers were anxious about the possibility of Shawn being acquitted, and Randy then having grounds to appeal. They decided to call Gail Cox as a witness. Peter George managed to track her down in the US and persuaded her to fly to Auckland.

Cox — who, when I met her, turned out to be a bubbly, warm-hearted person — told me, 'Peter said the magic words: "Randy and Shawn might get off." And the whole of the last seven years would have been for nothing, really, if Randy and Shawn got off.'

She went on, 'I'm doing it for [Belinda], really. She's the bravest little girl in the whole world. I know she's not a little girl any more, but she was so brave to come forward, and to still be sticking by it despite the way she's been treated by her family and the community. I'm so full of admiration for [Belinda], she's so strong. I'd like her to win the lottery and have a happy life for the rest of her life.'

In court, Cox was questioned about the procedures she had followed when taking Belinda's statement. Had an adult been present, as was legally required when a child was interviewed?

Adrian Cook cast doubt on Cox's assertion that Belinda's mother had been within earshot at all times. He asked her whether Belinda had had difficulty recalling details of the alleged rapes. Cox said that she had remembered almost everything clearly. She told the judge, 'I believed [Belinda]. Her story was very compelling.'

Shawn's police interview had been conducted by Peter George, who had questioned him on Pitcairn four years earlier about 11-year-old Caroline. Like Gail Cox, Belinda and Ricky Quinn, Shawn had played a key role in the genesis of Operation Unique.

On the tape, which was played to the court, he seemed eager to co-operate. Asked to name the Pitcairn girls with whom he had had sex, he giggled embarrassedly. What about Belinda?

'No, no, no.' Shawn shook his head.

Why would Belinda make up allegations against him?

'To be honest, I wouldn't have a clue,' said Shawn, his voice high-pitched and quavery. 'I'm as puzzled as you ... I'm also shocked as well, I'm also stunned.'

The next defence witness would be testifying from Pitcairn. Her face appeared on the video-link monitor. It was Belinda's mother.

The witness looked ill at ease, as well she might. The only purpose of her evidence was to undermine her daughter's case and help get her alleged rapist acquitted. She could have declined to testify. But as Kieran Raftery, one of the prosecutors, suggested, she was 'pulled two ways', since her own husband was an offender.

Belinda's mother had been called to tell the court that she was *not* present when Gail Cox took her daughter's statement. Then she was cross-examined. Raftery had been sharpening his knives, and he flung them at Belinda's mother, one after the other.

Wasn't it true, Raftery asked her, that she had told detectives early on that she was 'very proud of [Belinda] for coming forward'? Didn't she also remark that Randy and Shawn 'deserved all that they get'?

She replied, 'I may have, yes. I don't remember.'

Raftery asked, 'Do you support [Belinda] in these prosecutions?'

'Yes, I have,' said Belinda's mother. 'But I've also been informed by others that apparently I don't.'

Her loyalties were split between her husband and her daughter, weren't they?

'I thought that I was supporting all of my children.'

Did she still believe Randy and Shawn deserved all they got?

'I'm not a judge. It's not my job, and it would be wrong for me to come here and make opinions or suggestions.'

It was, I reflected as I watched this middle-aged woman sullenly answer questions, one of the lowest points of the whole Pitcairn saga.

By the time she had finished, it was nearly 5 p.m., a time when the court would normally adjourn. However, there was another witness standing by on Pitcairn, and the judge wanted his evidence heard while the satellite link was running. Special arrangements had been made to convey him to the public hall. The witness was sworn in, a uniformed corrections officer at his side.

Stevens Raymond Christian had been in jail for a month. He wore dark blue shorts and a dark blue T-shirt, the uniform of Her Majesty's Prison Pitcairn. His cheeks, usually covered in stubble, were clean-shaven; he looked gaunt in the face and generally thinner.

It was a dramatic moment. Steve had not testified at his own trial. This was the first opportunity to watch him being questioned by counsel. And the drama was barely lessened by the esoteric nature of the issue on which he had been called to speak.

A central plank of Adrian Cook's case was that Belinda could not have been raped near the sugar cane shed, as she claimed. The area was too exposed, the vegetation having been cleared when the islanders carved a track through it. The prosecution maintained that at the time of the alleged rape in mid-1995 the track had not yet been built. Steve was the man who would know for sure, for he had been the supervising engineer and 'number one tractor driver'.

As he told the court, 'I'm familiar with every road on Pitcairn. I could be responsible for putting nearly all the roads on the island.'

In the witness box, Steve initially appeared morose. But as he answered Cook's questions, he positively blossomed. It was as if he could forget, temporarily, the humiliation of being locked up on his own island. He was the community leader again, the man in charge.

Cook asked Steve whether he was acquainted with the area near the sugar cane shed. 'Well, I designed and built that molasses shed in the early '90s, so I should be,' Steve replied.

What about the all-important track?

'I cleared this road. I pushed the road through myself.'

And when had he carried out that work?

In January 1995.

With the aid of photographs provided by Adrian Cook, Steve showed the court around the alleged crime site, pointing out the bamboo grove, the big mango tree, the patch of wild beans. It was close to the Mission House, where Judge Lovell-Smith had lived for six weeks during the Pitcairn trials.

Then it was Simon Moore's turn to quiz Steve. As well as being in overall charge of the prosecution, Moore had led the Crown case against Steve. It was thanks to him that Steve was in jail, and Randy, too; now he was trying to get another of Steve's sons incarcerated. As well as persecuting Steve's family, as Steve no doubt saw it, Moore had dragged the island's name through the mud.

It was to be presumed that Moore was not Steve's favourite person.

As for Moore, this was his first chance to cross-examine Steve. I leant forward, pen poised. This was going to be interesting.

'Good evening, Mr Christian,' said Moore.

'Good evening,' Steve replied tersely.

Then it was on to the track. When had the track been put in?

Wasn't Steve talking about a different track? What were the names by which the various roads on the island were known? How old was that coconut palm in the middle of the photograph? Didn't the Pitcairn records indicate that the relevant track was built in 1996?

The cross-examination continued for two hours without a break. Steve stuck to his story; Simon Moore chipped away at it. The two men argued. They talked over each other. Steve glared at the screen, arms folded, no longer enjoying himself.

Steve turned Moore's questions back on him. What did I just tell you, he asked Moore insolently.

'I don't have to answer the questions, Mr Christian,' Moore responded. 'You tell us what it was you did as far as clearing that road was concerned.'

As a battle of wills, it was transfixing. But it was not sophisticated: it was like watching an arm-wrestle, or a pair of buffalo lock horns. A referee would have given the first couple of rounds to Steve and the match to Moore.

It was 8.20 p.m. in Auckland, 11.20 p.m. on Pitcairn, when a very obviously tired and sulky Steve stepped down from the witness box and returned to his prison cell.

The following morning, Shawn testified in his own defence — the only Pitcairn man yet to do so, bar Jay Warren. He stood in the box, hands behind his back, answering Adrian Cook's questions in his slightly whiney voice.

Again it was the spectacle, rather than the testimony itself, that was riveting. Cook helped Shawn to deny repeatedly that he had raped Belinda. Simon Moore grilled him about whether he and Randy had tipped each other off before they were interviewed. Moore reminded the court that Shawn's father, Steve, had been good friends with Leon Salt, and that at the time of Belinda's dislosures, Randy had been going out with Leon's daughter,

Rachel. Gail Cox, on the island, had kept in almost daily contact with Salt, and had sent Belinda's statement to him. Shawn said he was aware Rachel had told Randy about the allegations, but claimed that Randy did not pass that information on to him. In fact, Shawn had no inkling that anything was amiss until police arrived on his doorstep.

After interviewing Shawn, detectives flew to Norfolk Island and questioned Randy; Moore asked Shawn whether he had phoned his brother before police arrived.

No, said Shawn.

Really, asked Moore.

'I see no reason to. I know we didn't do anything, and why shouldn't I just let him tell his own story?'

Well, said Moore, Randy told police that Shawn did get in touch.

OK, said Shawn, but I didn't mention the investigation to Randy. And if I did, I only talked about myself: I didn't warn him that he was involved too.

Unlike his father, Shawn was no match for Moore. During a break in the proceedings he sat down in the witness box and placed his head in his hands. Giving evidence was, possibly, not the best decision he had ever taken.

Adrian Cook had planned to call not only Belinda's mother, but also her best friend from childhood, Karen. Curiously, Karen had agreed to speak up in Shawn's defence. But she had just delivered a baby and was still in hospital. Cook proceeded to his next witness: Belinda's aunt.

The aunt lived in New Zealand; a former complainant herself, she looked, as Belinda's mother had, uncomfortable in the witness box. She testified that Belinda had fallen down a well and nearly drowned when she was 18 months old; afterwards she 'could no longer walk and seemed to have regressed to a baby'. Belinda, who underwent lengthy medical treatment in New Zealand, had suffered brain damage, her aunt believed. She was afflicted by headaches and black-outs, had to take anti-epilepsy drugs, slept a lot and found it difficult to concentrate. As she grew older, she often spoke 'in an uninhibited and inappropriate way'.

Kieran Raftery asked Belinda's aunt why she had telephoned her niece after a gap of four years, just before she was due to testify at Randy's trial. The aunt insisted that she had spoken to her more recently and claimed the timing was coincidental. 'So,' said Raftery, 'your contacting or attempting to contact [Belinda] so shortly before her trial had nothing to do with trying to dissuade her from giving evidence?'

'No, it was not.'

The last defence witness was Leon Salt, an angular figure with a belligerent demeanour. Salt told the court that Peter George had telephoned him in 2000 after questioning Shawn and Randy. 'He told me that both the accused were convincing, and that they were believable,' he said.

During cross-examination, Simon Mount asked Salt how impartial he considered himself to be, as far as the prosecution was concerned.

'I don't believe I have a bias at all,' replied Salt.

Mount then read out some of the emails that Salt had written to Allen Cox, the former teacher.

Leon Salt scowled. He said, 'I had great difficulty with the process that was being followed.'

Jane Lovell-Smith already knew about Belinda's father's efforts to pressure her, and had just heard about a possible attempt by her aunt. Now Mount questioned Salt about a visit that he had paid to Belinda's workplace in 2003. Salt said he had gone there by arrangement, to collect a parcel to put on the ship to Pitcairn. He disagreed that Belinda might have felt 'intimidated and upset' by his presence.

Mount asked whether, in that case, Belinda's complaint to police had been the result of a misunderstanding.

Salt: 'I believe it's a deliberate set-up on the part of Karen Vaughan. Perhaps coaxed by your office.'

Once again, Simon Mount inquired how impartial Salt considered himself to be.

Salt took a deep breath, and let fly. 'I believe the entire process is fundamentally flawed ... I believe it's totally inappropriate to apply a system of justice designed for 50 million people to 50 people who are all related to one another. I believe it is incredibly unfair that people have been singled out to be charged ... And I believe that justice has not been served for anybody in this matter.'

The judge reserved her verdict until early January.

The following week Brian Young's trial started. Brian had a bit of a problem. During his police interview in 2000, he had owned up to just about everything he was accused of.

Specifically, Brian had admitted to raping three girls in the 1970s, when he was in his early 20s. He thought that Isobel had been about nine at the time, which meant that her sister, Jeanie, would have been seven. The third girl, Isobel's friend, Marion, had been 11. Brian had also confessed to having sex with 14-year-old Janet when he was in his 30s.

In her statement, Isobel said Brian had raped her 'countless times' — perhaps 30 or 40 times over two years, she estimated. Brian told police that, as far as he recalled, it had happened 'only' ten times, at most.

Asked how he felt about his behaviour, he told detectives, 'Fucking disgusting, totally disgusting ... If I could only make my

301

past different, it would definitely be different. It just shatters me to think what I did, you know, it's just bloody sick. But at the time, I must say I didn't think the same way as I feel now.'

How did he think it had affected his victims?

'Not too good, I would imagine,' said Brian. 'Not too good at all.'

In 2001, possibly at his wife's suggestion, Brian had voluntarily embarked on a two-year counselling course for child sex offenders. Despite all of this, he was pleading not guilty — a move that his counsel, Grant Illingworth, acknowledged might be 'a matter of puzzlement' to the trial judge, Charles Blackie. Illingworth attempted to elucidate the puzzle. While Brian accepted that he had 'done wrong', he told the court, and felt 'very great remorse', his version of events differed significantly from the complainants'.

Brian, 52, was charged with six counts of rape, two of indecent assault and one of gross indecency, all against Isobel and Jeanie. Several were specimen charges. The Janet charges had been withdrawn following the House of Lords judgement. Marion was to be dealt with at a separate trial. Brian's brother, Terry, had already been convicted of raping her.

Like Terry, Brian was a big, overweight man. He had greying hair, a dark moustache and coffee-coloured features. His wife, Kari, and daughter, Anette, were in the public gallery when the tape of his police interview was played. Kari looked pained as Brian described the things he did to the three little girls. Anette raised her eyes to the ceiling.

Jeanie settled into the witness box. She was in her late 30s, with collar-length brown hair. Brian leant forward, resting his elbows on the dock, and gazed directly across court at her.

Jeanie's family had moved to New Zealand when she was nine. However, she had a clear memory of her early childhood on the island. She recounted how Brian would call for her and Isobel, and ask their mother's permission to take them off on his motorbike. They were supposed to be helping him to collect firewood, but instead he would drive them to an old hut in an isolated location. Then 'either [Isobel] or myself would go first', while the other watched, Jeanie said.

Brian would lift Jeanie onto a work bench, remove her underwear and climb on top of her. He would rub his penis over her body and make her masturbate him. On one occasion he stuck his penis in her mouth. He would force open her legs and rape her. Then he would get her and Isobel to swap places.

Brian listened to all of this, head tilted, occasionally fingering his moustache.

Jeanie spoke in the present tense, as if she was reliving the assaults even as she described them. 'On one occasion it's in the bush ... but normally it's in the hut.'

The incidents occurred about once a week, Jeanie said. She and Isobel would 'run away [and hide]' if they saw Brian approaching. But their mother always ordered them to go with him, saying, 'Yes, go on, girls, go.' The sisters were scared to tell her what was happening, because Brian had warned them that, if they did, 'we're going to be in big trouble ... And it's all going to be my fault, and no one's going to listen ... No one's going to believe us.'

Jeanie added, speaking with quiet emphasis, that Brian was 'way bigger than me', and she was 'very scared of him ... It felt like he was in control.'

Could she have said no, asked Kieran Raftery.

'No, never ... It didn't even enter into our heads that we can say no.'

It was plain that Jeanie was as fragile as cut glass. Her voice trailed away at the end of sentences. She twisted a silver bangle on her wrist incessantly, as if, in its slim solidity, it was the only thing sustaining her.

I wondered why Brian was putting her through this, after making those damning admissions. Why was he obliging the women to give evidence?

As soon as Grant Illingworth began his cross-examination, it became evident that Brian intended to do his best to regain the considerable ground he had lost in his police interview. It was Brian's case, Illingworth told the judge, that Jeanie had been nine years old, not seven, when he assaulted her. The attacks had been infrequent and spanned just a few months, not two years. Was it possible, Illingworth asked Jeanie, that she was confusing Brian with other men who had abused her?

'Definitely not,' she replied.

Brian denied the masturbation and oral sex. He also denied having sexual intercourse with Jeanie. He might have appeared to admit to it when questioned by police, but he had actually been referring to something different, Illingworth said. He explained, 'Brian will say that there was a custom, if you like, amongst the men on Pitcairn of engaging in ... an artifcial form of intercourse where the penis did not go into the vagina but was rubbed between the thighs.'

That was what Brian had done to Jeanie, Grant Illingworth asserted; he had not penetrated her.

She responded, 'I can actually feel it, the pressure.'

'You've never found Brian to be a dishonest person, have you?' Illingworth inquired.

Jeanie said, 'All I can remember of Brian is the sexual abuse.'

Illingworth asked her why she had waited 22 years to make a complaint.

'Because there are people out here that want to listen, that will listen to my story and what happened to me back home on the island and will believe me,' Jeanie cried.

Illingworth ended his cross-examination on a surreal note, reading out an apology from Brian. 'I am truly sorry for what I did to the three girls, and realise I have been part of their bad memories from the island,' Brian said. 'My only excuse was that I was extremely uneducated. I did not realise what harm I had done, and I wish it had never happened.'

Isobel was two years older than Jeanie, and she told a similar story to her sister. But, poignantly, she told it with greater clarity and extra details, such as the fact that Brian's motorbike had a trailer. It reminded me how very young the girls had been — so young that a two-year age gap conspicuously affected what they remembered.

Isobel spoke so quietly that you had to strain to listen. It was not so much a whisper as a hum — like a voice on the radio with the volume turned down. She ended her sentences with 'erm', as if the 'erm' somehow insulated her from what they contained.

Although he had targeted both girls repeatedly, Brian had been more interested in Isobel, perhaps because she had been a little older. He was always finding pretexts to spirit her off: claiming that he needed her assistance to pick mandarins, for instance, or to hold a torch for him in his workshop. Most of the alleged rapes took place in the hut, with or without Jeanie. As Isobel spoke, she looked straight ahead, as if watching it all unfold in front of her.

Why didn't she resist, Grant Illingworth asked.

Isobel fiddled with the hem of her skirt. Eventually she replied, 'I don't know why I didn't stop him.' She seemed exasperated with her nine-year-old self for not standing up to Brian, and mystified by her own docility.

Isobel then gave a graphic account of the events that had led to her mother finding her soiled underwear. She had gone out to pick strawberries, she said, but Brian diverted her to the hut, and 'I knew what was expected of me to do, take my pants off, get on the bed'. While he was raping her, 'for some unknown reason', Isobel said, she began to weep. 'He said, "Stop your crying ... If you don't stop crying, I'm going to shit inside you." Meaning he was going to come inside me.'

Afterwards Brian was furious and he drove back to Adamstown at speed, 'taking lots of sharp turns and weaving from side to side', Isobel said. She tried to hang onto him, but he pushed her away. 'He was hoping that I would fall off, to make it look like that I'd hurt myself and that's why I was crying.'

A neighbour spotted them, and when Isobel arrived home, she said, 'My mother was standing on the porch and yelling [at] me where have I been, what have you done, and is it true that you let Brian interfere with you? ... She was thumping me on my shoulder and back and head, and said I shouldn't have let Brian do what he had done to me.'

During cross-examination, Isobel almost seemed to enter a trance. She answered Illingworth's questions only after very long pauses. But when he suggested that Brian had not actually had sex with her, but merely simulated it, Isobel suddenly woke up. 'Well, I'm telling you that he did,' she said. 'He definitely did.'

Illingworth started reading out the same apology, but Kieran Raftery interrupted him. It was nonsensical, he said, for Brian to apologise 'for conduct that's very different to the one that she's described'.

As Brian walked over to the witness box, I was struck anew by his size. He was a tall, thick-set, powerfully built man. He wore a crisp blue shirt and grey trousers.

When he was 17, Brian had gone to live in New Zealand for three years. On his return to Pitcairn, he met Kari, whom he subsequently married. They had two children, and raised their family on the island before emigrating to Auckland in 1994. Brian had been the Pitcairn magistrate for five years. Just before his trial opened, he had lost his job in the duty-free warehouse at Auckland airport.

Brian, it seems, had decided to take a gamble. He knew that he could not avoid a jail sentence; however, if he could convince the judge that the abuse had been less serious than the women were claiming, he might get off relatively lightly — more lightly than if he pleaded guilty, which courts always reward with a discount.

It turned out that Brian had been a victim of sexual abuse himself. When he was seven or eight, his family had lived in Auckland, he told the court, and the owner of a suburban grocery shop, a man named John, used to molest him and another boy at the back of the shop. One would wait out the front while the other was assaulted, then they changed places — just like Jeanie and Isobel, as Kieran Raftery noted. Earlier, at the age of six or seven, Brian had been abused by an older boy on the island: a relative of Jeanie's and Isobel's, in fact. The boy had forced Brian to give him oral sex and masturbate him, which was probably why 'these practices, I've never had a kick out of at all', he confided.

As the court was digesting these revelations, Grant Illingworth questioned Brian about the alleged Pitcairn custom of 'rubbing between the thighs'. Brian said that from a very young age he had seen this practised by couples — and while he now appreciated what sexual intercourse entailed, he had thought that police, when they interviewed him, had been referring to 'the rubbing thing'.

Brian claimed that, when he was in his 20s, he had known nothing about the concept or criminality of rape. He had never even heard the word used. 'I didn't know anything about that rape law, because that rape law is not in the Pitcairn law. We don't know that name on Pitcairn before it was invented for this case.' Brian took a swipe at the British government, which he accused of spurning the islanders' pleas for guidance on sexual matters. 'We're just taking the rap for what happened 100 years ago,' he declared, before adding hastily, at Illingworth's prompting, 'I'm not excusing myself at all for what I did.' For years, Brian said, he had been wanting to apologise to his victims.

During a break I chatted to Bill Haigh, who commented that he and Catherine had seen a very different Brian while living on Pitcairn in 1990. 'Brian was a bully boy and show-off, particularly when he was with the other guys,' he said. 'He was on a par with Steve in terms of being a dominant male and throwing his weight about.' Haigh related a story that appeared to illustrate Brian's clout, as well as the islanders' modus operandi. 'I remember one time going out to a ship with them, and the crew got a bit pissed off with the blokes because they were asking for too much from the stores. Brian got really annoyed, telling the others, "This is our livelihood, we've got to butter up these people."'

Next, Brian was cross-examined by Kieran Raftery. I was taken aback by Raftery's manner. He seemed almost angry with Brian. He fired off a volley of aggressive questions. Brian folded his arms and began tapping his foot nervously.

Before long Brian was agreeing with Raftery that 'rape and the wrongness of rape is something that the islanders have a concept of, and have known about all throughout your life'. Sheepishly, he also admitted that he had boasted to his mates about Isobel and Jeanie — although he had not mentioned his exploits to the girls' father. Raftery calmed down a little, but kept up the pressure. He had Brian by the scruff of his neck and shoved up against the wall, metaphorically. It was courtroom tactics: he was bullying the bully. The tactics were successful: Brian dropped his mask.

No longer was he the helpful witness, or the scarred victim of sexual abuse, or the reformed sex offender with all the right phrases at his fingertips. He was an angry, blustering, defensive man — and a man whose attitudes, despite two years of counselling, had not changed much.

Kieran Raftery asked him whether he had threatened to ejaculate inside Isobel.

Brian retorted, 'At that age, what's the chance of pregnancy? ... Why should you worry at that age?' He told the judge that neither of the sisters had protested. On Pitcairn, even younger girls 'throw themselves at men', he claimed.

'Are you suggesting that they actually did want this because they never protested?' demanded Raftery.

'No, I'm just saying how they are very flirtish with men on the island ... [and] strangers who come to the island.'

So in what way, exactly, had Isobel and Jeanie flirted with Brian?

'You talk to them and, like, they're very friendly back to you, and they're suggesting things as well, you know ... They wanted to come on the bike and things like that.'

Raftery asked, 'And you're saying that that was an invitation to abuse them?'

'Well, they did not protest,' Brian replied.

Kieran Raftery pointed out that Brian had been much older than the girls, and large enough to overpower any resistance.

'But I didn't,' said Brian.

'No, because you didn't have to, did you? Because you were an adult authority figure and big and powerful. So they just had to do what you wanted them to do. Just as you had to do what John wanted you to do.'

Lastly, Raftery probed the issue of Brian's remorse. Was he really sorry, or just sorry for himself — sorry that he had got caught? If he was really sorry, why had he fought extradition every step of the way, asked Raftery. Why was he denying all of the charges? Why had he not apologised years ago, as he claimed to have wanted to?

On legal advice, Brian repeated.

Why, asked Raftery, had he insisted on seeing new affidavits from the women, reiterating that they still planned to testify, before he would make up his mind whether to plead guilty or not?

After a pause, Brian said, 'I really need to get advice from my lawyer on that one.'

'Unfortunately you're not in a position to talk to him in the middle of your evidence,' Raftery told him.

Originally supportive of Operation Unique, Kari Boye Young had become a leading voice opposing it. She was better educated and more articulate than many Pitcairners. She told everyone that Brian's offending was 'at the very minor end of the scale', and just before his trial began sent out an email to friends and allies. 'Don't expect us to roll over and give up,' she warned. 'Alfred Dreyfus [the French–Jewish military officer wrongfully convicted of treason in a celebrated case in the late 19th century] would have rotted in his cell if his supporters had not kept on fighting.'

Testifying in her husband's defence, Kari said that she had been fascinated by Pitcairn from an early age, when she had watched *Mutiny on the Bounty*, starring Clark Gable. She had trained as a ship's radio officer, and eventually got herself to the island in 1973.

A middle-aged woman with a short grey bob, Kari recalled that Brian had been 'sexually ignorant' when they met. 'He didn't know what foreplay was, for example,' she told the court, with a girlish giggle. 'And neither [did] other Pitcairners, because I had relationship [sic] with two other Pitcairners before I married Brian.' In Scandinavia, children were educated about sex, Kari said.

'On Pitcairn, there was a lot of sex, but no sex education other than what they saw their elders do in the bush.'

Kari confirmed that Brian 'does not enjoy oral sex at all'. Nor did he enjoy being masturbated. Asked how she would characterise sexual standards on Pitcairn, she replied, 'Below standard. They didn't know anything about the ethics in sex at all. There was no such thing as being faithful ... I don't know any married couple on Pitcairn who were faithful to each other.'

Questioned about the episode where Isobel's mother had blamed Brian for the state of her daughter's knickers, Kari shrugged it off, saying it had not been 'a big issue to me'.

Lastly, Kari revealed that she and Brian had not had sex for five years. She explained, 'He does not have erection any more.'

There was, it appeared, nothing that Brian was not willing to own up to, apart from raping those two little girls.

Later that week Ron Christian, the third off-islander to go to court, was sentenced at Papakura. Ron, who lives in New Zealand, is Carol Warren's son and the former partner of Nadine Christian. He had pleaded guilty to three counts of indecently assaulting two girls, one of whom had been eight or nine years old. In each case he had crept into their bedroom at night and started molesting them while they were sleeping. Neither woman was prepared to give evidence against Ron.

Russell Johnson, the judge, took what he called the 'unusual step' of discharging Ron without conviction, merely ordering him to pay NZ$2000 (£700) in reparations. He acknowledged that such crimes would normally attract a jail sentence, but noted that, as well as pleading guilty, Ron had displayed remorse. What was more, one of his victims had provided a statement in which she called him 'a wonderful person not deserving of punishment'.

Johnson added, 'It is with regret that I read that it is still being said by some that what you were doing was something which was to do with the way of life which was accepted on Pitcairn.'

Three weeks later, in January 2007, the Pitcairn court sat to deliver judgement on Shawn Christian and Brian Young. I was back in Australia, but was given an eyewitness account of the proceedings.

The public gallery was full. Among those present were Shawn's partner, Michele; his aunt, Clarice Oates; his uncle, Kay Brown; his sister, Tania Christian; Kay's wife, Lorraine; Brian's wife, Kari; Leon Salt and his wife, Brenda; and Julie Christian, Dennis's sister. Two uniformed police officers flanked the dock. The first to occupy it was Brian, the most serious offender, allegedly, of all the men who had gone to trial.

Charles Blackie found Brian guilty of five rapes and one indecent assault, and not guilty of one specimen charge of rape. He acquitted Brian of gross indecency and one indecent assault, observing that while the latter charge — which concerned the oral sex allegation — was not irrefutably proved, 'I have strong suspicions as to the accused's conduct.'

The policemen escorted Brian through a door behind the dock which led down to the cells. He waved at Kari before he vanished.

Then it was Shawn's turn. The previous afternoon, Shawn and Michele had got married at a civil ceremony in Auckland. Adrian Cook, Shawn's defence counsel, gave away the bride.

Jane Lovell-Smith convicted Shawn on all three counts of rape. Shawn did not look particularly surprised or upset. Perhaps he and Brian had already resigned themselves to this outcome. As Shawn, too, was taken off to the cells, he mouthed 'I love you' at Michele. His sister, Tania, began to cry. So did Julie Christian and Shawn's uncle, Kay.

As soon as the court rose, Kari, Michele and Cook marched up to the prosecution table, where Kieran Raftery and Simon Mount were clearing away papers. Adrian Cook said, 'You've been very good to me personally, but this whole case is shit, and you know it.'

Michele told the lawyers, 'You two have made this the worst day of my life.'

Kari declared, 'This is corruption on a grand scale.'

Earlier, someone had overheard a conversation between Kari, Julie, Michele and Leon Salt. 'That Kathy Marks,' they were saying, 'she knew what these verdicts and sentences were going to be in 2000 ... It was all a set-up, and she was in on it.'

It seemed that no amount of evidence about the Pitcairn men's crimes — nor extensive admissions by Brian, nor guilty pleas by Dennis Christian, Dave Brown and Ron Christian — could penetrate the wall of loyalty constructed by their families and supporters.

Shawn and Brian were taken by van to Auckland's Mount Eden prison, a medium-security men's institution with a tough reputation, where they were segregated for their own safety. Sentencing had been put off until March for logistical reasons. Jail terms were inevitable, though, and the two men had already elected to serve them on Pitcairn, rather than in the Mount Eden sex offenders' unit. With bail withdrawn, the pair agreed to travel to the island. Graham Ford, the court registrar, drafted what was, in essence, a transportation order, 'to convey two convicted prisoners in custody from Papakura to Pitcairn Island by direct sea voyage for sentencing by satellite'. Ford says, 'There's been nothing like it since convicts were transported from the UK to Australia in 1788.'

Five days later, Brian and Shawn boarded the *Braveheart*, which was to carry them all the way to Pitcairn. They could not be flown via Tahiti, because that would have meant them leaving the jurisdiction, so a rough two-week passage across the Pacific was the only option. Four corrections officers accompanied the prisoners, who were supervised around the clock but allowed to stroll on deck during the day. Shawn was seasick, as were two of his jailors.

The *Braveheart* arrived off Pitcairn in late January 2007. The men were ushered up the hill and into the jail, where they joined Brian's brother, Terry, and Shawn's father and brother, Steve and Randy. A dozen islanders had gathered outside Big Fence, Shawn's family home, to watch them pass.

Later, in a written judgement, Jane Lovell-Smith said she had found Belinda a 'credible, honest and reliable witness' who 'never faltered with her evidence'. Shawn, by contrast, had been 'unconvincing and evasive', while Steve had been 'deliberately unhelpful and disingenuous in cross-examination'.

Of Brian, Charles Blackie wrote that it was 'abundantly clear that he wanted sexual activity with a young girl'. Referring to the assaults on Jeanie, the judge said, 'It was solely for his pleasure. He was a grown man in his 20s, she was a child ... His conduct was without a thought of her ... wellbeing, whether physical or mental, and without a thought to the consequences of what he was doing.'

In March 2007 Brian and Shawn were escorted to the public hall to be sentenced via satellite link. In Papakura, Grant Illingworth announced that Brian had changed his plea in relation to his third victim, Marion. He now admitted serially raping and assaulting her, and also forcing her to perform oral sex — a practice that, according to him, he'd 'never had a kick out of'.

The prosecution recommended 12 years in prison for Brian. Chief Justice Blackie addressed him sternly, saying, 'Three different individuals have had their lives devastated, or certainly seriously affected, by your conduct.' Despite that fact, he jailed Brian for just six and a half years.

Crown lawyers requested seven or eight years for Shawn. Jane Lovell-Smith gave him three and a half. As with Blackie, the judge's words were harsher than her actions. She told Shawn, 'This offending has almost destroyed this young woman [Belinda] . . . She has suffered persecution. She has suffered very significant emotional and psychological harm.'

The sentences were remarkably lenient, even by comparison with those handed down on the island. With Brian and Shawn, moreover, there had not been the supposed mitigating factor of their contribution to the community. Neither had lived on Pitcairn for years.

For some, though, even those penalties were too severe. Kari and Brian's daughter, Anette, lashed out at the prosecution lawyers, the police and, most of all, Tom and Betty Christian's family. In a widely circulated email, she expressed the hope that they all 'burn in hell', and concluded, 'NONE OF THOSE MEN DESERVE TO BE IN JAIL!'

CHAPTER 19

Reaping a sad legacy since *Bounty* times

It started as a routine chat about Pitcairn life with a woman who grew up there some decades ago. But after reminiscing about picnics and sports days and boat trips, Judith, as I will call her, suddenly broke off. 'It wasn't all ideal,' she said. 'There was sexual offending then too, and I was a victim.'

Judith, an eloquent, reflective woman, was not among those who took part in the trials. She did not wish to pursue her half-dozen assailants, and anyway, some of them were already dead. She seems to want to talk now. But she finds it hard to.

For years she had kept her memories hidden in a dark place. Then British police began excavating the past. Other women were telling their stories, and Judith could no longer ignore the insistent echo of her own experiences. 'You think, why me? What did I do wrong? Why was I picked on?' she says. 'It still makes me sick to think about it. How can guys behave like that? It's just disgusting.'

The conversation is taking place in a crowded coffee shop. Judith wipes her eyes on a paper napkin. 'I'm sorry,' she says. 'I don't mean to embarrass you.'

The abuse started when she was six or seven years old. Morris Christian would ambush her as she walked home from school. 'Mento [Morris] would chase you and grab you between the legs,' recalls Judith. 'He would rub himself up against you. It was horrible.' She did her best to stay safe, changing her route to avoid him and others who might be lying in wait. 'I tried to stick to the main road,' she says. 'As a child, I was scared to walk in the back lanes on my own, even in the middle of the day.'

But she was not secure at home either. Judith remembers sitting at the piano one day when she was 11 or 12. 'A neighbour came up behind me and put his hands around my chest. I was paralysed. I just waited for him to stop and go away.' That man, like others who molested her, was her father's age. When Judith began dating, one of her father's friends took her aside. He said, 'Listen, guys your age don't know what to do. You need to be broken in by one of us older guys.'

Judith told no one, not even her friends, what was happening. 'You didn't talk about these things back then,' she says. 'Sex was a dirty word. Anyway, who could you go to? Some of these guys were respected members of the community. There was no one to tell. So you just put up with it.'

Pausing, she gazes at her coffee. 'I don't understand it,' she says. 'People on the island seem to love kids, and if anything was done to them physically, there'd be hell to pay. But this is much more serious, and it hurts a lot more, even though you can't see it.'

As well as facing her own past, Judith is having to come to terms with the fact that her daughters were also abused. 'I didn't protect them,' she tells me, starting to weep. 'I had no idea this was still going on. I was naïve enough to think that once those old buggers died off, that was it. I have screwed up big time; I feel like I've failed as a mother. And they still haven't talked to me about it.'

When Judith had her first period, her mother scolded her, saying, 'You must have been going with boys.' Judith says, 'In her mind, apparently, the two things were connected.' Her mother grew up in the early 20th century, and seemingly had sex just before puberty, if not earlier. It is unlikely that she consented. She gave birth to her first child at a very young age.

Judith's grandmother was married to a much older man. Large age gaps were not uncommon then; nevertheless, it is reasonable to wonder how that relationship started.

Judith and her daughters, Judith's mother, and her mother before her. 'I think the abuse has always gone on,' she says. 'I think that sort of behaviour has carried on right since the *Bounty* days.'

Is she right? Did the sexual abuse begin with the mutineers and continue uninterrupted for more than two centuries, until it was halted (as far as is known) in 1999, when Belinda protested? It is impossible to be sure, of course. But what is certain is that the community was founded on sexual coercion. And there is anecdotal or documented evidence of abuse for much of the 20th century, at least.

After the mutiny, the *Bounty* returned to Tahiti to drop off 16 men who planned to stay there. Fletcher Christian invited some of the locals — mainly women — below deck, and while feasting was under way he cut the anchor cable. Only a few of the Tahitians were in on the plot. When the others realised that they were moving, one woman jumped overboard. Others tried to follow. The sailors put six older women ashore on a nearby island; that left a dozen females, including a girl of 14, for the 15 men.

Such is the basis on which Pitcairn was established: women abducted and shared out like rations of rum, then held captive, effectively, on a remote island 1,300 miles from home.

Next followed the John Adams era, with its adoption of Christian virtues, chief among them chastity and monogamy. Attitudes towards women had, on the face of it, changed overnight. However, some historians doubt all was as it appeared. If sexual morals were pristine, we only have Adams' word for it. Adams, who took three 'wives' after half of his fellow mutineers had been murdered. Adams, who lived in almost total isolation with nine women and 24 children, including a dozen girls aged under 12. Adams, whose stepdaughter accused him of killing her mother 'by his cruel treatment of her', according to the historian Caroline Alexander.

Then came the second generation: the children who had seen their fathers slaughtered and their mothers passed around, among them the growing boys for whom Adams was the only role model. The colony's blameless veneer was tarnished when Adams' own daughter, Dinah, gave birth to the first illegitimate child. His successor, John Buffett, an English sailor, married a local woman named Dorothy Young, but later took to drinking and 'seduced one of the young girls, by whom he has two children', according to William Waldegrave, the captain of a visiting British warship. In the decades that followed, persistent reports of 'immoral' behaviour trickled out.

In 1903 an Englishman, Walter Petsch, settled on the island with his Pitcairn-born wife, Maude Young. He became the school-teacher. Two years later Maude died. Within five weeks Petsch had remarried. The haste of it scandalised some islanders, and it was rumoured that he had poisoned his wife, or fed her crushed glass. But that was not all. One local wrote to a French colonial official in Mangareva that Maude had learnt about her husband's 'misdemeanour towards the girl (his scholar at school) ... Before she died one of her sisters told me she died of broken heart [sic].'

Albert Reeves, it seems, may not have been the first outsider who allegedly abused his position as teacher.

Six years earlier, Harry Christian had murdered his wife and baby girl. And what was his motive? Captain Henry Dyke of HMS *Comus* reported, 'It appears he had previously seduced her [his wife], but was anxious to get her out of the way so as to be lawfully married to another woman.' Or, as it was later explained, Christian was 'very jealous for a younger mate'.

In his police interview, Brian Young told detectives, 'You know, all the men on the island are doing things with girls ... [It's] one of the things that's been happening on Pitcairn ever since I was a kid. Actually, it probably goes right back to the *Bounty*'s time. I mean, the history speaks for itself.'

In police jargon, it is an 'Anacapa chart': a diagram illustrating the links in a complex criminal inquiry. The lines are not supposed to intersect; when it came to Pitcairn, though, the draughtsman was defeated. The chart, demonstrating who did what to whom on the island, is a tangle of crazily criss-crossing lines. It underscores the sheer scale of the sexual offending, as well as the nightmarish way in which relationships intertwined.

The diagram reminds us that the evidence heard during the nine recent trials represents only a fraction of what allegedly went on during one limited period in the island's history. Take Marion, a quietly spoken woman with a gentle demeanour, who was raped by Brian and Terry Young as a child. What she suffered at the brothers' hands was awful enough, but they were not Marion's only assailants. She named a number of other men, some of whom had died before the investigation began. Others she did not wish to be prosecuted. In fact, Marion had been raped so many times that when police asked her whether she was assaulted in the church on one occasion, as a friend claimed to have witnessed, she replied, 'I don't remember that ... [but] I'm not saying it didn't happen.'

Marion's friend, Jeanie, who gave evidence against Brian, was abused by other men too, most of them now dead. They included Oscar Clarke, Pitcairn's long-time postmaster, and Elwyn Christian.

It was Elwyn who had raped Elizabeth in the 1930s, leaving her unable to conceive. Forty years on he was still terrorising little girls, allegedly — in concert with his wife, Evelyn Totenhopfer. Evelyn had been the island's long-time nursing officer; an Australian Seventh-day Adventist, she was highly regarded for her mission work in the Solomon Islands. She was posted to Pitcairn in 1946 and settled there permanently, marrying Elwyn, who was more than a decade her junior.

Elwyn and Evelyn were childless. They invited children into their home. They gave them chocolate and nuts, and Evelyn would serve up delicious desserts. Among the girls who visited was Jeanie, who was about six at the time.

According to the girls, Elwyn would molest them in turn while his wife looked on from close quarters. The other children would also spectate. Sometimes the couple would have sex in front of them, or Evelyn would perform oral sex on Elwyn.

Elwyn was in his late 60s. Evelyn was nearly 80 and walked with a stick. They left pornographic magazines lying around. Jeanie told me 'Nurse would just sit there watching. At the time it seemed normal. I just went along with it.'

When Prince Philip visited Pitcairn in 1971, the Foreign Office provided him with a briefing paper about the place and personalities. Elwyn and Evelyn, he was informed, were 'a pleasant couple who live rather apart from the other islanders'.

Evelyn is the only woman implicated in the history of abuse on Pitcairn; both she and Elwyn went to the grave with their reputations intact. So did men such as Clinton Warren, Albert Young, Cairn Christian and Andrew Young, the long-time island secretary — all of them named by various women. Other alleged offenders were very old or very frail by the time of the police investigation. Andrew Young's son, Pervis, a former magistrate, died not long after it started, as did Fletcher Christian, Steve's elder brother. Apart from Catherine's mother, two other women told police that Fletcher had assaulted them. They were five or six at the time; he overpowered the struggling girls, who half a century on still remembered how petrified they had been of him.

Fletcher denied the allegations before he died.

His daughters, Vanda and Janine, both committed suicide in 1993.

Pervis's son, Daryl, had been one of the boys who allegedly held Jennifer down for Steve Christian. Police decided not to prosecute Daryl, who had only been ten or 11 at the time, or the man who had allegedly assisted him — Brian Young. Both men denied involvement in the incident.

Then there was Morris Christian, who appears to have emulated the behaviour that he saw around him. Nearly every Pitcairn woman from the past half-century has a tale about Morris, who was pouncing on young girls right up until his death in 1984 at the age of 80. Morris was also a kleptomaniac. He occasionally turned violent, and doctors warned he was capable of murder. In the mid-20th century British authorities considered putting him into care in Fiji. However, the Adventist Church declined to help, and British officials later pronounced him 'quite harmless'. Morris's half-brother and guardian was Elwyn Christian. He spent periods living with Elwyn and Evelyn.

Among Mento's victims was Jennifer. Now in her 50s, Jennifer was attacked by as many as a dozen men. Her entire childhood was disfigured by sexual abuse. She reached the point, she told police, where she was 'virtually hiding behind a tree, waiting for the next bloke to come along and rape her'. Only two of Jennifer's assailants have been prosecuted: Len Brown and Steve Christian. Another man, Cairn Christian, who raped her 'for a bet', wrote to her when he was elderly, claiming to have rediscovered his faith and asking for forgiveness. Jennifer burnt his letter, muttering to herself, 'Now you can burn in hell.' Cairn, who was Dennis Christian's uncle, evaded earthly justice, dying just before police descended.

With the exception of Len Brown and Jay Warren, those who went to court were charged with only a portion of their alleged crimes. Seven women named Steve Christian. Six named Randy Christian. Five named Shawn Christian. Six named Terry Young. Eight named Dave Brown, with one of those accusing him of a violent rape, which he denied. Even these figures — combined with the names of men who could not be prosecuted, for whatever reason — may not convey the full picture of abuse. Detectives estimate that they unearthed only 40 to 60 per cent of the offending from recent decades. Some women refused to be interviewed. Some did not divulge everything, police believe. Some could not be traced. Some of the crimes predated Britain's Sexual Offences Act taking effect on Pitcairn in 1959.

Among those accused but never charged is at least one man still living on the island.

One of the Pitcairn matriarchs who was critical of Operation Unique was 12 years old when she had her first child. Karen Vaughan spoke to her about it. 'Surely you weren't able to consent to sex when you were 11?' she asked. The woman smiled. 'You haven't done your homework, have you?' she replied. 'That was my second child. The first one died.'

Vaughan says, 'She can only have been nine or ten the first time she got pregnant.'

Information about the abuse of boys is frustratingly sparse. However, it seems inconceivable that it was not a feature of Pitcairn life too.

Brian Young told police about two island men as well as the Auckland shopkeeper. He was prepared to testify — until he was charged himself. According to Brian, the same assailants molested four other Pitcairn boys. Two of them have since been convicted of child sex offences. When questioned by detectives, three of them denied being victims. The fourth admitted it, but did not wish to make a statement.

That left police with no complaints to pursue, although Brian said he was sure other boys had been assaulted. How many will probably never be known, as few men are likely to own up to it. For Brian to do so, says Kari, 'was almost worse for him than admitting about what he had done with [the three girls]. Because he thought people would think he was queer.'

As for the girls, they endured an almost perpetual onslaught. Marion told the court that teenage boys and adult men 'took any opportunity available to them to touch or grab the young girls ... I didn't enjoy this but over time became used to it.' On Pitcairn, where children were supposed to be safe because no strangers could intrude, they were continually at risk. They were even attacked at home — by brothers, uncles, cousins and grandfathers. As far as is known, no father assaulted a daughter; perhaps that was the last taboo. A number of men who had committed incest avoided being prosecuted, as their victims were unwilling to give evidence.

It did not help to belong to a powerful family. Girls related to magistrates and other influential figures were targeted too. Men had virtually unrestricted access to young girls. On an overnight camping trip in the 1980s, Brian Young and Dave Brown were the only adults in charge. At home, no one bothered to lock doors and windows, for Pitcairn was, theoretically, crime-free. So at night, after the power had gone off, predators went in search of easy prey: girls asleep in bed.

During daylight hours, men would ask girls to 'go ride' or 'come here'. It was not so much a request as an instruction. Even girls of five or six knew what 'come here' meant, and what was about to happen. The men never showed any affection; in fact, they barely said a word. One woman told police that she had lost her virginity at a young age, but years later had never been kissed.

The background against which these events took place was one of general promiscuity. That is not a moral judgement: such is life in many small communities, and Pitcairn appears to be an extreme case. Sexual activity starts early and involves numerous partners. Marital infidelity is accepted and even joked about. Babies born of casual liaisons are absorbed into families, with the father's identity sometimes kept a mystery. Adoption is common. One woman was presented, as a small baby, to a couple who could not conceive — as a gift on their wedding day.

In addition, it seems, there has always been tolerance on Pitcairn of unconventional pairings. In 1898 one local 'had a child by her sister's son', an American missionary reported. In the 1950s a woman was engaged in 'intimate relations with an old widower' who regularly joined her family for meals. Her husband was 'not the slightest worried', according to the teacher, Roy Sanders, who was aware of two similar set-ups. More recently there was Steve Christian and his 'three wives', none of whom appeared to mind sharing him. A woman on the island has slept with her niece's husband. A middle-aged man has had an affair with his aunt.

As will have become obvious, there is little privacy on Pitcairn. According to many former residents, children watched adults having sex together and swapping partners. They heard them talking openly about sex. They viewed their parents' pornographic videos. From the age of five or six, children 'played' at sex. They would take off their clothes and touch each other's bodies. Sometimes it went beyond that. At seven, one girl began having sexual intercourse with a boy the same age. Not long afterwards she had sex with a second boy.

At the same time, girls were being abused by older men. That seemed to be part of life, and while it was extremely unpleasant, they resigned themselves to it. Girls were told, and excitedly told each other, that 12 was the age of consent. It was then that they would become women — although many were 'initiated' younger and consent rarely entered into it.

No wonder that, to visitors, young girls on Pitcairn appeared sexually provocative and precociously 'knowing'. No wonder that, for generations, the island's women have had an 'easy' reputation.

After being assaulted once or twice, girls were usually compliant. In a rough and ready way they were 'groomed'. One girl was molested when she was about eight. A few years later the same man raped her. It was agonisingly painful. A few months later he raped her again. This time she did not resist. The third time it did not hurt quite so much. She started to enjoy it, and gradually became infatuated with the man. Soon she was having sex with anyone who asked her. Men of all ages exploited her.

Such are the women whom Olive Christian has called 'these bitches that was put on the video link'. Olive proclaimed in an angry email, 'We all on Pitcairn know the history of these girls.'

Melva Evans wrote to the brother of Elizabeth, who as a girl had been raped by Elwyn Christian. Melva, who had spoken to her own mother, a contemporary of Elizabeth's, informed him, 'Your sister was a loose woman, known for her hospitality.'

There was sunshine and there was darkness in Jacqui Christian's childhood. She talks nostalgically about flying kites, sailing boats and climbing trees. 'We swam in the bay and the rock pools,' says Jacqui, the eldest of Tom and Betty's four daughters. 'I remember a big swing under the banyan trees, and sliding down the hill on coconut palm leaves.'

The darkness could descend at any time. Jacqui was three when she was first molested. By the age of 15, when she left for New Zealand, she had been assaulted by at least five men. 'I'm a fast learner, so I avoided being around adult males as much as possible,' she told me. 'From my experience, your immediate family, you were fine. But anything other than that, you were cautious, because you didn't know who to trust and who not.'

Jacqui says, 'It felt wrong. There was secrecy and fear, and being told not to say anything. You feel embarrassed and ashamed. You don't know who to talk to, so you don't talk to anyone.

'I didn't particularly like being a girl, because I thought if I wasn't a girl, it wouldn't happen.'

To what extent had it clouded her daily life, I asked Jacqui. 'You're always conscious of it, because if you weren't, how would you avoid it?' she replied. 'Of course, it can be hard to avoid people in a place like that. And I count myself lucky, because my experiences were not as terrible as some of the others I've heard about.'

In New Zealand, Jacqui boarded at a Seventh-day Adventist college in Palmerston North. She studied pharmacy, moved to Australia and, at the age of 20, got married. She told her husband, Peter, a little about her childhood. But it was not until her late 20s that she started dealing with it in earnest.

'A friend gave me books to read,' she says. 'It was then that I first became aware of the word "abuse". Initially I felt relief that it's not unique to me, a lot of other women go through it, and help was available.

'I started to feel that I didn't need to hide behind shame and feel guilty, that it wasn't my fault. I've always been quite a workaholic, trying to prove my worth through work and achievement and study. I started to think maybe I didn't need to work myself to death to try and prove that I was worthwhile.'

Jacqui sought counselling. She also addressed a chronic health problem, using acupuncture and massage. Gradually her anger and hatred evaporated. Around that time, her marriage collapsed. Soon afterwards the police investigation began, and Jacqui agreed to make a statement. Later she suffered nightmares and flashbacks. She then had to wait four years for the trials. Testifying by video link from Auckland brought her memories, still distressingly vivid, all back.

Now 35, she has 'forgiven the guys', Jacqui says, and 'processed the shame' of it. 'But it's taken 20 years of living in a different community. I've been hiding away for 20 years, really.' She is still feeling the after-effects of sexual abuse. 'I was never game to have children, because I was afraid I wouldn't be able to protect them. I guess it has affected my relationships. I'm going through a divorce again, so obviously I haven't figured it out yet.

'I can still mistrust people and have that misapprehension, particularly when I find myself alone with guys I don't know.'

Despite the upheaval caused by the prosecution, Jacqui — who spoke to me in her own name — is certain that she did the right thing. She says, 'I personally believe that probably every generation on the island has had abuse. I saw the trials as a chance to halt the destructive behaviour and make Pitcairn safe.'

Jacqui was one of eight women who gave evidence. A ninth, Linda, was standing by, but was not called because Dave Brown pleaded guilty. For some of those who testified, it was at great personal cost. Marion has been cut off by her family, and accused in letters — some anonymous, one from her sister — of testifying for money. Charlotte, one of Steve Christian's victims, is also estranged from her family. Like Marion, she is trying to rebuild relationships.

Most of the women who went to court were not seeking revenge. They wanted their abusers to acknowledge they had done wrong and say sorry. They wanted the culture on the island changed. Jeanie says, 'Hopefully the younger ones are growing up safe now. I'd like to think that I helped put a stop to it, stopped other kids from going through what I did.'

The men had predicted that these nine women, like the other complainants, would back out eventually. They underestimated their resilience and courage. After giving evidence, Marion was 'walking on air', according to Karen Vaughan.

Jeanie told me, 'I always remembered Brian Young as being really big and strong and terrifying, like a giant or monster-type person. When I saw him in court, he looked so small, and I suddenly realised he can't bully me any more, he can't tell me not to tell anyone . . . I'm not that little girl any more.'

In statements to the court, the women indicated how much they had suffered as a result of the abuse. Marion said that Brian had robbed her of her 'childhood innocence', and 'made it very hard for me to trust and be intimate with members of the opposite sex'. Thanks to him, sex meant 'something dirty and painful' to Marion. Another woman described how she used to spy on her husband while he was bathing or changing their children.

Jeanie's older sister, Jennifer, remains intensely frustrated that many of her abusers were dead by the time of Operation Unique.

She told the court, 'I often feel that my family would be better off if I were dead. I sometimes have an urge to drive into a brick wall and end the pain. I think these urges are mainly an expression of the enormous anger I feel.'

After settling in New Zealand with her family, Jeanie went through a series of abusive relationships. She repeatedly tried to harm herself. Her only clear memories of childhood on Pitcairn, she told me in an interview in Wellington in late 2007, are the sexual abuse — and the fact there was 'no one to stick up for you'.

Thirty years on, she 'can't bear' the sound of children screaming in the park, even in play. 'It sounds like they're crying out for help,' Jeanie says quietly. Recently she saw an advertisement in a New Zealand newspaper, seeking a teacher for the school on Pitcairn. She says, 'When I see the words "Pitcairn Island", I feel queasy in my stomach.' Jeanie has never been back to the island. Nor have her sisters, Jennifer and Isobel.

Belinda has not seen her father or brother for eight years. They have never met her partner or her two small children. Her mother and sister have visited her once in New Zealand. That was before her mother testified against her.

Without her grandparents, who looked after her devotedly, and her partner, whom she met several years ago, Belinda would probably have abandoned the court case. Without them, she might not have survived. She 'has felt like dying,' she told Shawn Christian's trial.

Belinda declined to be interviewed. She still finds it hard to talk, even to loved ones. Being rejected by her family, say those close to her, has been the most hurtful part of it — worse than being raped. She and her partner live in a little weatherboard house in a seaside town on the North Island. They have a little boy and a baby girl.

Belinda's grandmother lives opposite them. Her beloved grandfather died in 2006; it was a crushing loss.

In a statement before he died, her grandfather said Belinda had been 'in a very bad way' after being forced to leave Pitcairn. She had found it difficult to settle in New Zealand. She had dropped out of school. She had been tearful, homesick and suicidal, convinced that her father hated her, and feeling 'worthless and unloved by her people'.

Belinda told the court, 'At times I wish I had never made my complaint. That way I would not have been taken from my home and family. I have been told I have to stay in New Zealand. I am 3000 miles away from home ... I think of my family constantly ... I love them and miss them very much.

'I feel ostracised and cast out from the island. I feel disowned by my father. I wish my mum was with me to help me through this ... I feel abandoned. I cry about this a lot.'

More than anything, Belinda wants the men who raped her — Randy and Shawn Christian — to admit their guilt. 'She's being punished more than them,' says a friend. 'They may be in prison, but at least they're close to their families. She's lost everything: her home, her identity, her culture. Because of them, she'll never be able to go back to the island, and she'll probably never have a relationship with her family again.'

Her other grandfather has turned against Belinda, dismissing her as 'a slut'. She is no longer in touch with aunts and uncles in New Zealand, whom she once saw regularly. She remains, however, in intermittent phone and email contact with her mother and siblings.

Belinda hates being thought of as the person who set off the investigation. She detests media coverage of the case, which she considers sympathetic to the men. According to a relative, while waiting for the trials she frequently 'talked of forgetting the whole thing and getting on with her life'. Simon Moore told the court, 'She has often questioned the decision to come forward with her own story. She often regrets the decision to give evidence.'

Despite everything that has been thrown at her, Belinda kept going. Karen Vaughan says, 'She knows what's right and what's wrong. She knows what justice is, and what she should be doing for herself.'

Belinda has lived with the case for one-third of her short life. As I watched her give evidence twice, she struck me as a tragic figure, but a survivor. She told police in 2000, 'I want it to stop.' Since the legal process ended, Belinda has been 'walking with a lighter step', says a friend. He adds, 'I'm so proud of her. She's saved a lot of girls from what she went through.'

I sometimes imagine the island as a tapestry, woven from decades of secrecy and abuse. Belinda unpicked the first stitch. With each victim who came forward, a little more of the picture unravelled.

By the end of the police investigation, the tapestry was frayed. Since then, it has been patched up a little. Some of the women who spoke out recanted, judging the repercussions too great.

Others, too old or too compromised, stayed silent throughout.

Those who died before Operation Unique started never got the chance to speak.

Their sisters, nieces, daughters and granddaughters have spoken for them.

CHAPTER 20

Lord of the Flies?

It is wartime, and a plane carrying a group of British schoolboys crash-lands on a deserted island after being shot down over the Pacific. The boys discover that no adults survived. They must fend for themselves until they are rescued. At first they behave in a civilised manner, holding public meetings and voting on key decisions. They elect a sensible leader, Ralph, and agree on the importance of building shelters and keeping a signal fire burning.

But the fledgling community swiftly degenerates. Jack, formerly the head choirboy, starts hunting pigs, and other boys get hooked on the thrill of the chase. Most of them desert Ralph to join Jack's 'tribe'. In vain does Piggy, Ralph's ally, ask, 'Which is better — to have rules and agree, or to hunt and kill?'

The castaways fear that a 'Beast' is roaming the forest. Jack impales a sow's head on a stick to appease it. One of Ralph's followers, Simon, stumbles across the head, surrounded by buzzing flies, and hears it telling him, 'I'm the Beast ... I'm part of you.' When Simon returns, the boys are celebrating their bloodlust in a ritual dance. They fall on him in a frenzy and beat him to death. One of Jack's lieutenants, Roger, drops a boulder on Piggy, killing him.

Now Ralph is alone and being stalked. He knows Jack is planning to kill him. Fleeing to the beach, he meets an unexpected saviour: a British naval officer from a passing ship. 'I should have thought,' says the officer, 'that a pack of British boys would have been able to put up a better show than that.'

In the final scene of *Lord of the Flies*, William Golding's classic fable, Ralph weeps for 'the end of innocence' and 'the darkness of man's heart'.

Golding's message is clear: we are brutish and cruel, and it is only society's constraints that prevent us from behaving like animals. When those constraints are removed, along with the rule of law, we quickly descend from civilisation to savagery.

Pitcairn seems to confirm Golding's dark vision. Like his unnamed island, it was a social laboratory, but a real one — the site of a unique experiment thrown up by a confluence of historical events. Put 15 men, 12 women and a baby on a rock, leave them alone for 200 years, then take off the lid. We already know that the results were ugly, but were they inevitable? Would a different set of people, placed in the same circumstances, have acted the same way? Or were there, on Pitcairn, exceptional factors that helped determine this particular outcome?

Pitcairn is the world's most remote inhabited spot. Although there are islands that are more physically isolated, they possess superior communications. Easter Island, due east of Pitcairn, has an airport. Tristan da Cunha and St Helena, pinpricks in the South Atlantic that are British colonies too, are served by a scheduled boat service.

Furthermore, Pitcairn is the world's smallest territory. For the past 40 years, its population has hovered at or under 60 to 70 people. And it is a closed community — partly because of its location, but also at the islanders' wishes. Visitors cannot just turn up. They have to apply in writing. Most applications are rejected.

Tiny, sealed and cut off from the outside world: these are perfect conditions for a *Lord of the Flies* scenario. They produce the kind of crude power dynamics that favour dominant males, who given free rein will make up their own rules and tyrannise those who are weaker. All sorts of nastiness — violence, intimidation, abuse — can ensue in that environment.

While sexual abuse is found everywhere, it thrives in secluded places. It is furtive and shameful; it happens out of sight. And it is often linked with problems that are typical of isolated areas: poverty and ignorance, alienation, narrow cultural and social horizons.

Yet isolation does not itself breed abuse. There are plenty of examples of inaccessible communities where children are able to grow up in safety. Tikopia, for instance, an outlying island in the Solomons archipelago, in the Pacific, had little contact even with its closest neighbours until well into the 20th century. Today the traditional lifestyle remains more or less intact. Tikopia is a stable, well-ordered society.

Pitcairn is stable and well ordered, too. Children are fed and clothed and educated. The old and the sick are looked after. Adults carry out productive work. The island's leaders are democratically elected. There are no murders nowadays, or muggings or burglaries. There is an established religion, which nearly everyone used to follow and which is still influential.

Pitcairn is thoroughly civilised, except in one respect: until Britain stepped in, children were almost routinely raped and assaulted.

Speaking of 'civilisation', there are, of course, societies around the world with customs that may offend our Western notions of child protection. In some areas of New Guinea, for instance, young boys spend years closeted with adult men, performing oral sex on them — and ingesting their manhood, supposedly, with their semen.

We might recoil from such traditions, but they constitute some of the ingredients of an integrated belief system. They are publicly sanctioned and practised openly. On Pitcairn, the sexual activity involving young girls, and at least some boys, took place as part of a general free-for-all. It did not occur within a centuries-old ritualised framework. Nor, tellingly, was it out in the open.

The societies of New Guinea have been developing for thousands of years; Pitcairn, in its present incarnation, has existed for only 200 years — a blink of an eyelid, in evolutionary terms.

Pitcairn, moreover, has evolved on its own, with no external point of reference. Other remote islands with tiny populations mostly form part of a bigger network of communities with a common identity. In the Orkneys, for instance, off the north coast of Scotland, some of the outermost islands have as few as 18 inhabitants. Regular ferries connect them, however, and each island is bonded to the rest of the Orkneys, as well as to Scotland.

In the case of Pitcairn, its nearest neighbour is Mangareva, a French-speaking island with a South Pacific culture. The only sizeable expatriate populations are on Norfolk Island and in New Zealand, both thousands of miles away. While Pitcairn had input from Britain and the Seventh-day Adventist Church, the islanders, tucked away by themselves, mostly did their own thing.

Until recently there were no external controls, and 'with no external controls, the default behaviour is self-interest', says John Harré, the New Zealand anthropologist who visited Pitcairn in the 1960s. Harré explains, 'We move away from self-interest as we create social units, and establish value systems and norms that become embedded in society. Those systems and norms are often reinforced by religion — but on Pitcairn, religion was an arbitrary overlay without roots in the social system.'

In decades past, countless small communities had echoes of Pitcairn. In Welsh mining villages and Australian country towns, girls were 'broken in' by older men. Sometimes they were gang-raped by local youths, with the knowledge of community elders, who excused it as juvenile high spirits. Those customs have, to a large extent, died out. On Pitcairn, they just continued.

The dynamics governing island life are not much different from those of a prison or boarding school — any setting, in fact, that is its own little world, and where people can abuse power and authority. Another comparison might be communes or religious sects: self-contained, tightly controlled micro-societies. Like Pitcairn, such groups have artificial origins. Many have disintegrated amid revelations of financial and sexual exploitation.

In 1991 New Zealand police raided Centrepoint, a 'spiritual community' on 12 hectares of rural land outside Auckland. Six men including the commune's 'guru', Bert Potter, were subsequently convicted of raping and indecently assaulting children. Potter, a former vacuum-cleaner salesman, encouraged residents to swap partners in a quest for uninhibited self-expression. Rumours of sexual abuse had surrounded Centrepoint almost from its inception in the late 1970s.

The case was prosecuted by Christine Gordon, the Deputy Public Prosecutor in the Pitcairn trials. Karen Vaughan, the Wellington detective, says, 'Potter ruled that community with an iron fist. When social workers tried to go in, he resisted fiercely. It was like there was a big wall around it and no one else gets in. It was the same on Pitcairn, but the wall was the Pacific Ocean.'

It is not difficult to find other examples of children being abused in similar contexts. William Kamm, or 'Little Pebble', the founder of a doomsday cult in rural New South Wales, was jailed in 2005 for child sex offences. In late 2007 Warren Jeffs was convicted in Utah of assisting statutory rape. Jeffs was the 'prophet' of a renegade polygamist Mormon sect whose members took dozens of 'wives' — often girls as young as 12. Jeffs claimed to be the victim of religious persecution, in much the same way that the Pitcairn men complained that Britain was trampling their 'Pacific culture'. Another American polygamist leader was charged with molesting five of his daughters. They were pressured, like so many of the women in the Pitcairn case, into not giving evidence.

Robert Bropho, self-appointed leader of the Swan Valley Nyungah Camp in Perth, ruled the fenced community through fear and intimidation. Sexual abuse was rife inside the camp. Bropho and another prominent Aboriginal elder were jailed for child sex crimes in 2006, and Bropho was imprisoned again in 2008.

In small, closed societies, a strong individual can wield disproportionate influence, and aberrant behaviour can easily take root and become the norm. On Pitcairn, says Dea Birkett, the writer, who stayed there in the early 1990s, 'what was apparent was that society was dominated by a few Alpha males whom the others found it difficult to stand up to in any way'.

Although Pitcairn may have been sexually lawless, the island's hierarchy operated in this sphere, too. The leading men exercised *droit de seigneur*, picking off the most desirable girls — virgins in the nubile bloom of youth. The weaker men abused more vulnerable girls, while some socially awkward types who would probably never form adult relationships had sex with their sisters. Middle-aged and older men were sexually opportunistic, targeting girls they had heard were 'easy'.

It was partly about sex and partly about power — proving you were a 'real man', staking your claim to a place in the pecking order. When charges were laid, the islanders accused Britain of persecuting their able-bodied men in order to paralyse the community. It was those men, naturally, who had had all the power, and who had abused it in that particular fashion.

On Pitcairn, women and girls were — and still are — treated as sexual commodities: Randy Christian refers to them as 'pieces of meat'. One local says of him, 'He goes after females of any age, whether they are young girls or adults.' Randy once leant over a balcony during a party and pointed out two ten-year-olds. 'Those two are maturing well,' he remarked.

The men boast about their exploits, legitimising and encouraging each other. Brian Young told police, 'You hear the different chaps when we're doing public work, talking about this girl or that girl ... and you think, hey, well, if they're having so much fun ... why can't I have fun?'

At one time in his youth, Brian said, 'There was this chappie who was actually going around with five or six women at one time, and it was a big joke amongst the community.' That was a reference to Steve Christian. After the tape recorder was turned off, Brian told detectives, 'Steve was getting them as soon as they turned 11 or 12, so I decided I had to get them younger.'

'And so,' says Robert Vinson, one of the detectives who interviewed him, 'he went and found two girls for himself ... They were going to be his.' Those girls were Isobel and Jeanie.

Brian and the other men undoubtedly knew that, by any civilised yardstick, their actions were unacceptable. They had been brought up in a religion that, whatever its idiosyncrasies, was based on Christian ideas of right and wrong. They had all spent time in New Zealand, and some had voyaged further afield. As far back as

1940, British officials were reporting that 'practically everyone in Pitcairn visits New Zealand some time or other, and many spend a surprising amount of their time travelling to and fro'.

The outside world also came to Pitcairn. Although the island did not have a regular shipping service, ships called periodically throughout its history — almost weekly between the 1920s and the 1960s. The locals kept in touch with the world through their ham radios, and they always had outsiders living among them. Aware that different standards prevailed elsewhere, they tried to conceal certain aspects of their lifestyle, such as the high rate of illegitimate births.

When the police investigation began, one man had a specific fear, which was of being murdered in jail — presumably in New Zealand. (This was before the prison was built on Pitcairn.) Clearly he realised how crimes such as his were viewed by prison inmates generally.

Until Operation Unique, these men had never been challenged. Pitcairn was 'a society where the majority of adult males felt they were untouchable', says Max Davidson. It was a sexual predators' paradise, and when that paradise crumbled, the men blamed their misfortune on the girls. Brian Young, who had sex with a 14-year-old when in his early 30s, protested that 'she was very convincing . . . I was just like a dog being towed behind.'

As well as the girls, the men blamed the police. They blamed the British government. They blamed Tom and Betty Christian. And when their lawyers failed to get them acquitted, or to sway the Privy Council, they blamed them, too.

One outsider says, 'They remind me of a pampered child. But much more dangerous. Undoubtedly at times there is a palpable evil here.'

★ ★ ★

While the sexual abuse of children has been highlighted, it is only one manifestation of a wider bullying mentality that seems to pervade the community. Domestic violence is another. A woman was beaten unconscious the night before Christmas when Harry Shapiro, an American anthropologist, was on the island in 1934. Myrtle Warren, the first wife of Alwyn, whose second wife, Alta, had to enlist help from Britain in the 1950s, reportedly died with her throat 'black from bruises from being dragged about by the neck'.

Some wife-beaters were given a spell in jail; others were spoken to severely by their neighbours. According to Dennis McGookin, 'The women say there's always been this abuse, that all of them are physically abused, even the strongest ones, and they put up with it ... They're brought up almost as if it's in the culture of living on Pitcairn Island, and it's just something you have to face.'

Children and weaker men are bullied too. Terry Young was verbally — and possibly physically — abused in childhood. Dave Brown's parents are said to have favoured his younger brother, Kay. Dave was unpopular at school and later became a bully himself. Mike Lupton-Christian claims that Dave once attacked Brenda and her son, Andrew, in the square, gripping Brenda around the neck.

A female photographer who visited Pitcairn in the 1990s lodged with Dobrey Christian. One day Steve turned up at the house and put on a violent video. 'You're not frightened, are you?' he asked the woman.

Catherine Haigh, who has spent long periods living on the island with her husband, Bill, is convinced that the men regard the sexual abuse 'as a bit of bullying, at worst, and as far as they're concerned, bullying is part of life on Pitcairn'.

The Pitcairners were not merely isolated: isolation was burnt into their psyche. 'The mutineers deliberately chose the most remote place on earth,' says Caroline Alexander, the historian. 'The isolation was baggage that they carried around and passed from generation to generation. And every ship that called reinforced this sense of being removed and out of reach — beyond the arm of the law and the eyes of the world.'

Alexander told me in a phone interview, 'It's not the same as growing up on a South Pacific island as a South Pacific islander. They knew that when the last ship pulled away, they were in a place where no one was going to see what they were doing.'

The islanders were also conscious, from the moment Pitcairn was rediscovered, that they were part of a new and enthralling legend. 'They know they're a desirable romantic breed,' says Alexander, 'and people are flocking there to pay homage to them. It's very heady stuff.'

It is not surprising that the islanders developed an inflated idea of their own importance. It is not surprising that they came to feel a sense of entitlement: to British aid, to goods off the ships, to government stores of timber, to sex with young girls. It is not surprising that they considered themselves above the law — convinced that 'because they are Pitcairners ... they can get away with it', as Andrew Christian, Brenda's son, puts it.

Along with that went a sense of inferiority, because they were from such a tiny, faraway place and felt sure that everyone else was better educated than them, and more sophisticated.

It was a lethal combination.

Another key to the state of affairs uncovered in 2000 may lie in Pitcairn's bloody origins. Horrific scenes were witnessed by the women and children in those early years: five men wiped out in one day; a sixth, Matthew Quintal, hacked to death by two of his former shipmates. The new colony had collapsed into murder and mayhem. Just like *Lord of the Flies*.

Yet within a few years (or a few generations, the timing is not certain) a state of violence largely caused by sexual jealousy had been replaced by a virtual free-for-all. Men were having sex with each other's wives and daughters. And no one, apparently, minded. (Not the men, anyway.)

Could it be that those two situations are connected? Did the massacres influence the way the community evolved? Did they, perhaps, affect the children so profoundly that Pitcairn's men resolved never again to fight over women? Did the men, recognising that women would always be in short supply, decide they should become a common resource, to be shared in the interests of peaceful co-existence? Did they agree, tacitly or explicitly, that no man would ever again stand in the way of another man's sexual business, provided that all men could do exactly as they pleased?

If that was how the free-for-all came about, and this is merely conjecture, it would only have been a small step to extend the principle to female children — especially as there were periods during Pitcairn's history when men outnumbered adult women. Girls of 12 or 13 would have been regarded as young women anyway. Once the boundaries had melted, it would not have taken long for pre-pubertal girls to be included.

This theory that the mutineers' sons, or a later generation of men, reached some form of pragmatic accommodation in order to prevent further bloodshed is supported by several factors. First, sexual jealousy is rare on Pitcairn, despite the high incidence of infidelity. Secondly, no father retaliated on behalf of his daughter — the one known exception being in the Ricky Quinn case, but Karen's father, who quickly calmed down, was not brought up on Pitcairn. Thirdly, it is said that the men never use physical violence among themselves, however much provoked. Violence is reserved for women and children.

There is also evidence of how traumatised the first generation of young people was by childhood events. Invited to a meal below deck on a British warship in 1814, Fletcher Christian's eldest son, Thursday October, got up abruptly on seeing a West Indian crew member. He told his hosts, 'I don't like that black fellow. I must go.' He had grown up with the belief that dark-skinned men had murdered his father.

Pitcairn's founding women were not submissive characters. They played an active role in the civil strife and once they outnumbered the men, they rationed their sexual favours. But they could not leave the island. Ultimately they had to submit to their fate, and if there *was* an agreement among the men to pool the women, the women may have gone along with it — deciding that submission was preferable to risking another round of massacres.

It is true that marriage has always been popular on Pitcairn: a fact that undermines the theory of women being shared. However, often people married for practical and economic reasons, it appears, and afterwards both partners remained sexually available.

If there was a pact, it would have been handed down from father to son. In her book, Dea Birkett observes how Steve Christian's eldest son, Trent, 'obviously modelled his manhood on his parent, from the thick moustache to the way he stood solemnly at the helm of the rubber dinghy, as if he were at the wheel of a four-masted sailing schooner'. And since behaviour is cyclical, and Pitcairn is so isolated, the abuse of women and girls just went on and on.

At the same time, a process of desensitisation must have taken place, with the community numbing itself to the suffering of the girls who were the sacrificial lambs.

Robert Wade, now a professor at the London School of Economics, visited the island as a young student in the 1960s. Wade says, 'Pitcairn seems to me to be very much a cautionary tale about human nature. It shows the powerful urge of conformity within small groups. It tells us just how fragile is the behaviour that we call civilised, and how completely we can lose a sense of empathy and shared humanity.'

On the other hand, the Pitcairners were Christians, and Seventh-day Adventists to boot. Did their religion not act as a counterbalance? In the view of Roy Sanders, Adventism was a 'cultural accident'. The islanders resisted all attempts at 'moral uplift', he wrote in a letter home, adding, 'Mind you, I don't think the most noble efforts of any Church would be much more successful. They would break the heart of most of the vicars I know.'

The locals themselves, it appears, did not agonise about the gulf between their public professions of faith and their private conduct. On the contrary, they adroitly reconciled the two, according to John Harré, the anthropologist, who was on the island with Robert Wade. Harré recalls a sermon preached by Pervis Young, the then magistrate. 'Pervis said the Devil works hardest to get his claws into those who are trying hardest to follow Christ. In other words, the harder you're trying to be good, the more likely you are to be bad. It was a beautiful piece of casuistry.'

I asked Neville Tosen whether he believed that the islanders had ever been genuinely pious. 'I have my doubts,' he replied. 'This is the island that the Gospel changed, but I wonder whether Christianity really penetrated into their daily lives. Or was it simply a convenient cloak of respectability to cover up what was going on behind?'

★ ★ ★

After a few dozen Pitcairners returned from Norfolk Island in the mid-19th century, they were questioned by a British naval commander. He reported that they had found Norfolk 'so different from the life of freedom and irresponsibility ... that they had led at Pitcairn that they had a longing to be back to the island where no one could interfere with them'.

It should be remembered that those who quit Norfolk, turning their backs on an easier lifestyle with better opportunities, did so out of choice — just like those who stayed on Pitcairn during the 20th century. The latter did not *have* to battle the elements and risk their lives just to unload basic supplies. They could have moved to New Zealand, where they had the right to reside and work, and shopped at the supermarket. There was something about Pitcairn life that suited them.

Visitors spoke of the islanders' wish to 'limit outside inter-ference' and ensure 'freedom from intrusion'. After Harry Maude, a colonial official, redrafted the Pitcairn legal code in 1941, one local asked, 'What did that white man want to come here for, interfering with our laws?'

Several of the convicted men, as well as other men who have been implicated, had spells living in New Zealand, which is home to several hundred Pitcairn expatriates. They did not offend while they were overseas, apart from a very few incidents, all of which involved Pitcairn girls. It was the island that furnished the congenial atmosphere.

The community that has grown up on Norfolk, meanwhile, manifests many of Pitcairn's characteristics, albeit in greatly diluted form. The people who migrated there were very isolated too: left to themselves until Australians and New Zealanders started to settle in the 1950s and established a tourism industry. Even in the 1970s, horses were still the main form of transport on

Norfolk, and there were few telephones; television did not reach the island until 1987.

The 800 or so Pitcairn descendants, who make up about 40 per cent of the population, are fiercely proud of their roots and to a large extent keep themselves apart from the 'mainlanders'. Locals described to me a hard-drinking, male-dominated society where domestic violence is entrenched, and stalking and sexual harassment are commonplace. And not just harassment: the case of Stephen Nobbs, a leading businessman convicted in 2000 of sexually assaulting two girls, was said to be indicative of a much wider phenomenon. Indeed, when the islanders heard about Operation Unique, 'there was a fair bit of fear that if the same inquiry was conducted on Norfolk, it would be just as bad, if not worse', according to one woman. A man with impeccable Pitcairn origins told me, 'There's a culture of it here, too. I think it's a genetic thing. I think it's in the blood.'

In a foreshadowing of the strikingly light penalties handed out to the Pitcairn men, Nobbs was sentenced by an Australian magistrate to 48 periods of weekend detention at the local police station. It was also reported, in the *Sydney Morning Herald*, that elders of the Seventh-day Adventist Church, of which he was a deacon, had tried to cover up his actions — a claim that the Church denied. A judge who heard Nobbs' appeal, quashing one charge, noted that he 'retains the respect and belief of a significant portion of the population'.

Neville Tosen says, 'I think there's a pattern. I think they took the same mentality with them to Norfolk. Maybe on Norfolk they were exposed to more outside influences, so the problem was not so intense. But it still remained, and it breaks out every now and again.' A businesswoman on Norfolk expressed similar sentiments, remarking to me, 'You've read *Lord of the Flies*? What happened on

Pitcairn and here on Norfolk are not much different. It's a wonderful example of how people revert once some of the restrictions are taken away. We're savages at heart. Not that far removed from the apes, unfortunately.'

As on Pitcairn, anyone who disturbs the status quo on Norfolk risks intimidation and reprisals, which in Norfolk's case include arson attacks. However, despite all the parallels, Pitcairn — minuscule, formidably isolated and barely watered down by outsiders — is in a category of its own. It is a place where 'it's difficult to be good', says one islander. Dave Brown's brother, Kay, when interviewed about his relationship with a much younger girl, told police, 'I think being on a rock like that, you get rock fever and you don't tend to think too straight … It's almost like something else is taking control of you.'

The climate appears to have been infectious. While only a few visitors went so far as to join in the abuse, allegedly, many outsiders talk of the strange pull that Pitcairn exerts. Yet many are bruised by the experience of living there. One woman declined to be reinterviewed, saying our previous conversation had left her 'emotionally exhausted … Pitcairn remains a very upsetting memory for me.' Another woman talked at length but had nightmares that night, grinding her teeth so hard that she broke a cap. Neville Tosen says, 'There's an aftermath that stays with you, and it's negative. It still eats us on occasions.'

Despite the way women and children were treated, the community survived. But the population declined steadily, and by the time of Operation Unique a whole generation of women — 20 to 50 years old — was missing. Hardly any children were being born on the island, and only a handful of adults under 30 remained there. Were it not for the dramatic intervention seen recently, it is debatable whether there would have been, in a few years' time, much of a community left.

The islanders were leaving for all the usual reasons that people leave small, out of the way places. The child abuse was a major element, though: most of the girls who went away did not come back. In that sense, it could be argued, Pitcairn was slowly imploding as a result of the men's actions.

Nonetheless, the way things turned out there was not preordained, as William Golding would have us believe. Human nature has a capacity for altruism as well as cruelty. On Pitcairn, both were displayed. And in every generation there were men who did not molest children.

Robin Fox, an anthropology professor at Rutgers University in New Jersey, says, 'Just because it's isolated, and people are stuck there, doesn't mean you get that outcome. If a bunch of Tahitians had settled on Pitcairn voluntarily with their pigs and their women, they would have set up a recognisable Polynesian society, and it would have been a different story.'

The outcome that did eventuate was much more likely in that setting, however, and there must be other such secluded places that, if they were subjected to the same degree of scrutiny, would yield similar results. Sexual abuse is found in big cities, of course, but in pockets. It does not infect the whole environment and insinuate itself into the culture. There are competing influences at play, and people travelling in and out. There is information, and a means of escape.

Once the factors unique to Pitcairn are added to the mix, there *is* an inevitability about what happened. A community established by desperate men and abducted women who know little of each other's backgrounds or even language. An outbreak of terrible violence. A long period of the islanders living enclosed in their own minute world, worshipped and mythologised by outsiders.

Only the scale and duration of what transpired are unusual. All societies are driven by power, money and sex. Those goals just seem to be pursued more nakedly on Pitcairn, where life is lived in the raw, and human instincts are stripped down to the basics.

The Pitcairn story makes us shiver. We recognise that hellish little universe, and we recognise ourselves. The island offers a glimpse of the darkness that lies within every one of us.

A male friend says, 'I don't see the fun in raping children, but is that because of the way I'm conditioned? Maybe it's only a question of degree, a line that most people don't cross. If it was acceptable, would you feel differently?'

Another friend, a gentle, good-natured photographer, exclaims, 'If it's in them, it's in me! Pitcairn is me!' He jabs himself in the chest.

Again I remember how ordinary the island men appeared to be. The philosopher and journalist Hannah Arendt wrote famously of 'the banality of evil' in relation to the Nazi leader Adolf Eichmann. It is a phrase that applies equally to Pitcairn.

CHAPTER 21

The last throw of the dice

Pitcairn has changed beyond recognition in the last few years. A new school opened in 2006. The islanders have television, including CNN, and an affordable telephone system; there will be 24-hour electricity once a wind turbine scheme is complete. Work starts in 2008 on a breakwater that could treble the number of cruise ships visiting. There will soon be a regular passenger service to and from Mangareva; Pitcairn may even get its own boat. Britain is spending nearly £2 million a year on a population of 54: surely one of the highest per capita expenditures on any community, anywhere in the world. It has also provided £4.5 million to upgrade infrastructure and communications; the breakwater will cost another NZ$13.5 million (£5.8 million), at least.

It might seem odd that so much money is being ploughed into a society that has just been exposed as deeply dysfunctional. But once the trials had focused attention on Pitcairn, Britain's only option — given its commitment to maintain its Overseas Territories — was to compensate for past neglect. The island had to be made safe, which meant sending out social workers, police and diplomats. If it was to have a solid future, living conditions had to be improved and new sources of income created. Crucially, ways had to be found to reduce its isolation and the likelihood of such behaviour recurring.

Pitcairn is at a crossroads. Ironically, its prospects have never been brighter. The rule of law has been established, in theory at least, and officials in London, Wellington and Auckland are working hard to make the community viable. The European Union is contributing to projects such as the breakwater. For Pitcairn, there is an almost unlimited fund of goodwill, money and ideas.

What it needs more than anything else is people: new immigrants who will boost the population and transform the social climate. Britain's hope is that a revitalised economy, new jobs and better transport links will tempt Pitcairners living in New Zealand and elsewhere to come home. But before they do, expatriates will want to be sure that the sexual abuse of children has stopped — and that the mindset that allowed the abuse to thrive no longer predominates.

Some have already affirmed their faith. Jacqui Christian moved back to the island in late 2006, just after Steve and Randy Christian were jailed. Jacqui calls it her 'mission': making a new life for herself on Pitcairn while participating, she hopes, in the communal healing process. A pharmacist with an interest in herbalism and alternative therapies, she has trained in acupuncture and massage, and would like to open a health retreat. 'This is such a unique place, such a beautiful place,' she says. 'You can get away from the rat race, but you have everything here that you need: fresh air, great food, great fish. You can go fishing and bush walking, all the nice time out things.

'I've always felt very blessed to be able to go away and get an education, and travel and learn so much. I'm interested in just helping the community and giving back with any skills that I have. I see so much opportunity here.'

Clever and articulate, Jacqui could play a leading role in a reborn Pitcairn. However, most locals regard her as a traitor, and her homecoming was preceded by a flood of vindictive emails. 'I knew it would be really difficult to come home, and it *is* difficult,' she says. 'When I agreed to give evidence, I knew exactly how the community would react. There's been some verbal abuse and gestures, but mainly people are ignoring me. Anything that I have anything to do with, they boycott.'

In mid-2007 Jacqui publicly apologised to Jay Warren and his family, saying that she must have mistaken his identity when she accused him of molesting her. Her admission caused an uproar, with Kari Boye Young fuming that 'it only served to cast more doubt on the legal process and the sincerity of the victims ... This might lead to other victims rethinking.'

Jacqui has no doubts about the other men who assaulted her. And she has no regrets about taking part in the legal process. 'I think the trials had to happen,' she says. 'I believe in a strong future for Pitcairn, but you can't have that if there's any risk to children. If we can make it better for the little kids growing up now, and the generations after them, then it will all have been worthwhile.'

As for her own bad memories of childhood, and the challenge of living among men who abused her, Jacqui says, 'There are locations here which, when I drive past, there's still a sense of foreboding about them. But I don't feel any resentment or hate towards any of those men. The hate that people here are trying to dump on me, I feel sorry for them. Once you let it go, it's so much easier.'

To those islanders — the majority — who still believe their men are the real victims, the sight of Jacqui is a daily irritation. So, too, is the large building with the high metal fence in the area known as Bob's Valley: Her Majesty's Prison Pitcairn.

The prison's inmates — three at the time of writing; there were originally five — are unlocked every morning at 7 a.m. They have to clean their cells and have them inspected. Randy Christian then cooks breakfast. The men do their laundry and carry out maintenance work around the prison.

The Pitcairn equivalent of sewing mailbags was supposed to be making wooden souvenirs. The plan was for the proceeds to be split between the prisoners' families and the British government, as a contribution to the men's upkeep. But the scheme was judged too complex to administer. And Steve Christian refused to have anything to do with it. Instead, the prison inmates perform work around the island under the supervision of corrections officers. They clear the tracks of undergrowth and crush rocks for the roads. They have constructed a new boathouse and put up swings at the school. They have carved steps down to St Paul's Pool and up to Christian's Cave, and laid a new pathway leading to Garnets Ridge.

The men get out as often as three to four days a week; occasionally they crew on the longboats when manpower is short. Their relatives sometimes see them pass on a tractor on their way to work — and they run outside, 'shouting and waving as if greeting heroes', according to Kari. Randy cooks dinner for the prisoners in the evening. From 8 p.m. they are locked up.

In their recreation time the men carve curios for their families to sell. They exercise in the concrete compound or the new multi-gym. They watch DVDs. During weekly visiting hours most of the island converges on the jail, and, says Kari, 'It's just like party time ... [with everyone] sitting in chairs on the floor ... kids running around yelling and playing, people laughing and joking.'

Other islanders support the men's families, particularly Randy's, by supplying them with firewood and catching fish for them. Nadine has four children to look after, including a baby, Adrianna — named after Adrian Cook, the QC. Dennis Christian, the postmaster, delivers mail to the prison three mornings a week. The Pitcairners are prolific correspondents: the jail's occupants receive up to 200 letters a month, some decorated with fresh hibiscus blooms.

The corrections officers are supposed to keep their distance from the community, including the prisoners' families. On Pitcairn, though, it's hard not to socialise. One female guard struck up a relationship with an islander. Some prison officers have become entangled in island politics. Others have voiced doubts about the criminal case, even professing their belief in the innocence of the men they are guarding. One officer described them as 'a top bunch of guys', adding that it was 'a shame they've been hit with this'.

For Randy Christian, and for brothers Brian and Terry Young, it's not a bad life. They are close to their loved ones. Labouring in the open air and making carvings in their spare time is not so different from their normal routine. They can't go home, of course, and there are no Friday night parties. But unlike most incarcerated child sex offenders, they are not in any danger. Their fellow inmates are friends and family members.

For Steve Christian and his youngest son, Shawn, it's an even better life. Their membership of the 'Bob's Valley Five', as the prisoners used to be known, was short-lived. In August 2007, after just nine months in jail, Steve requested permission to serve the rest of his three-year term on home detention. And the parole board agreed — despite noting that he 'maintains denial to this day that he committed any offence, including rape'.

Shawn spent just under a year behind bars before being released into home detention shortly before Christmas 2007. In February 2008, Steve was granted parole. However, for father as for son, home detention was not too confining. They could leave the house for funerals, longboat emergencies and public work. They could visit Randy in prison and receive visitors themselves. Steve helped Olive to run a café and bar at Big Fence, which they had opened with the aid of a low-interest loan from the British government.

Even when he was 'inside', Steve got out regularly. He is the only person on the island with dentistry, explosives and radiography expertise. He filled a tooth for the teacher, Susan Davey, and blasted rocks for concrete for the prison yard. In jail, says one source, he was 'constantly pushing the boundaries to see how far he could go ... He was demanding and manipulative, challenging the prison regulations and trying to get the corrections officers on side. He was still trying to be in control.'

And he may have succeeded, to a degree. Leslie Jaques, who spent much of 2007 on Pitcairn, went into the prison regularly to update the men about Britain's plans. When Steve found out about a new longboat training scheme, he was incensed. Jaques made a special visit just to placate him. Steve also put word out from jail that Jay Warren was 'making a bad job of' being mayor.

As for the others, Len Brown was granted parole in December 2007, while Terry and Randy were due to apply for home detention in 2008. Brian would not be far behind them.

The spectacle of child sex offenders serving their sentences at worst in a highly congenial prison environment, at best in their own homes makes one unnamed British official despondent. 'I feel as though we've done the victims an injustice by putting them through that traumatic process — and for what?' he says. 'They were lenient sentences to start with, and the situation now is a joke.

I don't see the point of what we're doing out there any more. I think we've failed people, in a way.'

Jeanie, one of Brian's victims, agrees. 'Punishment-wise, this case has not been taken seriously,' she says. 'Steve's already out of that hotel they call a jail, and Brian will be following suit. But the victims are serving a life sentence.'

There are few signs yet that jail is proving a salutary experience, or that a sex offender treatment programme conducted by a New Zealand clinical psychologist has had any more of an impact than the one Brian underwent before his trial. The prisoners continue to rail against the 'injustice' of their situation. They complain that other men were not jailed, and still others were not prosecuted at all. 'They think they got a bum deal,' says one insider. 'There's no acknowledgement that anyone did anything wrong. They just see it as what blokes do, a bit of fun in their youth.'

Perhaps the only exception is Dennis, who back in 2000 pinned a definition of child abuse up on his wall at home. The pastor, Ray Codling, has been visiting Brian, who claims to have rediscovered his faith behind bars. Sometime ago, Dennis and Dave completed their community service, which involved mainly road clearing as well as construction and drainage work.

Outside the prison, the community remains fractured and fractious. Anger and resentment continue to boil. On Bounty Day 2007, for the first time in Pitcairn's history, two separate celebrations were staged. A minority of islanders — those who might be called realists — burnt a boat off The Landing, as is traditional. Families and supporters of the convicted men held their own event at Tedside, on the other side of the island.

On Mutiny Day, a few months later, festivities were once again split. The 'old guard' had a barbecue at Highest Point. The others marked the anniversary in the public hall.

In February 2007 Jacob Warren, Jay and Meralda's father, died at the age of 86. The family sent Pastor Codling to let Tom and Betty Christian know they were not welcome at his funeral. In October, 79-year-old Vula Young, Brian and Terry's mother, followed Jacob to the grave. This time the funeral ban extended to Mike Lupton-Christian, as well as Tom and Betty. Refreshments were served at the jail, all four inmates (as they then were) having attended the burial.

If the trials have been cathartic for the wider community, there is little sign of that yet. 'There's no sense of people accepting that stuff went on and needed to be stopped,' says one outsider. 'It's just seen as outside interference.'

There is bitterness, too, about the accolades given to the police and diplomats involved in the case. Matthew Forbes was made an OBE in the 2007 New Year Honours; Peter George and Robert Vinson were made MBEs in 2008. Karen Vaughan received a Queen's Service Medal. Each award triggered a volley of angry emails.

On a more positive note, Pitcairn has spruced itself up in expectation of tourists. The locals have created an eco-trail that incorporates endemic plant species, some so rare that they have not yet been named. The islanders have a new museum. They can offer trips to Henderson and Oeno Islands, the habitat of more rare flora and birds. Some have used interest-free loans to build guest houses or renovate their homes for paying visitors.

In early 2008 there was still no reliable means of getting people on and off the island. It was hoped, however, that by August passengers would be able to travel on a bi-monthly chartered boat that brings supplies from Mangareva. There was also talk of a joint bid with French Polynesia for a European Union grant to buy a vessel. An airstrip has been ruled out as expensive and impractical.

What will revolutionise the place is the breakwater, with two big stone jetties turning Bounty Bay into a more or less sheltered harbour. At present, only a dozen of the 40 ships that ply between Easter Island and Tahiti stop at Pitcairn; many others would do so if they could lower their own tenders safely. The landing fees alone would yield a substantial income for the community.

As well as more day-trippers off the cruise ships, the island aims to attract botanists, ornithologists and other scientists, along with tourists interested enough in the history and ecology — and wealthy enough — to visit for a week or two. In the meantime, niche industries such as honey production are being developed. Pitcairn's honey is one of the few allowed into New Zealand and Europe. It is being exported to Japan and to Partridges, the Queen's grocer, in London. There are plans to quadruple output.

Not everyone is impressed by these schemes. The partner of one complainant is aghast at the amount of money being pumped into the island. 'It's almost like rewarding them,' he says. 'What about the women? They're getting nothing.'

It's true. Pitcairn is not covered by Britain's criminal injuries compensation scheme, nor by a parallel New Zealand scheme. The British government has refused to make special provision to compensate women who were sexually abused in its long neglected territory. Yet between 2000 and late 2007 Britain spent at least £15 million on Pitcairn, and even that figure is a conservative estimate; some officials suggest it may be twice that.

Pitcairn still faces major challenges. If the island is to move forward, the old power structure will have to be smashed. Already the 'jobs for the boys' mentality has gone. Commissioner Jaques, in tandem with local officials, oversees the allocation of government positions; there is a formal appointment procedure, followed by monthly audits and performance appraisals. This has led to a more equitable spread of jobs. In addition, training to man the longboats and operate heavy machinery is now given to anyone who wants it. Fourteen people have taken up the offer of longboat training, including Jacqui Christian and Pawl Warren. Pawl remarked, 'I've waited 14 years for this.'

At the last count, there were 17 outsiders on the island — nearly one-third again of the local population. They included seven prison officers, one community constable, two social workers, the doctor, teacher and pastor, the Governor's Representative and various spouses. Their presence significantly altered the power dynamics while providing a stabilising influence, British officials believe. Pitcairn will have social workers and a doctor for the foreseeable future. A Governor's Representative will be there for as long as the prison is open. In 2007 the MDPs were replaced by Malcolm Gilbert, a retired Scottish police officer, and his wife. There will be outside policing on the island indefinitely.

Thanks to cheaper satellite communications, the Governor or Deputy Governor can attend monthly council meetings by video link. They can telephone the mayor. Local officials are, in theory, subjected to greater scrutiny, and the decision-making process is more transparent.

The men who received prison sentences will not be able to hold public office for five years from the date when they began those sentences. Nevertheless, there is no one who believes that old habits have disappeared, or that Steve — once again able to brief his followers at Big Fence — is not still the main player. Recognising that he cannot deal Steve out of the equation, Leslie Jaques says he hopes he will be part of Pitcairn's future. 'He has lots of skills,' Jaques says. 'He is a leader and an orator.'

The December 2007 elections saw a further consolidation of Steve's position. Cookie Warren, a close ally, replaced Jay Warren as mayor, while Dave Brown — already eligible to stand for office thanks to a fit of generosity by the Governor — was elected internal committee chairman. In early 2008 Steve, while still on home detention, was appointed to a six-person group reviewing Pitcairn's system of governance. So was Shawn, who like his father was still serving a sentence for child rape.

The population has increased since the trials. Shawn Christian and Brian Young came home to go to jail — and may well have to stay, since neither the Australian nor New Zealand immigration service looks kindly on convicted child sex offenders. Their respective partners, and Brian's son and daughter-in-law, are also on the island for now. Brian has a British passport and could live in Norway. Pitcairn-based offenders such as Steve will encounter major obstacles if they try to resume their customary jaunts to New Zealand or Norfolk Island; they may even have difficulty entering New Zealand for medical treatment. Other new arrivals, apart from Jacqui Christian, include Brenda Christian's son, Andrew, who came back from university; Daphne Warren's husband, Kean; and Kerry Young, an expatriate Pitcairner who has settled on the island with his New Zealand partner, Heather Menzies.

Britain hopes that others will follow, bringing new blood, new ideas, new expertise — and, most importantly, new attitudes. Only then, probably, will the culture change: when Pitcairn has a critical mass of people who have grown up overseas and can bring a different outlook to bear. If that happens, those who insist on clinging to the old ways will be outnumbered and marginalised. Young families are seen as particularly desirable immigrants. There are only four children at the school, and only a few women of child-bearing age. Jaques aims to improve standards of education, acknowledging that in the past Pitcairn children have lagged well behind their New Zealand counterparts.

The island's population is not much bigger now than when the mutineers settled, or when a few families returned from Norfolk. On both occasions the community built itself up. Britain has set its sights on a population of 100, at least. The Governor, George Fergusson, says, 'I hope we can get to the position in seven or eight years of somewhere between 70 to 90 people, with ten children at the school. That would enable the place to become a rather more relaxed society.'

The critical question is whether the cycle of abuse has been broken. Simon Moore says, 'I can't see it's likely that anyone's going to offend again. And if they did, they would be looking at big penalties, without the inevitable leniency of this case. The fact that there's now a proven commitment to set up a court, appoint lawyers and bring judges across the water to mete out justice shows there's no way you'll get away with it again.'

Others are less optimistic. Fresh allegations have emerged in the last couple of years, including claims of children being abused by an older child. There are wider concerns about juvenile behaviour. Of the men, Peter George says, 'I don't believe a lot has changed. I'm sure that if police and social workers were to go away, the sexual abuse would be back within five to ten years.' Karen Vaughan agrees. 'We can't assume the abuse has stopped. Some perpetrators get a real thrill from carrying on after authority has intervened.'

One social worker warns, 'If abuse did recur, we wouldn't find out about it from a disclosure. I don't believe a child would speak up now, not after the way the community has reacted in recent years.'

The case has been shattering for the island — but that was an inevitable side-effect of the law being imposed on a lawless community. Matthew Forbes is certain that trials were needed. 'You had to draw a line,' he says. 'I don't think anything would have changed if we'd had truth and reconciliation. If it had been going on so long, there had to be consequences of serious criminal behaviour.'

Forbes' predecessor as Deputy Governor, Karen Wolstenholme, who was in post at the time Belinda spoke up, says, 'In a community that size, to come forward and make these allegations was hugely brave. I thought the most important thing was to see justice done for the people who had come forward.

'If this has achieved nothing else, the islanders will realise they can't do whatever they want, there's a law and it applies to them.'

Many people feel it is regrettable, though, that the case was allowed to become so protracted. Their views were perhaps summed up by a contributor to an internet chat room in 2005, who wrote, 'They've [the men] tried every trick in the book except to say that the rapes were done by Little Green Men from Mars . . . These Pitcairn guys and their families have gotten every break known to western jurisprudence.'

Graham Ford, the Pitcairn court registrar, says, 'This case has had more kinks and turns than most people accumulate in a lifetime. Law students and academics will feast off the scores of decisions and judgements for years to come.' And the legal saga has continued.

In early 2007 Steve Christian filed a complaint with the European Court of Human Rights, which was expected to be heard sometime in 2008.

In April 2007 the charges against Albert Reeves were dropped. Reeves, 82, was suffering from emphysema and cognitive impairment, and geriatricians said there was no prospect of his standing trial. Jennifer, who fervently wanted him brought to justice, was crushed by the news. She was also disgusted that Steve, who had been convicted of raping her four times, was already on home detention.

In August, a Crown appeal against the brevity of Shawn Christian's and Brian Young's sentences was dismissed, and one of Shawn's rape charges was quashed.

In October, Randy Christian appealed once more against his convictions, arguing that his case had been tainted by 'impermissible prejudice'. The appeal was dismissed in December.

Pitcairn and its inhabitants are still being mythologised. A new documentary, *Dem Tul Pitcairn*, made by an American production company, was due to be broadcast in 2008. On their website, the film-makers ask, 'Will this unique, tiny island be able to survive modern-day pressures and technologies? Or will its simple, happy lifestyle be lost forever?'

Media reports of the case continue to state that the men were convicted of 'under-age sex' offences, and that they pleaded Tahitian culture in their defence. (That was never mentioned in court.) Their crimes are routinely described as 'historic', although the last one was committed in 1999.

And while some of the island's admirers now grudgingly recognise that unsavoury things did happen on Pitcairn, they pin the blame on recent generations of men — determined to view child sexual abuse as a temporary aberration, rather than a long-entrenched tradition.

Simon Moore says, 'The irony is that we've got convictions for really serious offending and had them confirmed on appeal, and these people are locked up for really serious sexual crimes, and yet their supporters will still come out and say that it's all cultural. Which, apart from being not true, is offensive and racist and patronising.'

Pitcairn, says Moore, 'will always be remembered for the prosecution of a wistful island community for minor offences, which failed to take into account the cultural values of the community'.

Tiny signs indicate that divisions on the island may be melting. More community events are being held, and more people are participating. Olive Christian has set up a hairdressing and beauty salon with Michele Christian, Shawn's wife, and has welcomed both Jacqui and Betty Christian as clients. On Friday nights, most of the island congregates at Steve and Olive's café. Carol Warren has started a takeaway food service, offering fish balls and boiled goat meat, while Dave Brown is baking bread commercially. A honey co-operative has been re-formed, and while it is beset by splits, members are working together.

In early 2008, Steve cleared some land for Jacqui to build a house — a strikingly conciliatory gesture. Jacqui is working with Steve and Shawn on the committee reviewing Pitcairn's future, and only narrowly missed being elected to the council. Brenda Christian was elected, in an indication that her fellow islanders are beginning to recognise her worth.

'There's a feeling that people have had enough of conflict,' says one outsider. 'Nobody wins. People are starting to co-exist a bit more. Small bridges are being built.'

Betty Christian says, 'I'm optimistic about Pitcairn's future, with all the projects and hard work that are going on. This is probably the most critical time ever for the island. In some ways I feel we've come full circle from the early days, with all the murder and mayhem.'

Pitcairn does have a history of resilience. It has survived two mass emigrations. Adversity is part of the islanders' psyche. Some people speak of 'miracles' in the past: a light shining through fog to guide a longboat crew home, a child rescued in impossible circumstances.

Matthew Forbes says, 'This is a real watershed for Pitcairn. The future depends on the islanders themselves. If they start working co-operatively together, and accepting other people who come to the island, then it does have a future.'

Leslie Jaques says, 'If we don't get it right this time, if mindsets don't change, Pitcairn will die with these people. No one will come home, and if no one comes home, this will be the last generation. The old people will die and the young people will leave. This is the last throw of the dice for Pitcairn.'

EPILOGUE

Isobel's story

It is mid-2007, and Isobel greets me with a hesitant smile at the door of her family's cottage in a semi-rural area outside Wellington. A year ago, when Karen Vaughan tried to deliver a letter requesting an interview, she refused even to take it, snatching her hand away. Now, with the trials over and her main tormentor in prison, she has agreed to talk.

This is not the nervy, anguished-looking woman I saw in court at Papakura. Isobel seems calm and relaxed. She is a bubbly, sweet-natured person, with a quiet self-confidence that is newly won. 'Ask me whatever you like,' she says. 'I can talk about it now without getting upset. I've done enough of that in the past.'

Isobel settles into a sofa. She speaks in little bursts, punctuating her answers with sharp intakes of breath and the occasional shudder. She talks about her mother, who sought to pierce the bubble protecting the Pitcairn men but more or less gave up after the fiasco with Isobel's underwear. For Isobel, there was nowhere else to turn. She had already tried confiding in another adult, an older woman, who, she says, 'just laughed at me, saying, "You're making things up."'

All that Isobel's mother could do was urge her and her younger sister, Jeanie, to keep away from Brian Young. 'And we did our best,' says Isobel. 'But he always ended up doing the same thing. Because the men could. They knew we were easy pickings.'

When she was 11, the family moved to New Zealand, and Isobel's mother gave the girls a warning. 'She said, "Now we're out here, whatever happened there on the island is never to be mentioned." Otherwise, we'd be blamed, we'd be had up for slander, we'd be the ones that would get into trouble.'

As she became a teenager, then a young adult, Isobel followed her mother's advice. She tried to forget the horrors of Pitcairn, where she had lived in dread of the sound of Brian's motorbike, and where 'we were taught in church that it's wrong to steal and wrong to blaspheme, but not that it's wrong to touch kids, and there was no one to say, "This shouldn't be happening to you."' Isobel recalls, 'We came out here and you learn to move on. It was, like, that's my past on the island, that's left behind now, which I thought it was. And I would watch the news, and see different ones here being prosecuted for that stuff. But I always thought that, being from such a small island, nothing could be done about it. Because who would care?'

By the time the investigation started, Isobel was married with four children. She was astonished to learn that action was finally being taken. But she had no hesitation about speaking to police. 'I'd heard about a young girl on the island who'd made a complaint and was being ostracised,' she explains. 'And I felt really bad for her. I knew exactly how she would be feeling, because I'd been in her shoes.

'I felt, something's got to be done about this, or it will just keep carrying on. Because obviously it still *was* going on and had never been stopped. I knew there would be other young kids there, and they'd grow up and have the same thing happen to them. Someone had to put a stop to it.'

At the police station, Isobel panicked. 'I thought, what have you done? I thought, surely they're not going to believe all this. Then I thought, hang on, I'm in my 30s now, why is it that we can't do something about the abuse on the island, but that out here things get done?'

The police believed her. And so did Isobel's husband, who was hearing for the first time her story of being abused by a succession of men. 'My husband went through everything with me,' she says. 'It was a total shock to him, but he's stood by me all the way through and I've had some real crap times. He's been a rock, really.'

Isobel twists her dark, wavy hair into coils. 'After going to the police, I started getting these frightening feelings, because I thought, is my mother right, am I going to get myself into trouble, has she predicted it all? I got really scared then, and I had nightmares countless nights, dreams that I'm in line and we're going to be taken out of New Zealand and shipped back to the island. There's these men with coats and guns, and it would be the men that's doing the prosecuting, and it would be me that's on trial.'

During daylight hours, meanwhile, she says, 'I had all these memories coming back ... Things that you've buried so deep down are coming to the surface. I'd be vacuuming and it would all come back to me, and it's like you're reliving it over and over. I hit rock bottom then, and my husband was in despair. He must have thought I was going to end up in a loony bin.

'There were times I thought it would be better to end it all. Once I just walked out into the traffic. I didn't care what happened to me. Then I thought about my kids. I want to be here to protect my kids, to make sure this doesn't happen to them.'

A hospital care giver, Isobel began working every shift on offer, in an effort to escape from herself. 'When I wasn't working, I was horrible. I was on edge all the time. I was snappy with everyone. I would hate anyone else to have to experience what I've gone through. The stress and strain it puts on your family is unbelievable.'

Those stresses were magnified by the drawn-out legal process and the seemingly endless appeals. 'The men were doing their damnedest to stop this case from going ahead at all,' says Isobel. 'They were desperate. It was really frustrating, and it wasn't fair. Because for us it was another torment. All I wanted to do was have it over and done with. I didn't want all these years of waiting. I felt like these men were getting special treatment. They were treated too softly by the courts. It was always "poor them". What about the victims that's having to go through all this waiting and constant worry and wondering where's this going to take us, is it going to get thrown out?'

And throughout those years Isobel had to listen to the islanders and their allies attacking the prosecution and the women. She says, 'These outsiders who visit Pitcairn and then get on the band-wagon, saying it's not true and making excuses for the men ... I think, how pathetic they are, wake up, you're only seeing the good things, they're putting on a really good show for you. These people haven't got a clue. Just because they've been there and experienced a bit of island life, they think it's a wonderful place. They've not experienced the reality behind that.'

At times Isobel wondered if it was worth it. 'Then I kept thinking about that first girl, and I thought no, I'm doing it for her, and anybody else that's there in the future. Somebody has got to stand up to these people. And if I gave up, these bastards would win and they're going to get away with it again. So even though it was bloody hard, I held on.

'I had this phase of wanting to get hold of them, all these offenders, and line them up and put them through torture. I wanted them to feel the pain of what they did to us. If I had my way, I'd have them slowly tortured every day. I thought, yeah, you bastards, you'll suffer for the rest of your life and I won't let you die. I wanted them to feel as helpless as I was, and frightened, and don't know what's coming next. I just wanted revenge, really.'

She breaks off to fetch us some lunch. In the living room, where a fire is blazing and the walls are covered in modern artworks, Isobel talks about the run-up to the trials. 'It was really daunting. My stomach was churning, and you're just praying you'll be believed. After all this time it would be a shame, it would be devastating, if you'd gone through hell for not being believed.'

In 2004 Dave Brown was acquitted of indecently assaulting her. It was a heavy blow. Two years later came Brian's trial. 'Leading up to it, I was a total mess,' she says. 'I was crying and really doubting myself, thinking it's going to be a complete waste of time. Then as I was walking to the court, something came over me. It was like a protective shield. I just felt confident. I walked in and I was determined to eyeball him. When he looked up, I looked him straight in the eye. Many occasions I actually stared him down and I felt really good about it.

'At times I felt like getting off that chair and giving him a bloody slap. He was shaking his head, and I thought, you bastard, how dare you?

'And I wanted to say to him, "This is revenge for what you did to me. Do you remember what you did to me back then?"'

Brian's attempt to apologise infuriated Isobel. 'I already told the police, I'll never forgive him. No amount of apology would give me those innocent times back. You can never replace what you've had taken away from you, your innocence.'

I mention that Brian claimed she and Jeanie flirted with him. 'Flirted?' Isobel looks at me, momentarily dumbstruck. Then she shakes her head and laughs. 'An 11-year-old flirting? He is obviously sick. That's just typical of the Pitcairn men. You can send them to counselling, but that will never change them. Because that's how they are. That's their mindset.'

When the guilty verdicts came back, she was elated and relieved. She read the newspaper reports and the judge's comments 'over and over again, for it to sink in'. She kept the papers for a while, and then she threw them on the fire. 'It was like purifying myself.'

After a pause, Isobel says, 'I'm glad to see justice done, but that sentence, it's like a slap in the face. And the jail out there, to me it feels like a mockery, really. They need to be in jail out here in the real world, having to watch their backs every time they move around. That's paradise, what they're in, they're laughing. It's not a jail really.'

Still, it's highly unlikely they'll be allowed to live in Australia or New Zealand again, or even visit, I point out, not with a conviction for child sex offences.

'Really?' Isobel beams delightedly. 'So they're stuck on Pitcairn? That's brilliant. That's a real prison sentence for all of them.'

Personally, she would not go back 'for many millions of dollars'. Watching a documentary recently, she noted how much Pitcairn — where she was born and spent much of her childhood, but has not set foot for nearly 30 years — has changed. 'There are things I miss about it,' Isobel admits. 'It's a pretty island. I miss the ruggedness of it, the rough sea. Fishing in rock pools, the freshness of the fish. Just going up to a tree and picking a fresh mango.

'But seeing all the people there, and them still denying it, it just makes my skin crawl. Maybe if it was a different set of people. I feel sorry for them, really, particularly the women. I don't think they want to face the truth.'

Since the case began, Isobel has severed most of her links with the Pitcairn community, including her family. She no longer sees her two elder brothers; her parents died some years ago, and she has grown apart from her elder sister, Jennifer, who lives in England. She keeps in touch only with Jeanie and Jeanie's friend, Marion. 'In a way, I've cut off that part of my identity,' she says. 'I totally refuse to speak Pitkern. My sisters still speak it. My older sister says you should be proud of who you are and where you're from, but how can I? I feel ashamed of it, because of what's happened there.

'I think after all this the people shouldn't be allowed to stay on Pitcairn. If they don't want to come to New Zealand, put them on Norfolk Island. Because really, all the money Britain's putting in is for what? What are they keeping it for? I mean, what future has the island got?'

For herself, as far as the trials are concerned, Isobel feels it has all been worthwhile. 'I've been heard and I've been believed,' she says. 'And hopefully people will know now that if they go there, they've got to be very careful. Personally I'll always find it hard to be trusting of the island. Those men, they've come to New Zealand and they knew they're not going to get away with it. But Pitcairn's a small island, not very well known. It's ideal for paedophiles.'

Since the verdicts Isobel has given up the counselling sessions that helped to sustain her over recent years. She still gets flashbacks. 'It's always there in your mind, the abuse. It won't ever go away. But you learn to say it's in the past.'

One of her daughters returns from a shopping trip and dances around the room, showing off her new clothes. Her mother looks at her with love. As we say goodbye, Isobel tells me, 'It's a new era now. I'm getting on with my life.'

Her strength is inspiring.

Acknowledgements

Many of the people who helped me most with this book did so backstage. While they have to remain nameless, I am extremely grateful for their assistance, and for their leap of faith in trusting me.

For the historical sections, I have drawn on the work of Trevor Lummis, Glynn Christian, Caroline Alexander and David Silverman.

I owe a special debt to *The Independent* for sending me to Pitcairn; to David Hardaker and Bronwen Reid for urging me to write the book; to Mark Dapin, Claire Harvey and Helen O'Neill for reading early drafts; to Sue Ingram and Ewart Barnsley for supplying their uncut interviews; to John Harré and others who gave me photographs; to Leslie Jaques for his help with factual queries; to my agent, Lyn Tranter; to Amruta Slee and Anne Reilly at HarperCollins; and to close friends and family, particularly Terry Cutcliffe, for their unconditional support.

In addition, I would like to thank those islanders who showed me and my colleagues great kindness during our stay. Lastly, I salute the brave women of Pitcairn, particularly the woman whom I have given the pseudonym Belinda.